CAPTAIN SOCCEROO

the PAUL WADE story

CAPTAIN SOCCEROO

the PAUL WADE story

HarperSports

An imprint of HarperCollinsPublishers

PHOTO CREDITS

Special thanks to the following photo libraries, who provided many of the photographs
in Captain Socceroo.

Australia Picture Library/Allsport: 133 (top left).

News Limited: 65, 67 (bottom), 68, 70 (top), 72 (top), 74 (top), 76 (top and bottom),
77 (top and bottom), 78 (bottom), 79 (all pics).

Sport: The Library: 73, 131, 132 (top and bottom), 133 (top right, bottom left, bottom right).

Sporting Pix: 134 (top).

The Photo Library: 134 (bottom).

Harper*Sports*

An imprint of HarperCollins*Publishers*, Australia

First published in Australia in 1995

Text copyright © Wade Promotions Pty Ltd 1995

HarperCollins*Publishers*
25 Ryde Road, Pymble, Sydney NSW 2073, Australia
31 View Road, Glenfield, Auckland 10, New Zealand
77–85 Fulham Palace Road, London W6 8JB, United Kingdom
Hazelton Lanes, 55 Avenue Road, Suite 2900, Toronto, Ontario M5R 3L2
and 1995 Markham Road, Scarborough, Ontario, M1B 5M8, Canada
10 East 53rd Street, New York NY 10022, USA

National Library of Australia Cataloguing-in-Publication data:

Wade, Paul, 1962–
    Captain Socceroo: the Paul Wade story.

    ISBN 0 7322 5175 3.
    Includes index.
    1. Wade, Paul, 1962–. 2. Soccer – Australia. 3. Soccer players – Australia – Biography.
    I. Patterson, Kyle, 1960–. II. Title.

796.334092

Front cover photograph: Australia v Argentina (SFS, October 1993) © Sporting Pix
Back cover photograph (lower): Australia v Argentina (SFS, October 1993) © Joe Mann,
Australian Picture Library
Printed in Australia by Pirie Press

9 8 7 6 5 4 3 2 1
98 97 96 95

CONTENTS

FOREWORD

by George Negus

ONE MEETING WITH HIM at the historic OzSoccer Summit 95 in Melbourne earlier this year and my eight-year-old — the proud striker for the Bellingen soccer club — was talking of Paul Wade as 'my mate Wadey'.

To soccer-adoring Ned, Paul Wade is a fine player, a good guy and a hero. Normally, as a professional sceptic, I would discourage Ned from the whole idea of heroes — soccer or otherwise. Heroism is not a concept with which I've ever been all that comfortable. More often than not, 'would-be-if-they-could-be's' artificially elevated to that sort of pedestal let us down by their all-too-human imperfections and fallibility. But in this case, I don't mind young Ned and his mates seeing Paul that way. If he's got to have a hero, then the guy in the No. 6 gold and green strip, the guy with the ferocious header, will definitely do!

The others have their Meningas, Campeses and Abletts. We in the Australian soccer family have Paul — and our growing constellation of stars like him. Paul Wade is a born leader. If we have one, he's the face of Australian soccer.

Paul's in the evening of his illustrious playing career — a massive 100-plus matches with the Socceroos. It would be an unmitigated disgrace if his talent, commitment, experience, personal charm and personality and his communication skills were to be lost to the game when he pulls off the No. 6 for the last time. As an individual, that loss would sadden me; as the Soccer Australia Commissioner responsible for the advancement of the game, it would frustrate and annoy me profoundly.

In a very real way, how we do — or don't do — the proverbial 'right thing' by Paul Wade at this seminal point in his career will be a measure of whether we make sure OzSoccer rockets into the 21st century — or whether it drags itself in apologetically as a second-class sporting citizen, unrecognised for its true worth. In the past, we've let our legends and greats wander off from the game into sporting oblivion, never to be seen or heard of again. Unforgivable stuff!! Wadey

— and all those Socceroos and club stars, past and present, whom we admire so much — have a vital role in the future of the game in this country. It would be irresponsible (no, it would be plain stupid!) if we didn't invite as many of them as is feasible to contribute — indeed, pay them to do so; it should be official Soccer Australia and club policy. They don't hang up their brains and knowledge when they hang up their boots. Let's exploit them, in the nicest possible way and to all our benefits!

Wadey, don't walk away. Australian soccer has given you much. You still have heaps to give Australian soccer.

There are good and bad advertisements for all sorts of things. Paul Wade is about as good an advertisement for the soccer product as we can get. Australian soccer officialdom needs to properly acknowledge this. For reasons that defy soccer logic (or any other kind of logic!) Paul has never really been accorded the plaudits he deserves, either as an exponent or as an ambassador of the World Game in this country. This timely autobiography should rectify that anomaly.

Put together by Paul Wade with the help of SBS's Kyle Patterson, *Captain Socceroo* is a terrific read. The opening chapter, 'My Duel With Diego', is quite splendid — looking over Paul's shoulder at the Sydney Football Stadium and the River Plate is the closest encounter the rest of us are going to have with 'the Picasso of sport' ... or maybe that should be 'the Salvador Dali of sport'!

Soccer in Australia is on a cusp. With the right administration, financial backing, club competition, promotion and marketing currently in the offing — if we get our house in order — it is about to take off, locally and internationally, in the way its millions of players and fans have dreamed one day it might. Paul Wade — 'Captain Socceroo' — should and will be part of that reinvention of the game in this country.

September 1995

My Duel

with Diego

PLAYING IN FRONT OF a home crowd of 42,000, plus two million Australian TV viewers and 400 million worldwide, is enough to make you scared if you think about it for too long. Playing man-on-man with the world's greatest soccer player in front of all those people is enough to create a personal crisis. And when the game is the biggest event in Australian soccer for almost 20 years, a World Cup showdown against the former world champions, the pressure is enough to make you want to run and hide. When my time came, I'd been through fear, anxiety and a hundred other emotions, and I just wanted to get on with it.

The worst thing about any big game is the waiting, and the waiting for this game, on Sunday, October 31, 1993, felt like forever. As I led the Socceroos out of the dressingroom, I saw our opponents in the tunnel, waiting in line, so we would enter the stadium together. I walked down past the light blue and white shirts of Argentina. Walking past players I'd only ever seen on TV: Batistuta, Goycochea, Balbo. Players I had watched in World Cup finals and in Europe's best leagues, a million miles away from the modest surroundings of Australian soccer. Now they were here in our backyard.

At the head of the line, there he was. Diego Armando Maradona, the captain of Argentina and the world's most famous and controversial footballer. I stopped next to him and waited for the signal for both teams to enter the field. The first thing that struck me was his stature. I couldn't believe how small he was! The top of his head came up no further than halfway between my elbow and shoulder. I'm just over six feet tall, about 183 centimetres, and I had read that he was 168 centimetres, about five feet six, but that seemed a bit generous. He would need to be on tip-toes to make five feet six. He had on his captain's armband, with pictures of his daughters on it. The day before was his 33rd birthday and his daughters were in Sydney to help him celebrate. I had two daughters, like him, and I decided there and then that if we qualified for the USA '94 World Cup finals I would have an arm-band with my daughters' pictures on it.

I'll admit, I was totally in awe of Maradona. He is a legend, a kid from the slums of Buenos Aires who became a millionaire because he played the game like no other player on the planet. A tubby little guy who did amazing things with a soccer ball, things mere mortals like me hadn't thought possible, and he didn't save the tricks for the beach — he pulled them out in World Cup finals! He was idolised by millions around the world. Who was I to be taking him on? I was 31, a battler who'd gone further than I had ever dared to dream. A part-time player in a country where soccer is the No. 3 football code. A midfielder of modest skills whose game is about never giving up.

As I stood nervously waiting, it hit me. In a few minutes the contest would begin, a World Cup play-off, with qualification for the USA '94 World Cup for the winner and nothing but hard luck stories for the loser. Argentina, world champions in 1978 and 1986, and runners-up in 1990, among the giants of world soccer. Australia, despite all the progress we've made, a minnow.

Why did we have to play them?

Thanks to the political wheeling and dealing within FIFA, world soccer's governing body, the winner of the Oceania group got no favours. We were too small to have any clout, and that meant our path to the World Cup was long and hard. We knew we had to play a team from Central or North America and, if we won, then play a South American nation. We sneaked past the Canadians, and thought we'd play Colombia, Paraguay or Peru. They were in the South American Group A with Argentina, who were certain to win the group. We had to play the runners-up, so we didn't even think about Argentina. Well, that all changed on September 5, 1993, when Argentina was thrashed 5–0 by Colombia in front of their own fans in Buenos Aires. It was one of the biggest upsets in the history of the game and meant the proud Argentinians had finished second. Now they had to beat us over two games to qualify for the USA '94 World Cup finals.

I'm sure they thought the Socceroos were a bunch of nobodies, a part of soccer's Third World, but they couldn't be sure, could they? We had beaten Argentina in Sydney during the 1988 Bicentennial Gold Cup. They might have thought it was a fluke, but anyone who underestimates the Aussie spirit is asking for trouble. When Argentina was humiliated by Colombia, Diego Maradona was watching and weeping in the grandstand. In May, 1991, he was banned from international soccer for 15 months for testing positive to cocaine in Italy. Maradona the playboy forgot about Maradona the footballer. He was the greatest player of world football's modern era, but he got caught and had to do the time. He'd won the World Cup almost single-handedly in 1986 and somehow carried Argentina to the final in 1990, but when someone gets caught doing drugs people forget all the good things.

Maradona's comeback to club football in Spain in September, 1992, was an expensive flop, but there were still clubs queueing up to sign him. Clubs were willing to pay millions to get him because he was the best. In fact, more than A$40 million has changed hands between soccer clubs who've acquired his services, not to mention the millions he was paid. He was just starting another comeback in club football at home in Argentina when the national team was thumped by Colombia. The millions of soccer fans in Argentina needed a saviour, and Maradona was it.

So on top of all the other challenges for the Socceroos, we had the international comeback of Diego Maradona. There I was standing next to the guy in the tunnel at the Sydney Football Stadium, carrying the hopes of thousands of fellow Australians. I didn't know how to act. Should I stare straight ahead and look tough? Should I shout some inspiring words to my team mates? Instead, I turned to Maradona and said, 'Happy Birthday', and shook his hand. He didn't say anything, but I figure he knows some English because he closed his eyes and bowed his head, as if to say 'thanks very much'. Straight away I thought, 'I shouldn't have done that!' Was I sending the wrong message? Was I being too nice? It was a reflex thing, but I was starting to think that maybe I was psyching myself out.

When we left the tunnel there was a huge reaction from the 42,000 fans. There was green and gold everywhere, but in the grandstand directly opposite the players' tunnel there was a sea of light blue and white: the Argentinian expats, about 5000 of them. They really pissed me off. They were Australians, or at the very least Australian residents, and they were supporting the enemy. My nerves disappeared there and then, and were replaced by feelings of anger. I was determined to shove it up them. The teams lined up for the national anthems and that's when the Aussie fans did us proud. I don't think I've heard 'Advance Australia Fair' sung with such pride or volume in ten years as a Socceroo. Even people who don't normally go to soccer went that night and sang their lungs out. I reckon it would have been heard in Wagga, it was so loud. Just to hear the wall of sound bounce back off the stands and swirl around the stadium was inspiring. I had a flashback to how I learnt 'Advance Australia Fair'. I did it with one of those shower song-books — I sang a new line each morning until I knew it off by heart. To hear thousands of others singing with the same national spirit was brilliant.

The anthem was over and we gathered for the team photos. For Diego and his team, three dozen cameras were flashing away. The Socceroos had maybe half a dozen photographers shooting and that was another slap in the face. Maybe the media thought we were only there to make up the numbers, and maybe there were 5000 Australians who paid money to see us lose, but I was determined to show the lot of them they were wrong. The custom is for the captains to exchange pennants before the toss of the coin. Again, it wasn't me they wanted to photograph; it was the little bloke beside me. It was front-page news around the world. The flashbulbs were going a million miles an hour. It was like being an inch away from destiny and that was scary.

There was no doubt that on that night, the focus of the sports world was on Sydney, Australia. The legendary Diego was back. That was big. It was all another reminder (as if I needed one!) that my opponent was no ordinary player. He was Diego Maradona and all the world wanted a piece of him. This was his comeback game and we were playing for a place in the World Cup finals. I was marking the great Maradona. It was my 90 minutes of fame.

B EFORE MY DUEL WITH Diego I was bombarded with images of Maradona, the multi-media superstar. There had been seven weeks between the time we learned we had to play Argentina and the actual game. Seven weeks of reading Maradona comeback stories. Seven weeks of TV reports showing the personal training sessions helping to get him back into shape. Seven weeks of almost daily reminders that Maradona was coming. The Socceroo squad was in Adelaide for a training camp in early October, 1993, two weeks before the first game against Argentina, in Sydney.

Argentina's squad arrived in Sydney late one night. The next day in our Adelaide hotel we scanned the TV news services. The coverage showed a sea of people in blue and white at Sydney airport. It looked like a carnival, with drums and horns going full blast. There was a split-second shot of a little dark-haired figure. The Australian media were straight onto the Maradona bandwagon. We had been preparing for the Argentinians for weeks, but no one expected the blanket media coverage. It was all happening. Everything was about Maradona. It was as though the rest of the players were just there to make up the numbers. The next evening we saw the news coverage of Argentina's first training session in Sydney. Diego was juggling the ball with his bootlaces undone — the rest of us can't even walk with our laces undone, and here he is running, juggling and scoring goals with boots barely on his feet!

The Socceroo training camp in Adelaide finished, and all the players went back to their clubs for the opening round of the National Soccer League (NSL) on Sunday, October 24. On Monday we went back into camp in Sydney, at the Novotel on Botany Bay, to begin the serious preparations. We started to find out more about Argentina, mainly from the Socceroo assistant coach, Raul Blanco. He was Argentinian-born and so had plenty of knowledge and contacts. It became obvious that Mehmet Durakovic of South Melbourne and Alex Tobin of

Adelaide City, the two Socceroo centre backs, would be busy marking Abel Balbo and Gabriel Batistuta, the two forwards that Argentina was likely to play. These two played their football in Italy; Balbo with Roma and Batistuta with Fiorentina. It was another case of torture by television. We could watch these guys on TV every week, playing in Italy's Serie A, the best club competiton in Europe, and listen to all the stories of how Batistuta had a US$20 million price tag. It was a different world from ours.

I desperately wanted to play, but even though I was the captain of the Socceroos, I was no certainty. Three months earlier, in July, 1993, the Socceroo coach, Eddie Thomson, had dropped me for the World Cup qualifier against Canada. I had the dubious honour of being the first Socceroo captain to be axed from the starting eleven. After that setback I had just concentrated on training hard to convince Thommo I was worth a spot again, so I had no thoughts about marking Maradona. Before I worried about Diego's comeback I had to worry about my own. A few weeks before I was certain Durakovic would mark Maradona. He had shadowed the England captain, Gary Lineker, in an international in 1991 and hadn't let him have a kick, let alone score a goal. That was what we needed to do to Maradona if we were to beat Argentina.

Suddenly things changed. Thommo and Blanco figured that Maradona would play midfield rather than as a forward, and now all the speculation was around which of the Socceroo midfielders would mark him. Someone had to mark him. If you give Maradona any space, he'll destroy any team in the world. Even in a comeback game. I looked around the squad and figured I was in the running for the job. Instead of just watching all the coverage of Maradona, as any other fan would, it was starting to hit me between the eyes. I watched the TV news and thought, 'Maybe it's me, maybe I've got to mark him.' Even thinking about it was daunting.

We had a behind-closed-doors session at the Sydney Football Stadium the day before the game. Eddie Thomson announced the starting eleven and I was in it. It was a tremendous feeling — I'd worked hard for three months to get back into the Socceroo team and all the work had paid off. A lot of critics thought I was finished when Thommo dropped me for the Canada game in July, so I felt a lot of satisfaction. There was more to come. Thommo hadn't yet discussed marking Maradona, but announced his decision in a team talk. I would be marking Maradona! No one said a thing, but immediately I felt the pressure. It was the job everyone in the team and the media had been talking about.

We went out onto the ground for a training game. Raul Blanco was in the other team acting as Maradona, which is not bad because he's Argentinian and the same shape! Thommo and Raul gave me direct instructions: 'We want you to mark Maradona, but we don't want you to play your game. We want you to play his game.' In the practice session I had to forget about making runs forward or getting into the penalty area. I had to stay with Raul. For twenty-five minutes Raul hardly moved and neither did I. Raul said Maradona wouldn't do much running. Great — I'd made a name for myself as a player capable of covering every blade of grass and competing flat out for 90 minutes and now I'm told not to worry about running! I have always played football with 100 per cent commitment. If I'm not running, tackling and involved in almost every pass, then I'll try to support my team mates by shouting instructions or encouragement.

Now I had to forget about my usual game. A couple of times in the practice game my natural instincts took over. I would receive a ball, play it forward, then dash off in support. After only a few paces Raul would bellow, 'Wadey, where the hell do you think you're going?' I would quickly retreat to mark Blanco. 'If he goes to the loo, you go with him.' He kept saying I was to be Maradona's Siamese twin. That went against everything I had done in my 20-odd years of playing football. It was against every principle I had been taught. All the times my dad said to me as a youngster, 'Move yourself.' All the times he would say, 'You have to be quicker, you have to want the ball.' Coaches throughout my career have told me, 'You have to want the ball to be a good footballer.' It all went out the window.

I soon realised it wasn't such a negative role. I'd be playing side by side with a legend before the eyes of the soccer world. I was immediately nervous, but I kept telling myself, 'Why am I worried? If he tears me to pieces with his skill, then that's what he's meant to do. He's the best player in the world. And if I do a half-decent job I'm a hero.' So all the pressure was on him. But your mind still plays tricks. I kept thinking of the goal Maradona scored against England in the 1986 World Cup quarter-final when he beat half the team and then sold a dummy to Peter Shilton, one of the world's best keepers. And the goal that he scored for Napoli (his Italian team) from near the halfway line with a volley. All these super-human feats. Bending free kicks around walls. Unbelievable passes. I had to stop thinking about it. All these images built him into a superman.

Until then, I'd never really thought about a contest between Diego Maradona and Paul Wade. It was Australia v Argentina. Now it was shaping up as a game within a game. Diego Maradona, a genius with a soccer ball, versus Paul Wade, a part-time footballer with modest skills. I didn't have to get forward to help Graham Arnold, the Socceroos' lone striker. I didn't have to go back in the wall for free kicks to help the defence. I just had to stay with Maradona and be snapping at his heels when he got the ball. Even when the ball was at the other end I had to stand next to him. Blanco said he expected Maradona to play a lot of first-time passes. My job was to make sure that that first touch was a pass backwards or sideways, not a telling through ball. I had to do my job within the rules and the spirit of the game. Maradona has been hacked by defenders all over the world, but I wasn't going to resort to anything like that. In fact, the instructions from the coaches warned me against rushing in to tackle Maradona. If I could get to the ball first, or as it arrived at his feet, that was fine, but I was under strict instructions not to rely on tackles to contain Maradona. The more I thought about it, the more nervous I became. You keep thinking about things that could go wrong.

And this was no ordinary game. At one closed-door training session we were rehearsing our set pieces, free kicks and corners. Someone noticed a shadowy figure at the top of the grandstand. All hell broke loose. There were coaches and officials shouting at whoever it was to get out. It might have been a curious fan or it could have been an Argentinian spy. It just added to the tension. In the days leading up to the game it was Maradona this and Maradona that, all over the media. And then I learned I was the one who had to stop this legend! I was starting to pysch myself out of things. So I went to church.

I'm no Bible-basher. I had a Catholic education and I was brought up a Catholic. If ever I needed help, it was now. On the Saturday afternoon before the game I went to the Catholic church near our hotel on Botany Bay. It was St Thomas More's of Brighton Le Sands. It was too early for the Saturday Mass and the church was empty. I sat there, just me and Him. I said a prayer. I just hoped He heard and was on my side, but then I thought, 'Diego is a Catholic, too!' Whose side will He be on? In any case, I felt a little bit more at ease. I returned to the Novotel and we had an early dinner before all the Socceroo players and officials went to Marconi Stadium to watch Marconi Fairfield play Sydney United in an NSL game.

I didn't want to go, because I'm one of those people who need an early night before a game or I'll feel mentally tired. But I went anyway. My heart was working overtime. I was half watching the game and half thinking about the World Cup. 'It's D-Day for the Socceroos.' Imagine the pressure I was putting myself under. I'm marking Argentina's No. 10, I'm the captain of the ship, carrying the hopes of 17 million in front of a worldwide audience of 400 million. I wanted to be anywhere but there that night. And I wanted to be anyone but Paul Wade. The anxiety was getting out of hand and it was time to draw on some experience. I'd played against the best in the world before and never been disgraced. I had to wipe the worry slate clean and use my 'Que Sera, Sera' calm-down method. I kept telling myself, 'Whatever will be, will be.'

MATCH DAY finally arrived. I had slept well and felt refreshed on the morning of the game, despite the anxiety of the previous evening. On Sunday, October 31, 1993, I was back where I wanted to be after a pretty traumatic few months. I was in the starting eleven, and I had the captain's armband on once more. When I got dropped for the game against Canada in Edmonton the starting eleven seemed a million miles away. Now I was back and feeling great. I tried to prepare as normal, as if this day was like any other match day. I didn't want to get too hyped up.

I don't recall things being any different from the usual routine. The dressingroom was the same as always. Some guys get ready in a very quiet way, others, mainly Robbie Slater and Graham Arnold, make a bit of noise. They're always having a crack at each other or ganging up to take the piss out of someone else.

Within seconds of the kick-off I was there next to Diego Maradona. Despite all the preparation and instructions from Thommo and Blanco I still felt unsure about what Maradona would do and how he would play. In the weeks before the game he'd lost a lot of weight, maybe as much as six kilograms. He looked super-fit and very sharp. The stadium was full of screaming fans and the atmosphere was electric. As Blanco had predicted, Maradona wasn't interested in running. I wanted to run and be involved, but there I was standing next to this guy who looked totally unfussed by it all and gave the impression that if he didn't get the ball it would be no big deal. There was no way in the world he was going to run too far to get into the play. The play had to come to him, instead.

A full five minutes must have passed before Maradona had a real touch of the ball. The first time he received the ball, I could hardly believe how he acted. Coaches tell players to call a name or an instruction when they want the ball. 'Give it short, Micky', or something like that. Not Diego Maradona. He whistles for the ball. No names, no instructions. The only time he ever calls for the ball he shouts 'Hey', with all the arrogance a human can muster. And sure enough, when he whistles or calls 'Hey', the ball arrives. Most of the time he didn't make a sound and still received the ball. As soon as he was open for a pass they gave it to him straight away because they were confident that no matter where I was, Diego would keep possession.

We went to the touchline when Argentina had a throw-in and he was just standing there and I knew what the player throwing the ball was going to do. He was going to throw it to Maradona. But even though I knew where the ball was going, it didn't help much. I couldn't very well get in front of him to try to intercept the throw because I could lose him, and that would have been too risky. So I had to stay behind him and make sure I was goalside, with him and the ball in front of me. I'd try to get a toe to the ball and poke it away. Fat chance. I remember trying to push his arms and give him a shove to put him off, but he didn't move one inch.

Even though I was a lot taller, our weights were pretty close. I weighed 75 kilos in peak condition and even after losing a lot of weight for his comeback Maradona was said to weigh 71 kilos. It was like pushing a brick wall, he was so strong. He put his arms to his side and knew exactly where I was. He didn't exactly grab my shirt, just sort of made a bumper bar with his solid arms and there was no way in the world I could get past. I couldn't move and I could not see the ball with his low frame. He just hid the ball from me. My height advantage didn't help one bit either. He kept hiding the ball, and then he would just flick it with the outside of his foot. Early in the game there were a couple of times when I felt helpless. Most of the 42,000 crowd, and especially that sea of light blue and white, wanted to see some Maradona magic, at Paul Wade's expense. It's like being handcuffed to somebody and then having a ball and chain around your ankle and being told, 'Okay, you can play now.' It was so frustrating.

In the early part of the game, Maradona played just the way Raul Blanco had said he would: not much running, first-time passes. I was doing as I'd been instructed, making sure I was snapping at his heels, without committing myself. I was able to make some contribution, apart from my job on Diego, by tidying up loose balls in the midfield and helping other defenders cover their men. After 15 minutes I was happy that the Socceroos had settled quickly and Maradona had had no real influence. I kept hoping the game would open up. I'm nothing if not a competitor and if I could get the ball from him and play a telling pass myself, or have a crack at goal, I was going to do it. But even when the ball was at the other end I had to be next to Argentina's No. 10.

SBS TV had a camera just filming Diego, so it caught behind-the-play incidents. On one occasion I had arrived a fraction of a second late to challenge Maradona and bowled him over. There was no foul and the ball moved away as the play continued. I made a gesture to say, 'Sorry, mate, that was an accident.' From the Socceroos' 1985 World Cup qualifier against Scotland in Glasgow, I remembered someone going down the back of the great Kenny Dalglish's legs in a late tackle. I cringed. Dalglish was a genius with the ball and trying to stop him by kicking him was a prehistoric tactic. Today's Socceroos are better than that. That's why I made the gesture to Maradona. Not because I was being too nice, but because I think I'm better than that. I wanted him to know I wasn't going to resort to dirty tactics. He got up and shrugged his shoulders, and I knew he understood. It was going to be a good clean battle.

There was one tackle in the first half, right in the middle of the stadium, when I was sliding in to win a ball. My foot didn't make contact with Maradona, but in the tangle my shins and knees collected him and the referee awarded a free kick. It probably looked worse than it really was. In any case, I ended up on the deck with Maradona, thinking to myself again, 'Come on, Wadey, that was crap, you're better than that.' It was sheer desperation to win the ball and contribute that forced me to compete for a ball I had little chance of winning, but that's me, always pushing the limits. Never in my career have I gone out to hurt another player and I wasn't about to try to injure Diego Maradona. I apologised once more and some media commentators bagged me for doing it.

Football writer Tommy Anderson, talking on an SBS TV show, said I was too nice to Maradona, picking him up after tackles. That was nonsense. I've never tried harder to win a game for Australia than I did that night. If I made a mistake, or misjudged a tackle, I wanted to make sure Maradona knew it wasn't malicious. I was busting my guts for my country, trying to help us get to the World Cup finals.

It was another slide tackle, a clean and effective one this time, that brought the moment I'd worked so hard to avoid. It started from an Argentina throw-in, after about 35 minutes of the first half. This time Diego gave me the slip for a moment. I chased back and won the ball with a sliding tackle, guiding it to Milan Ivanovic, the Socceroo sweeper. I thought I'd done my job and the danger had been removed. My confidence was growing. I thought, 'Yeah, there's another one for Wadey.' Then in a split second, Maradona was back on his feet and closing on Ivanovic. Milan tried to go past Maradona, but Diego got a toe to the ball and won possession about five metres from the touchline, adjacent to the penalty area. He pivoted with the ball, then sent over a cross with that renowned left foot. Even then I thought to myself, 'That's a pretty ordinary cross.' It wasn't really deep enough to cause us real problems, but I didn't bank on Abel Balbo. He met the ball in front of the near post and somehow fired his header between goalkeeper Mark Bosnich and the post. It was an unbelievable header. I didn't realise just how good it was until I saw the TV replays. I was devastated. Argentina was 1–0 up and that was an away goal, which counts as double if the scores are tied after two games. All the Argentina players hugged Diego as if he was their saviour.

I guess our big mistake was letting Maradona get the ball anywhere near goal. That was my greatest fear, that with one or two touches of the ball he could win the game. I felt for Milan Ivanovic. You could usually count on one hand the number of times he gives possession away in 90 minutes, but this time he had lost it to Maradona and we were now a goal down. I think I was actually shocked that Maradona had got up from my tackle and gone over to challenge Milan. I had stretched a long way, from a sort of 45 degree angle behind him, to get my toe in to push it out to Ivanovic, and in the tangle Maradona had half fallen over. Normally he would sit on his bum and put his hands in the air as if to say, 'If you don't mind, referee!' That's the sort of feeling he gives me every time he goes down from a tackle. When he got up and went across to Milan Ivanovic and won it back again I think Milan was as shocked as I was that Diego was actually putting the pressure on him.

I have always said that I don't mind people making mistakes, even those that might cost us. I give the ball away plenty of times and I can handle mistakes. It's how you react to mistakes that really matters, because they happen dozens of times every game. Despite the setback, no Socceroos dropped their heads.

We'd played well until then and our confidence was high, even now that we were behind.

The home support was brilliant, and before half-time we gave them something to really cheer about. Playmaker Ned Zelic sent a brilliant pass to the overlapping Tony Vidmar. He fired a shot that I thought was mistimed, but that turned into a good cross, and his brother Aurelio was there dead in front to flick it home. We were back in it! I rushed over to Ned Zelic and picked him up. I really felt this was it, we were going to pinch this game. We had worried Argentina with our pace on the ball. Robbie Slater had made a couple of great, driving runs. Graham Arnold had run hard at the Argentinian defence and generally our defensive pressure all over the ground had unsettled them. We went out 1–1 at half-time, feeling the game was there for the taking.

At the break Thommo said he was proud of the way we were playing. Our tactics, to keep the wings open for the full-backs Tony Vidmar and Jason Van Blerk, were working perfectly and that is where our goal came from. During the interval the Sydney Football Stadium floodlights went off. If anything, the extra time waiting for the lights to come back on helped Argentina regroup. We couldn't quite find the same momentum and Argentina were better going forward in the second half and then seemed content to hold on to the draw.

We had created a couple of great chances in the first half, both falling to Arnie. Unfortunately for him, he didn't make the most of the openings and later came under fire. Some critics reckoned he was below par, but the way we played, Arnie had the hardest job of all. He was the lone striker, having to cover 70 metres across the ground and hold the ball while waiting for support. I thought he was brilliant.

The only trouble was that a bit of tiredness took the edge off us in the second half. When we threw David Mitchell on as a second striker he was in the referee's bad books straight away and kept giving away fouls. We didn't create as many chances, and that was disappointing. And in the second half, Maradona decided to run, for one of the very few times in the match. The ball broke nicely for him and he was away on a run of 40 metres or so. The through ball at the end of it was too strong and nothing came of the attack, but for once he got into his stride. That was the first and probably last time he really moved. Other than that, he played short one-two passes and didn't clock up too many minutes in possession. If his role was to be the playmaker for Argentina, I had stopped him. It was a case of me applying maximum pressure in order to restrict Maradona to minimum damage. His moment of genius, apart from the cross that led to Balbo's goal, came with a second-half free kick. He chipped over the top of the wall to Balbo, whose back-heel sent the ball bobbling into the six-yard box. Luckily for us, the rest of the Argentinians were just as surprised as we were, and no one was there to score.

Even when the game finished at 1–1, we were still in the hunt for the USA '94 World Cup finals. Yet again we'd proved we could play at the highest level. Robbie Slater was our best player, making some great runs from deep in the midfield and troubling Argentina with his pace and strength on the ball. Tobin and Durakovic had kept Batistuta and Balbo quiet, apart from the freakish goal. Tony Vidmar and Jason Van Blerk had defended well and provided plenty of support in attack. Ned Zelic had a great game against Fernando Redondo in midfield. SBS TV put together a story on the Wade/Maradona thing and their video showed that I hardly touched the ball. When I looked at the video of the entire 90 minutes, I'd done my job to the letter. If there was a fear Diego would win the game single-handed, I'd made sure it didn't happen. The tactic of man-marking Maradona worked perfectly and the Socceroos played world-class football that night. I reckoned the Argentinians would have gone away more worried about us than we about them. Going to Buenos Aires for the second leg with the score at 1–1 wasn't the big deal that everyone else seemed to be making it. Playing away from home was never a big deal for me.

In the minutes after the final whistle I went over to Maradona and asked to swap shirts. Usually I don't like to swap my Socceroo shirt. I get all the team to sign the shirt and then make it available as a present for a youngster. It means so much to them. But this was the famous No. 10 shirt of Diego Maradona, so I had to have it. I approached him, shook his hand and gestured that we should swap shirts. He said, 'No.' I couldn't believe it. He pointed to the sky. I was trying to work out what the problem was. Had he promised it to somebody else? Was there one coming down from above? Because he'd obviously said his prayers, too. He shook his head. I was thinking, 'Gee, I know I mistimed a few of those tackles, but I am the captain. The least you could do was swap shirts.' At the time I didn't know Maradona wore two shirts, one for each half.

I went up the tunnel. I was happy about the way we had played on this big night, but it still niggled me that I didn't have Maradona's shirt. I decided to dig my heels in. The dressingroom doors are only a few paces apart at the top of the tunnel. I waited outside. I wasn't moving until I got that shirt. An Argentinian team official came out and I gave him the message about the shirt. He mumbled something in broken English. By now all the Argentinian team and officials were inside and I was still standing guard outside. That's when I realised that I wasn't going to get it. I went back into our dressingroom, still in my strip and boots. The boys were talking. The room was abuzz, which is a sign that everyone was on a high. We had played well. A post-game dressingroom is deathly silent when you don't do well. I sat down and everyone started asking, 'Did you get it?' Graham Arnold came over and said, 'You must have got it.' Robbie Slater couldn't believe it either — he had been given one of Maradona's shirts because Diego had decided Slater was our best player and deserved it.

Suddenly the shirt became a big issue. After changing and heading to the bus through the crowds I found myself thinking more and more about the bloody shirt. We arrived back at the Novotel. As I climbed down the steps, feeling proud of what we had done, Tony Labbozzetta, the Socceroos' Head of Delegation, came up and said, 'There you are, Wadey, I got it for you.' It was drenched in sweat but, sure enough, it was the No.10 shirt.

The first thing I did was put it on, right outside the hotel. Corinne Blatter, the daughter of FIFA Secretary-General Sepp Blatter, was there. Straight away she wanted a photo. So there I was in the foyer of the hotel with a sweaty Maradona shirt on. Everyone was milling around. Word spread and soon the boys were heading for my room. Without fail the first thing everyone said was, 'He ain't very big, is he?' The shirt was very small. It was starting to smell as the perspiration took over.

I had dinner at the hotel with my mum and dad, Jim and Elaine, and my father-in-law Frank and my wife Valerie, but I couldn't eat much. My body was still racing. I was still wearing my Maradona shirt and some of the boys gave me a hard time about it. 'Wadey, you idiot', was the general cry. I suppose it was one thing to idolise the guy, but to wear his sweaty shirt to dinner? There had to be a limit. But I didn't care, I was loving it. I thought about the tunnel before the game when I wished Diego Happy Birthday. Looking back, I've got no regrets. I'm glad I did it. I shook hands with one of the world's greats and I thoroughly enjoyed the moment. It really had nothing to do with the 90 minutes; I was there to lead my country, he to lead his. I wanted to savour the occasion.

As for the great Maradona, he's had as much attention for his off-field misdemeanours as for his on-field brilliance. I saw what I hoped was the real Maradona when we were at the Auckland airport en route to South America for the return leg. The Young Socceroos, Australia's under-20 team, were on the same plane, heading to Venezuela for a youth tournament. In the transit lounge Diego was surrounded, but seemed relaxed. He signed every autograph. He signed Milan Blagojevic's Socceroo shorts and anything else that was thrust in front of him.

It seems every day of his life Diego Maradona is hounded by the media and his fans, but in that transit lounge, among fellow soccer players, he was, it seemed, showing his true self. By the way, I didn't get an autograph.

Getting ready for the return game in Buenos Aires was an enormous struggle. The Socceroos had gone to a training camp in Santiago, Chile. The reason for going there was simple. Go anywhere in South America outside Argentina, and people will hate the Argentinians. They're regarded as arrogant. The fact that we were trying to beat the hated Argentina made us heroes in Chile. Everywhere we went in Santiago the people were so friendly and helpful.

We were using the training facilities of Colo Colo, Chile's biggest club, and the conditions were perfect.

However, that didn't help me much. In one of our first sessions I was running for a ball near the touchline when reserve midfielder Jason Polak challenged from behind. As a result I rolled my right ankle badly. It blew up straight away and it turned out I'd torn the ankle ligaments. It was an injury that usually needed three weeks of recovery. I had ten days to get ready for a World Cup qualifier. What followed was the most intensive treatment I've ever had. Pedro Ruz was the Socceroo physio. Once he diagnosed the problem, he set up a program to get me ready. Never once did he say, 'You're in danger of missing the game.' He was so sure he could get me right. Pedro spent hours every day treating my ankle and supervising my recovery. It was a painful experience. One day he set up a test on a treadmill in the hotel gym. I slowly began to jog on the treadmill. The pain was killing me. There were mirrors on the walls and I could clearly see I had a limp. It was like having a nail hammered into my ankle. My brain was crying out for my body to stop, but then Eddie Thomson arrived for his daily exercise. Thommo works hard on his fitness and had decided to do some time on the treadmill next to me. He asked how my ankle was feeling. 'Fine', I said, trying not to show the discomfort I was in. Then Pedro decided it was time to increase the pace of the treadmill. The pain was getting worse, but I knew I couldn't stop. If I wanted to play in Buenos Aires I had to get used to the pain. I increased my pace to match the treadmill. I must have run for about 10 minutes, but it's hard to remember anything other than the excruciating pain. Finally, Pedro said I'd done enough. I'd made it. I knew then I could play at the River Plate. I felt like I'd gone through a mental barrier, and was able to cope with the pain.

There was more to come. I needed two cortisone injections and Dr Siri Kanangra, the Socceroo medico, had a huge needle to inject the stuff. At other times a needle was used to drain fluid from the ankle joint. I tell you what, I'll never forget Jason Polak! To this day I give him a hard time. 'Jay, I know you wanted a place in the team, but you didn't have to kill me to get it!' The recovery went according to schedule, although having cortisone injections meant I had to rest the ankle for 24 hours. Picking the best time to rest without affecting the rehabilitation was a tricky decision. In the end I had a day off in Santiago and was able to take part in the final team sessions before we left for Buenos Aires.

Then it was goodbye to Santiago and a lot of friendly people, and hello Buenos Aires, where we were expecting a frosty reception. We'd been warned about walking the streets or leaving the hotel and I think we all expected the Argentinians to be hostile. After all, we were trying to kick them out of the World Cup. When we arrived in Buenos Aires airport, we found out there was a large crowd of fans and media waiting. The security people arranged for us to bypass the normal exit and go straight from the plane to the team bus. It was only a short trip into the city and when we arrived at the Sheraton we could hardly believe our eyes. There were hundreds of screaming girls, waving to us, asking for autographs and treating us like idols. For two minutes we felt like superstars, then one of the hotel porters broke the news. Jon Bon Jovi, the rock singer, was staying in the hotel and the girls were hanging out for him! Oh well, it was good while it lasted.

Anyway, it changed our views of the Argentinian people. We had no hassles, as far as hostility goes. In fact, the only problem for the Socceroos was being too popular. As part of the security precautions, players were told not to wear any Socceroo clothing, such as tracksuits, when we went out shopping or walking. Of course, some people like being different. Robbie Slater was already something of a cult figure in Argentina, thanks to the rave reviews from his mate Diego Maradona. On one morning when we had some free time, because it was quite cold, he grabbed his Socceroo jacket with the huge 'Australia' on the back. Within minutes, Slater was surrounded by fans who wanted to shake his hand or kiss him or just talk about the game. Graham Arnold saw what was going on and quickly doubled back to the hotel to get his Socceroo top. Good one, guys. It was like that for the three days before the game. The Argentinian fans are incredibly passionate about their football.

Our biggest problem was injuries. Ned Zelic and Mark Bosnich had both returned to Europe after the first leg and hurt themselves in club games, so they wouldn't be travelling to Buenos Aires. Even so, all the pressure was on Argentina, because it was their first game back at the River Plate since the 5–0 defeat to Colombia in September that had forced them into the play-off with Australia. We trained at the stadium the night before the game and got a surprise. The pitch was a disgrace. There had been a Madonna concert not long before and the surface had been relaid right down the middle of one half of the pitch. It was bumpy and soggy from rain. Just what my ankle needed!

MATCH DAY WAS COLD and wet. The kick off was 9 pm so we had all day to watch the rain tumbling down. We made it to the stadium through a massive traffic jam. It was time to take a look at the pitch and get a feel of the atmosphere. It was a weird feeling entering the stadium, because they set up an inflatable tunnel. There's a huge fan and they blow air down it and they close it at the other end so it stays up. It's to allow the players to enter and leave the field under some protection. I remember walking out there when we first arrived at the River Plate. We had our tracksuits on so the fans knew who we were. This would be my 65th full international — beating Peter Wilson's record.

It was about an hour and a half before kick-off and the stadium was about three-quarters full. The top tiers were definitely full because I remember looking up and seeing masses of people. There weren't any seats and the fans were jumping up and down on one another. It was an incredible sight, but it looked dangerous, these thousands of bodies nine storeys high jumping up and down as if they were in the (former) Kop at Anfield. They were like the fans behind the goals at Middle Park, South Melbourne (gone, too, to make way for a Grand Prix track). I could see that if they weren't too careful, people could easily be pushed off. Obviously they had done this dozens of times before, but I was just amazed at the height of the grandstand and the open terracing. Once they saw some Australians they began whistling and shouting 'Kangaroo'. They didn't know much about us, but it just shows how well known the old kangaroo is.

My instructions about Maradona were exactly the same as they were in Sydney. That's why I got a new nickname in Buenos Aires. They called me 'the dancing Aussie'. I would be behind Diego Maradona with my arms out, my legs spread, balanced, and all I was doing while Maradona had the ball at his feet was jockeying behind him in a similar pose, moving every way he moved. I had been given clear instructions: 'Don't dive in. Don't sell yourself or this guy will tear you apart.' At one time at the River Plate, almost everybody was up the other end of the ground or over one side, and Diego was just walking back as though he wasn't interested in what was going on. He was the best player in the world and he didn't seem to give a stuff.

He just walked around and knew that Fernando Redondo, or Diego Simone, or whoever had it at the time, would give the ball to him. He didn't have to chase it .Whenever he wanted it, he would get it, with the usual 'hey'. He would move no more than five metres in a hurry and that's when he would start doing his stuff, but there was no way in the world he would leg it back into midfield so that he could get it again. He would walk and shuffle about. Inside I was pleading with him to run because I wanted to get involved in the game. Maradona had to take me to the action, but again, half the time he was doing absolutely nothing.

Having said all that, my performance in the second leg wasn't as effective. Because of the terrible surface, I slipped a couple of times and he got away and created a few chances. Early in the game he sent a great cross to Batistuta, who had a free header but, thank heavens, missed the target. Diego did a few different things. At one stage he went and stood near Mehmet Durakovic and I thought the Argentinians had sussed out a way to break up my marking of Maradona. I did a reasonable job on the best player in the world in the Sydney game and they must have known I would mark him in the return leg. Several times Diego walked over to Durakovic so there were two Australian players marking him. While there were two of us marking him, plus the sweeper Milan Ivanovic, that meant that there were two extra Argentinian players floating around somewhere else. I was thinking I should tell Mehmet to pick him up while I push forward in midfield and go and do my stuff, but I knew that the only way you get results at international level is by being disciplined. The tactics you talk about during the week and at training sessions must be carried out even though you are dying to go and do something else. The one time you leave your job or don't do it or pass the responsibility on to somebody else, bang, it all comes undone and four years of a World Cup campaign can go down the drain. That's why I was standing there next to Maradona and saying, 'Come on, please move. Do something, so I can be involved.'

And sure enough, it would happen in a split second. Maradona would receive the ball and flick it away in almost one movement. It's so hard to turn on and off like that, particularly for a player like myself who's used to being involved all the time. Usually I will run around for 90 minutes and I will lose 10 balls, but I will have been in possession or have been involved in 40 or 50 different plays. In the Australia versus Argentina World Cup qualifiers, Diego was involved in 10 plays and nine out of the 10 produced something: goalscoring opportunities, some brilliant bit of magic or a pass that opened up the play for his team. I'm sure the free kick in Sydney, when he chipped the ball over the wall to Balbo, would have had the whole soccer world talking for the next couple of days, had it resulted in a goal.

Our mission at the River Plate was to win. Because of the 1–1 result in the first leg, a 0–0 result was enough for Argentina to win on the away goals rule. Then again, a 2–2 draw at the River Plate would see us through. In any case, we had to score at least once to be in the hunt. Early in the game it looked on. Graham Arnold put some pressure on Sergio Vasquez, the big centre half, and won the ball. Arnie was away, and got past Oscar Ruggeri, their last man in defence. Ruggeri grabbed his shirt and pulled him down. It had to be a red card, but the referee, Danish official Peter Mikkelsen, only gave him a yellow card. That really hurt.

There was to be only one goal at the River Plate and it came about 15 minutes into the second half. Alex Tobin closed down Batistuta in the penalty area, near the goal-line, and the Argentinian turned and crossed it. The ball flicked off Tobin's foot and as it went up in the air, goalkeeper Robert Zabica and I were at the near post. I remember Robby saying, 'Oh shit!' as it went over both of our heads. I turned around to see Durakovic trying valiantly to clear it, but it bounced into the roof of the net.

We had been warned about what to expect from the River Plate crowd. Quite a few of us had played there in 1992 in a friendly international against Argentina, when the crowd was about 40,000. This time it was around 65,000. Raul Blanco had said, 'You wait until you first go out there and you wait and see if they score a goal. You'll feel nothing like it and you will remember it for the rest of your life.' He was right. If I thought the noise was deafening when we went out to start the game, the reaction to the goal was like standing next to a jumbo jet when it's about to take off, and paper started to cascade down from the grandstands. I don't know who the paper manufacturers are over there, but they must make a fortune from football games!

Anyway, that was the ball game for the Socceroos. I recall being so focused in the last 30 minutes of the game that I couldn't hear the crowd any more. We were desperately chasing an equaliser. Everyone was giving 100 per cent. It wasn't until very late in the game, when Carl Veart, who had come on as a sub, had a shot that went wide, that I realised we weren't going to make it. I felt totally empty. Another World Cup campaign was over, without the ultimate success of qualification. The goal Argentina scored was such a fluke. We lost 2–1 on aggregate.

On the final whistle both sets of players were overcome by emotion. I looked around and saw that half the Argentinian players were on their knees, relieved that the pressure was over. Others were embracing each other, some were in tears. The Socceroos were shattered, as it hit everyone that we were finally out of the World Cup, but we did our best to console each other and congratulate our opponents.

Arnie took it really hard. Of all players in Europe who have come back and played for their country, no one is prouder of wearing that green and gold shirt than Arnie. He never had any hesitation when he was called up for the Socceroos and wouldn't give a damn who he would upset in Europe to play for his country. There are a few Aussies abroad who wouldn't do that and it's quite understandable. In some of the cases clubs put the players under enormous pressure to stay in Europe and play club football, rather than join their national team. Graham Arnold never thought twice about the green and gold and I can understand why he was so emotional in Buenos Aires. He put in so much and was the captain for the games against Canada when I was left out. He was criticised by some supporters back in Australia, but I thought he did another great job for his country. Arnie busted his gut in both games and with a bit of luck could've had a goal.

I was feeling pretty emotional, too. A few minutes after the finish I was doing an interview on SBS TV that was going live back home. I was thinking about the Australian public and the fantastic support they'd given us in Sydney and all the messages and faxes that had come from around the country. I hoped we hadn't let them down.

I went back to the pitch and crossed paths with Fernando Redondo. I shook hands and congratulated him and he replied, 'Do you want to swap shirts?', in quite comfortable English. I remember saying to him, 'No thanks, I'm going to get Maradona's.' What a mistake! To be honest, I was really impressed by Redondo over the two games. He was a mountain of a man. He was all left foot and seemed to be able to have time and space to do whatever he wanted with the ball. I just cannot believe how silly I was in refusing his offer. Redondo put his hand up to say, 'Okay, if that's the way you feel', and walked off. I chased Maradona because I wasn't too far away from him. I asked to swap shirts and he said, 'No, no, no', and tried to explain by grabbing his shirt at the chest and putting his hands out to the side as if to say, 'Look, buddy, I can't give you this, I have already given you one.' I found out later he gave it to Fidel Castro, the Cuban leader. So I shook Diego's hand and started looking for my mate Redondo. Too late. He'd already swapped his shirt. Gee, I'm brain dead at times.

Reflecting on my own performance, at least I can say Maradona hadn't scored. For the Aussies, Robbie Slater did another excellent job, but the real star was Robert Zabica. I thought he played absolutely brilliantly. There was so much talk about Bosnich being injured and what a loss he would be and we all felt for Zabica. He went through so much to get there.

I remembered a tournament in Indonesia when we played Kuwait and Zabby let one in — he expected the ball to bounce but it didn't; it rolled through his legs and into the back of the net. After that catastrophe, we heard that on Adelaide radio Eddie Thomson had more or less said that Zabica would never play again. To see him come back and play so well at the River Plate, and pull off so many brilliant saves, was great. I thought he was all class. I really felt happy for him.

Our strategy for the matches was, I believe, the right one. The tactic of marking Maradona so closely was the only choice. In the second leg there might have been a case to play zone defence, where the nearest player goes to Maradona, but if you give him half a yard he is going to do something with it. He had to be watched so carefully. There was plenty of criticism about supposedly playing with only one striker. However, as I've said, Graham Arnold did a great job for us. The system was the right one, given the players we had. The whole idea is to support the front man from deep. Players like Aurelio Vidmar and Robbie Slater are brilliant at making late runs forward. In modern soccer that's the best way to break down defences. The only time it didn't look so good was late in the game when players became tired, but in both the home and away legs we finished the game with two strikers, Arnold and Dave Mitchell in the home game and Arnold and Carl Veart in Buenos Aires.

Silence. That's what I remember most about the hours after the game in Buenos Aires. We were too devastated to talk. The guys who'd played the game didn't want to talk, and the rest daren't say a thing. By the time we got back to the hotel it was almost one in the morning. The game had started at 9 pm and we weren't off the park until after 11 pm. We went to the dining room. No one said a word. From the coaches' and officials' table there were a few murmurs, but nothing from the players. It wasn't until we went back up to our rooms to get changed from tracksuits to some going-out gear that people started talking.

We were all going out to drown our sorrows. We'd been invited to an exclusive nightclub in Buenos Aires, called 'Tramps'. We grabbed taxis and headed off. Milan Blagojevic and I walked in and went to the bar. I ordered a beer and Milan wanted a Southern Comfort and Coke. We went to pay, but the barman refused to take our money. He shook his head and pointed to someone away in the distance. The nightclub was pretty dark and smoky. We looked for a moment and then it all made sense. In a corner of the club, surrounded by people, we could see that little dark-haired guy. Diego Maradona was shouting the drinks. All night. Of course, one Aussie was part of Diego's inner circle. Robbie Slater. What a suck! We were really giving it to Slater. Ever since the days before the game in Sydney, when Maradona gave Slater such a big wrap in the media, Robbie was Diego's boy. We really hammered him, but he didn't care. The guy loves the attention. When we left the nightclub it was six in the morning and the sun was up. Diego picked up the tab which, we found out later, came to US$10,000.

The next night Raul Blanco was on Argentina's top TV soccer show talking about the game. They interrupted the show to hear from a viewer who'd called on the phone. It was Diego Maradona. He thanked the panellists for all the kind things they'd said about him. Argentina was going to the World Cup and Diego was getting a lot of the credit for restoring morale to the national team after the 5–0 thrashing by Colombia. Finally, he addressed Raul Blanco. He urged the Socceroos not to shed tears over the failure to reach the USA '94 World Cup finals. Diego said we had fought and lost, but our pride shone through. He thanked us for showing Argentina how to fight with dignity. Raul admitted afterwards he was close to tears. We left Argentina feeling we hadn't lost a thing.

FOOTNOTE: If at the end of this chapter you are fed up reading about the great man, Argentina's No. 10, Diego Armando, etc., imagine what I was going through for two weeks in 1993! And to cap off his controversial career, Diego went to the USA '94 World Cup finals, scored a brilliant goal in Argentina's first-up 4–0 victory over Greece, but then tested positive to stimulants and copped another 15-month ban.

THE LANCASHIRE LAD

THE WAR OF THE Roses is always a thorny issue in the Wade family. My parents, Jim and Elaine, were born and bred in Barnsley, deep in the heart of Yorkshire, in the north of England, where they went to school together. The Wade children, however, regarded Lancashire as 'home', and Lancashire was enemy territory to any Yorkshireman. My dad was an electrical engineer in the glass industry and his work took him all over the place. By the time the Wade children started to arrive, Dad was working in Altrincham, Cheshire. That's where I was born on March 20, 1962, the first of four children.

My first words, apart from 'Mum' and 'Dad', were 'kick it'. Dad bought me a small sheepskin ball with a bell and as soon as I could stand up I was learning to pass. I can't remember much about Altrincham because we didn't stay there for too long. We were a sort of nomadic family because of Dad's work and it wasn't long before the Wade entourage was getting bigger. My brother Mick was born in May, 1963, at home in Timperley, Cheshire. Phil was born in May, 1965, in Kettering, Northamptonshire, and my sister Claire arrived in November, 1966, in Corby, Northamptonshire. My mum had given birth four times in five years, with just a year off between Mick and Phil.

My birthplace, Altrincham, is just outside Manchester, and soccer people can't believe that I don't support either Manchester United or Manchester City. The reason is simple. By the time I was six we were living in St Helens, near Liverpool, in Lancashire. That's the place I think of as my home in England. That's where the Wade kids grew up, so we felt we were Lancastrians. The rivalry between Yorkshire and Lancashire is still pretty fierce today. The football fans of Leeds United in Yorkshire and Manchester United in Lancashire make sure there's an occasional re-enactment of the War of the Roses, which goes back to the 1450s, on the terraces. Some things never change in England.

So Paul Wade, raised in Lancashire with Yorkshire blood, had to tip-toe carefully across the Pennines, the famous hills that separate the two English counties. At home we were always having a go at each other, Lancashire versus Yorkshire across the moors. It was all in good fun because Dad had a dark secret. This Yorkshireman actually supported the enemy, Manchester United, and in his youth would cross the Pennines to Old Trafford to watch his heroes — Bobby Charlton, Denis Law and Nobby Stiles. He is a well-educated man and spent many years at university; in fact it was at uni that a Manchester United fan made him a convert.

After years on the move we settled down in St Helens. While we were looking for a house we lived in a little flat above a betting shop, the six of us. We'd moved so many times! I can recall the kids sleeping four in a bed, head to toe, at our Grandma's place when we were in between addresses. Our beginnings were very down-to-earth. There was no silver spoon in my mouth, but we all got on just fine. We had our blues, as everybody else does, but my mum would probably say we had more than our fair share. After six months in the flat we had a new home in Chain Lane, Blackbrook, St Helens, Lancashire. It was fortunate for my football career that we moved into that street because, although St Helens is mostly a rugby league stronghold, in my street, if you didn't play soccer (or football, as it was to me then), you didn't have any mates.

When we first arrived in Chain Lane, ours was the last house on the street. It backed onto a paddock and cows used to come right up to our back door. We thought that was brilliant, but as time went on a shopping centre was built on the paddock and a pub was built next door. The pub had a big car park so the neighbourhood really became a concrete jungle. My brothers and I would spend hours on the car park playing football and the whole of the street would join in. If we weren't at school or asleep we'd be playing football.

We used to play silly little games: one of my favourites was called 'Spot'. On the pub wall there was a valve for a fire hydrant. It stuck out from the middle of the wall and we'd try and hit it. Somebody would have a shot and if they missed it would come back off the wall and somebody else would have a go. If you hit the valve the first time you got the letter 'S' and another shot. Another direct hit got you 'p' and so on. You couldn't take two touches of the ball, so it was great for developing skills.

Bitumen was the most common playing surface because the north of England was freezing cold and wet most of the time. We always had a game on the pub car park on Sunday afternoon because the pub would close at midday and we'd have it to ourselves. We'd rush our Sunday roast and make Mum mad by running around with a full stomach. When it wasn't too damp, our backyard garden was the pitch. By the end of the football season there wouldn't be one blade of grass left because my brothers and I and our mates would be playing cup finals every day. We'd get so dirty, I don't know how my mum put up with all the washing.

Our other grass pitch was a strip of green in front of the pub. It would have been only 20 metres by 10 metres and had a wall on one side that stopped the ball going onto the road. By the end of the soccer season there wasn't any grass left on the pub's lawn, either. The car park had a small brick fence at one end with an entrance that was used as the goal. The trouble was that scoring a goal sent the ball across the road and into the front garden of a non-football house. The owner would often come out, pick up our ball and go indoors. As there was only one decent ball for the whole street that would be the end of things for the day.

From a very early age I knew I had something that could keep me going longer than other kids. I'd stay out in the backyard as long as someone would play. Dad used to put in hours with me because my brothers Mick and Phil would get tired or lose interest. At St Mary's school, down the bottom of Chain Lane, I was captain of the Grade Five team and also played in the Grade Six team. After one game the teacher in charge grabbed me by the scruff of the neck, turned me around to face the rest of the team and said, 'This is the way I want you to come off the ground every time you play for this school.' I was covered in mud from top to toe and had been involved in everything. 'This is the sort of commitment and dedication I want to see from every single one of you.' I'll never forget that. It set a standard that I wanted to reach every game. I had the natural stamina to run all day and I made sure I pushed myself hard.

From what I can remember, I was a good student as far as behaviour goes. You didn't answer back in class, because you'd get a clip around the ear there, and at home. I think that's why I'm so easy to get on with. I never got away with anything when I was young: if you were cheeky or rude to anybody you were whacked, it was as simple as that. As the Socceroo captain I've met all sorts of people, from the Prime Minister of Australia to the fan in the street, and I like to think I treat everyone with the same respect.

Like any youngster, I ended up in a few scrapes. I was in deep trouble one time because my enthusiasm for Guy Fawkes night went too far. Guy Fawkes night was always a big deal in St Helens. Chain Lane had a bonfire and we competed against other streets for the biggest fire and the loudest crackers. To raise money for the crackers the kids would go doorknocking, saying, 'Penny for the Guy?' We'd have our stuffed Guy Fawkes in a wheelbarrow. We did a roaring trade outside the pub on a Saturday night when all the drinkers were about. One year we couldn't be bothered making the stuffed Guy Fawkes so we found a big coat. My mates put me inside it and had bits of paper and straw hanging out. I sat down, slumped against the wall of the pub, and by the end of the night we had 15 quid in coins, enough for a couple of dozen boxes of fireworks. We also needed wood for the bonfire so we raided a building site.

Usually we'd gather off-cuts, but we got so carried away that night we nicked loads of quality timber. The police usually patrol on Guy Fawkes night, on the look-out for thieves like us, something we discovered when they came down Chain Lane to inspect our booty. Fortunately, we escaped with just a telling off for taking the timber and for our 'entrepreneurial' money-raising scheme, but at the age of nine, even that made me feel like a criminal.

One thing St Mary's didn't teach me was tidiness. My bedroom was always an absolute mess. I would leave cups of tea under the bed until they'd turn into mould experiments. No matter how hard Mum tried, she could never get us boys to keep our rooms clean. It's the same today. When I'm travelling with the Socceroos, my side of the hotel room is total chaos. I don't know why I do it, when over the years I've roomed with four of the most spotless footballers you'd ever meet; Andrew Zinni, Micky Petersen, Paul Trimboli and Milan Blagojevic.

St Helens, even though it was a rugby league town, was still split between Liverpool's two most famous clubs, Liverpool and Everton. Most of my mates supported Liverpool, but I followed Everton. However, I pretty soon changed allegiances, because Liverpool was winning everything. In our car park football games I'd pretend I was Alun Evans, Liverpool's centre forward. (Ironically, Alun Evans didn't last very long at Liverpool and ended up heading Down Under and playing for South Melbourne at the end of his career.) We'd dribble and commentate at the same time and there'd be crowd noises after a goal. At the age of nine I went to Anfield, Liverpool's famous home ground, for the first time. Liverpool was playing Stoke City and I wanted to see Ray Clemence (Liverpool) and Gordon Banks (Stoke City), the best goalkeepers in the world.

Football was everything to me in those days, even though it meant going through some pain. On one freezing winter's day in St Helens, my fingers seized up in the cold. My mum was watching the game and told me to do up my bootlaces and pull up my socks. As I said, I'm not the tidy sort. I tried to fix my bootlaces and socks, but couldn't. A few minutes later Mum shouted again and I ended up in tears. The coach took me off and when Mum realised my fingers were blue with the cold I was rushed away to thaw out. I don't know which was worse: the painful fingers or getting dragged off before the game was over!

My football career was always top priority. At age 11 I was picked to play for St Helens Town, a representative team, but it didn't mean much to me — I didn't really care who I was playing for in those days, as long as I was playing. The game was all that mattered, not honours. Then out of the blue, Dad arrived home from work one night and asked us kids, 'Who'd like to go to Australia?' In fact, he'd already made up his mind we were going. My first question was, 'Do they play football in Australia?' Like every other 11-year-old footballer, I had dreams. I wanted to play for Liverpool. I wanted to be a midfielder supplying the superb forwards Steve Heighway, Kevin Keegan and John

Toshack with perfect passes. I was a bit concerned about whether I'd find a football team in Australia. Maybe there weren't any. The St Helens Town coach had told Mum that 'England was losing a promising footballer'.

Now my dad wanted to take me to a place I'd never heard of. I looked at a map of Australia and located Melbourne, where Dad had a job waiting. An Aussie visitor to St Helens, whose accent was really weird, told us all about Frankston, where he'd lived. He made it sound like a glorious tropical beach, more like Florida than the Peninsula. I'd been doing a bit of swimming at school and decided when I arrived in Melbourne I'd swim over to the little island I could see at the bottom of the map. The island was Tasmania! Just shows you how little minds work!

When it did eventually come time to leave, the emotion among our family was heart-wrenching. Mum absolutely cracked up. She was bawling her eyes out. My grandmas and aunts and uncles were crying as well. To the kids it was like going on a holiday. We didn't realise how permanent it was. We took a bus to London and flew to Tehran, Bahrain, Singapore then Melbourne. It took 36 hours, I couldn't sleep and the food was awful. I was thinking, 'This Australia had better be good.'

In October, 1973, the Wade family moved into a flat in David Street, Dandenong, in Melbourne's southeast. Glass had brought us to Australia. Dad had a job with Pilkingtons ACI Glassworks in South Dandenong. The contract was for two years. If he stayed for two years he didn't have to pay back the airfares. It had cost us 10 pounds to travel halfway around the world and we were no different from the hundreds of thousands of people who've migrated to Australia over the years.

In October the school year was almost over, so I didn't start until the next year. I had one helluva summer holiday. My first surprise was the rain. I couldn't believe how warm the rain was. I was used to the freezing cold rain of England. It was raining and I was warm! I thought, 'This is brilliant. I can't believe this.' So much for my concerns about football. I wasn't playing and didn't miss it at all. There were so many new and exciting things: the weather, the mountains, the beach. Soccer, as the Aussies call it, took a back seat. I didn't care and my soccer ball stayed packed away. It was a long, lazy summer; no school and no soccer.

Eventually, though, my brothers and I got a bit toey, so out came the soccer ball. Dad located the Dandenong City juniors and got us motivated; if ever I wanted to kick a ball and there was nobody else around, he would find the time. Once I started training, my love of the game was back. After one session the coach wanted me in his team, but the registration took a little while to sort out. I went to watch my new team and came away disappointed. 'They don't know how to play', I told Mum afterwards. 'You'd better show 'em, then', was her reply. Our coach was a Mr Jennings, the father of one of the boys in the team. Training was a couple of shirts down one end and another couple at the other and away we'd go in a game. In England I had been taught how to balance in defence and had been given some real coaching, but at Dandenong there were players who'd never kicked a ball before. But pretty soon it didn't matter that I was more advanced than my new team mates. I was enjoying myself, even though we were getting hammered quite often. The Dandenong City under-11s were underdogs and something in me made the challenge enjoyable. I reckon that's where my 'underdog' spirit was born.

I started my career in Australian soccer as a left winger. I was naturally right-footed, but at nine years of age a coach in St Helens had warned me, 'Wadey, if you're ever going to make a professional footballer, you have to be able to kick with both feet.' For two months I did nothing but kick with my left foot and that's how I learned. Eventually it became as strong as my natural right foot. Mick, Phil and I were in different age groups, so on Sundays Mum and Dad would watch three separate games. My sister Claire played netball, so the whole weekend was taken up watching us play sport.

Dad was never directly involved in coaching our teams, but every now and again he would shout something like, 'Move yourself, Wadey!' When you hear your father's voice it stands out among all the others. Dad was never satisfied with the way any football team played. 'You were all rubbish, today', was often his summary. I would be thinking, 'We did alright, because we won.' That wasn't good enough for Dad. Manchester United could beat Liverpool and Dad would say, 'What a load of rubbish.' I would wonder what football was like in his day. Was it that much better or was he just hard to please? I was forever trying to fulfil his expectations and it seemed that maybe I was never going to do it. There wasn't any praise, but this didn't really worry me, because I knew when I had done well and I could tell when Dad agreed. Then he would say nothing. Silence was golden. It meant Dad hadn't seen anything to complain about.

His interest kept me going through all those junior years. There were distractions that could have taken me away from soccer, but if your mum and dad are so interested it's all worthwhile. I wasn't playing for any State teams or winning heaps of medals. I might have made a regional representative team once, but in the end I was a keen soccer player because Mum and Dad made it part of the family's life. School was also back on the agenda. I started in Grade Five at St Mary's, Dandenong, a school with the same name as the one I'd left in St Helens. Nothing else was the same and I couldn't settle down. I had to re-do Grade Six before I finally made it to St John's Regional College in Dandenong.

I still wasn't at all sure about education, and I recall a mathematics exam that scared the life out of me. Mum told me to do something about it, like study. I swotted away and ended up getting 89 per cent. It was a breakthrough and I realised I could be a decent student as well as a decent soccer player, if I put my mind to it.

I'd left Dandenong City by this time, after two years, and joined Doveton, where one of my school mates played. Doveton under-14s were full of stars. The coach was Ian Sweeney, a player from the Doveton senior team. He was massive, about 6 feet 3 inches. He could kick the ball miles. I was playing sweeper and didn't have a problem. My natural ability and stamina were good enough, but halfway through the season I asked to go back in the midfield. We were a good team and always attacking and I was sick of standing at the back watching everyone else. I wanted to run.

My education was now steaming along. Until Form 2 I was an A+ student, but then St John's Regional College was made co-educational in Form 3. Girls! It was too much. Your body is going through a transformation anyway and they throw girls into the equation. I was on an emotional rollercoaster, and that tipped it over the edge. I couldn't do maths or English or anything. At the age of 15 I started getting pimples, and not just ordinary pimples. I had pimples on my pimples! They were bad. My face was covered, and to have girls in my life as well, all of a sudden, was traumatic. I went from A+ to C+ and D overnight. My life was absolute chaos. In a science class one day my mates were saying, 'Jane likes you, she really does', and I said something stupid to her, like 'Go away, you're ugly'. She wasn't ugly at all, but I just couldn't handle the pressure.

In the middle of this chaos, along came Cindy. We got on really well, but I think she really fancied this surfie guy in the class, Shane, who was huge, had blonde hair that went right down his back, and looked very cool. On the weekends, while he was surfing, which was cool, I was playing soccer, which was very uncool. On Sunday nights I'd go to dancing lessons at St Gerrard's in North Dandenong because my mate was going. It was fun and my regular dancing partner was Edith. She was a pretty blonde and the very uncool Paul Wade, after plenty of prompting from her friends, built up the courage to ask, 'Do you want to go with me?' She said, 'Okay.' At 16 I had my first date. There was never any kissing or anything. We would dance together at St Gerrard's and I wouldn't see her for the rest of the week.

But Cindy was always there in the classroom and started to show more interest in me, I thought. I decided to drop Edith. 'I don't want to go with you any more, you're dropped', I said, just like that, cool, cold and callous. Cindy was the girl for me, and we both went on the school camping trip soon after that. I was waiting for the right time to ask her to 'go with me'. I was walking down one of the beaches with a couple of mates and it was dark. I had a torch and we came across a couple in a sleeping bag, except they weren't there to sleep. I flashed the torchlight and, to my horror, it was Cindy and the blonde surfie!

I was absolutely devastated. I had dropped Edith for this Cindy and she was in the sack with another guy.

I had misunderstood all the vibes from Cindy. This girl business was too complicated. I couldn't read signals from women, so I decided, 'That's it. I've had enough.' I continued to be embarrassed by my pimples and I used to wash my face three or four times a day, to no avail. I would do stupid things like lie in the back garden in the sun to dry my skin up. I'd get blisters from the sunburn to kill the pimples. It used to work for about three days then the moisture would come back into my skin and, bang, all the pimples would appear again. I was continually standing in front of mirrors at home squeezing them. It scarred me. So did my first experiences with women, so I gave up. I didn't have another girlfriend until I was 20 years old, when I met my wife, Valerie. I was happy just to play football from then on because I had tried women, and I just couldn't handle them. I devoted even more time and energy to soccer and other sports. I played a game for the St John's College Aussie Rules team and even won an award for being the best team man.

By Form 5 the thought of doing the dreaded Higher School Certificate (HSC) was scaring the living daylights out of me. All the stories were that you never saw daylight for a year, that you spent all your time studying for exams. That was a serious threat to my soccer career. I had been talent-spotted by Prahran Slavia, a Victorian State League club. In 1978 the Slavia reserve coach, Harry Chalkitis, invited four of us from Doveton to join their under-16 team. We were called Slavia Colts. Midway through the season there was a big kerfuffle in the club and most of the senior players went on strike over money. To make up the numbers, the four of us played senior soccer in the State League reserves on a Sunday after playing for the under-16 Colts on a Saturday. It was then that I discovered Slavia was full of Scousers, guys from Liverpool. There were lots of English players and quite a few Irish and Scots. I felt right at home. There was no way I could study, I just didn't have the time or the interest. I just had to leave school.

I wanted to be a full-time footballer, but that was just a dream. If I had to work, architecture was attractive, but at a careers day I discovered architecture meant the HSC plus years at university. No way. I wanted to do something with art, but I didn't want to study. That didn't leave too many options. Mum found a newspaper ad for a job at A.E. Smith Engineering as a trainee draftsman and at the job interview I showed work from my Form 5 graphics class. The guy loved my work. I was always good at perspective drawings and he was so impressed he didn't bother looking at my Form 5 report card, which was littered with Cs and Ds. In graphics I was a B student so I guess I'd found my calling in life. Now I was a trainee mechanical draftsman designing air conditioning systems for buildings.

I couldn't avoid night school, but I was torn between classes and soccer training on a Thursday night. I'd miss most of my classes in the soccer season and kiss goodbye to the 10 per cent of marks awarded for attendance. I had no life outside work, soccer and home. My weekly wage was paid by cheque and I would put it in my wallet and weeks later go to the bank to deposit eight or nine cheques. I was spending hardly any money because I wasn't doing anything. My day began with a 6 am alarm and an early morning train ride of 45 minutes from Dandenong to the A.E. Smith office in Burnley, an inner-city suburb of Melbourne. After work I'd get a lift to Orrong Road to train with Prahran Slavia. After training I'd walk to Toorak station and travel all the way back on the train to Dandenong and phone Mum, who'd pick me up at about 10 pm. It was a long day, but that was my life.

After a season in the under-16s and the reserves, Harry Chalkitis was made senior coach and promoted me to the firsts in 1979. I was 17 years old and the Victorian State League felt like the big time. We had Air India as a sponsor and lots of seasoned pros. Slavia operated a bit of a meat market, bringing out players from Britain, most of them Scousers, for $2000 (airfares and fees) and selling the best to other Australian clubs for $20,000. My time at Slavia reinforced my Pommy accent because almost the entire playing staff was English.

That wasn't the only thing I picked up from the Scousers: I was tending to think like a Pom and put on the accent to be part of the gang. All they ever did was play, drink and joke. They were all big drinkers. They loved a bevvy. Jamie Paton loved a drink, but on the weekend he would still go on the park and look as sharp as a razor. He was a Scot and Slavia made a tidy profit when he was sold to Heidelberg United for $20,000. (John Yzendoorn went the same way — to Heidelberg for big money.) I was caught up in the atmosphere. I thought there was no reason why you couldn't have a drink and still make it as a footballer. I was having a few beers and thought there was no harm in it.

Looking back, it was a dangerous time. My brothers Mick and Phil were playing soccer until they were about 15 or 16 and I honestly believe they were better footballers than me. Phil had much more determination than I ever did and Mick had all the skill in the world, but didn't really have a big heart when it came to getting crunched. They didn't play senior soccer, mainly because they discovered girls and alcohol. I'd had my brush with women and had given them up, but alcohol was waiting to trap me.

At 17 I made my State League debut as a left back. I was playing against some top players, like Tommy Cumming of Essendon Lions, who went on to play for the Socceroos. Slavia had tons of quality players, like Jimmy Williams, Cliff Whiteside, Steve Aldridge and Paul Cook. Cliff was an Irishman and I used to go to his flat to kill a few hours before training started. His wife, Margaret, was a gorgeous brunette, who wasn't a bad cook, either. Being an impressionable teenager, I fell for her home-made shortbread biscuits and her good looks. To this day we've remained good friends and we share a laugh about my crush on her. We had plenty of good guys and plenty of headbangers at Slavia, but that was half the fun. I learnt so much, and I felt I was growing up really quickly.

One hard lesson came from my first serious injury. In 1979 I got a kick in the face and my nose was broken. At that time Mum had been nagging me about getting some ambulance cover, but I hadn't got around to it. As I was getting carted off all I could say was, 'Whatever you do, don't call an ambulance.' I was still an amateur player and only earning trainee wages at A.E. Smith, so I couldn't afford an expensive ambulance ride.

At the end of the season, in October 1979, Harry Chalkitis, the coach who gave me my big break, was sacked and replaced by Tony Vrzina for the 1980 season, but Slavia was on the slide. All the best players had been sold and there were new restrictions on bringing players from overseas, so Slavia was in trouble. I played the season in midfield and at 18 years of age was able to handle the physical side of senior soccer.

I must have done okay because at the end of the 1980 season I was offered my first contract. Getting paid to play football? Now that's my kind of job. An official from Croydon City, another Victorian State League club, said he'd heard that Slavia was going to fold and that it was a good time for me to move.

HAVING NEVER RECEIVED ONE cent to play football, my negotiations with Croydon City for the 1981 season were a big test. The money was set at $80 per game, but I was more concerned about controlling my destiny. I'd seen at Slavia how clubs could treat players as if they were only objects to be bought and sold, and I wanted to avoid that. I made sure it was only a one-year agreement with no option for the club to renew the contract. I also negotiated a maximum transfer fee of $1000 so that if I wanted to leave Croydon after one season there was a reasonable price on my head.

The best thing that happened to me at Croydon City was playing with Jimmy Rooney. He'd come from Scotland, played 100 times for the Socceroos and was in the Rale Rasic-coached team that made the World Cup finals in 1974. His career was winding down at Croydon, but he was so professional. After training he'd go into the social club, say hello, have one beer and then disappear. What! I was used to players at Slavia drinking for hours after training or games. Jimmy could see I needed to be set straight. He pulled me aside and said, 'Wadey, whatever you do, don't let the drink rule your career, otherwise it will be a very short one.' That was it for me. It wasn't as though I was a big boozer, but that warning was enough for me to switch to lemonade. I had a lot of respect for Jimmy and what he had achieved. Of all the players I'd come across until then he had the biggest influence on my career.

Ian Dobson was another professional, who'd joined Croydon City after playing more than 150 games with Hull City in England. He'd turn up on match day in a suit and a tie and I was amazed. We made fun of the guy. 'This is a game of football, Dobbo, we're not going to a wedding!' Dobbo was always serious on match day and would say, 'The way you think about yourself and the way you present yourself sets the attitude you take out onto the park.' The message sank in, and within a few months, most of the Croydon City players were turning up in suits and ties.

Dobbo also always paid attention to detail. He was such a small centre half and even though he was brilliant in the air he didn't want anybody, particularly opposition centre forwards, to know just how short he was. In our team photo Dobbo was standing on tip-toes to make himself look bigger. I always used to laugh at him, but at the same time I learnt heaps. Moving to Croydon City meant a change in travel plans. I was old enough for a driver's licence, but I hadn't got around to having a lesson or buying a car. I was still on the early morning train to Burnley and after work another train to Croydon, about 50 minutes away. Then I was stuck, because there was no direct public transport from Croydon to Dandenong. A Scouser came to the rescue. Steve McCoombe, a big centre half who had played for Slavia before joining Croydon, would drop me home. We had a super playing staff at Croydon, with Gus McLeod, Steve Irvine, Peter Loughnane, Ian Loughnane, Mickey Edwards in goal and the cagey Jimmy Rooney.

Jimmy had been there, done that. All he'd do at training was nutmeg people, just knock the ball between players' legs and nip past them to collect it. Getting nutmegged is a player's nightmare, but it didn't matter how hard we tried to prevent it, Jimmy Rooney would get us. I played next to him in midfield and he'd execute quite a few nutmegs in a game. I did all the legwork getting up and down the park while Jimmy would calmly play the ball around as if it was a social game. He made it look easy. Next to him I was a raw, young kid. My hair was down to my shoulders, my face was covered in pimples — I wasn't a pretty sight. I didn't bother buying the lastest fashions. At that time I didn't care. I didn't have a girlfriend, I didn't go out to nightclubs so I didn't have to look good. I was a footballer and that was all that mattered.

However, I started to get to know Valerie Pegg, a gorgeous blonde whose family was involved at Croydon. In my first year I won the best and fairest award. At the presentation dinner, everyone was having a good time. My family had come and my sister was on my left and my mum was on my right. Valerie leaned over, kissed me on the cheek and said, 'Congratulations!' My heart missed a beat. It was the only kiss I'd ever been given by a girl. True. I tried to say something in response, but all I could manage was, 'Thanks.' She left and I was blushing. Her dad, Frank, was the team manager and from then on he'd often say, 'Wadey, Val says hello.' You beauty! I would tell Frank to say hello back. This went on for weeks, but I didn't suss out that maybe this girl liked me and that I should give her a call.

Val finally took matters into her own hands. At a pre-season function she casually walked over and said, 'Well, when are you taking me out, then?' I looked over my shoulder and looked down the line of other players. There were some good-looking guys in our team. I thought, 'She's not talking to me. Surely not.' I said, 'Sorry?', because I couldn't believe my ears. 'When are you going to take me out, then?' She said it again! I panicked and said, 'Arrh, umm … do you play squash?' As soon as I said it I thought, 'What an idiot. I'm a complete nightmare.' Valerie was very cool and polite. She was 17, I was 20, but I felt about 12. 'No, I don't play, but I'll have a go if you want to.' My heart was racing again. I wanted to go out with her, but I was scared that I'd just embarrass myself.

We organised a date to go to the local squash centre near Croydon station, then real panic started. I'd bought a beat-up Morris Minor that could only do 30 kilometres per hour (22 miles per hour) at full speed. I thought, 'I can't pick her up in this heap.' I asked my dad for a loan of his Kingswood. It was an automatic, so I wouldn't have to worry about crunching the gears. I was getting so nervous that I rang my mate Des Shannon, who'd played soccer with me at Croydon, Slavia and Doveton. He was my natural back up. I said, 'Des I've got to take this girl out to play squash, will you come with me?' He made a very good point. 'You can only get two on a squash court, Wadey.' I said, 'Bring your brother and you can play him while I play Valerie.' Like a true mate, he agreed. I picked up Val. She wasn't impressed about going out with a gang of blokes. I still had no idea how to handle women. We played the game and I dropped her home. The next time I invited her to play squash I promised it would be just the two of us.

So our first couple of dates were games of squash. We might have kept on playing squash forever, but Val said, 'I think I've played enough games of squash. Why don't we go out for a drink?' It was panic stations again. I borrowed the Kingswood. I had to go on my own, because she'd warned me about bringing my mates along. I rolled up to her house and I knocked on the door. I'll never forget the sight as long as I live. Valerie was standing there in a black, sequined dress, cut low, with her blonde hair absolutely shining. I froze. Her dad was standing just behind her so I kept looking into her eyes, even though I had an urge to check out the rest. I didn't know what to say or do, but somehow I managed not to make a complete ass of myself. We were off to the Matthew Flinders Hotel in Warrigal Road, Chadstone. I'd told Des to meet me there! I needed the moral support. The first drink I bought for Valerie was a Black Russian, because I'd seen a girl at a work function order a Black Russian and it sounded like a good drink. She thoroughly enjoyed the drink and I had a couple of beers to settle down.

That was it, for me and Valerie Pegg. I'd finally stopped being a nervous git. I was cool, and our relationship just went on from there. Val had to knock me into shape, though. She took me shopping and bought me a whole new range of clothes. Until then, I was the worst-dressed man in town. She educated me and took me under her wing. It was just as well she did, too.

I HAD THREE VERY happy years with Croydon City, but it was time for a bigger challenge. Jimmy Rooney was appointed coach of Green Gully Ajax, which had been accepted into the new Southern Division of the National Soccer League and wanted to sign me. Jimmy said, 'It's time to break into the national league.' It's everyone's ambition to play in the national league and how could I refuse an invitation from someone like Jimmy Rooney? The people at Croydon were urging me to go. Some were saying, 'You'll play for Australia one day, but not if you stay here.' My transfer was going to be straightforward, I thought, because I had the $1000 maximum clause and Green Gully was happy to pay. It wasn't to be. Jimmy rang and said, 'Croydon has pulled a bit of a swifty on you.' I was stunned. 'They can't stuff me around because I've got it all in writing.' The trouble was the wording. It read, 'The player (Paul Wade) shall be available for transfer for the duration of this contract upon payment of a fee not more than $1000.' Croydon claimed the maximum only applied during the contract, not at the expiry. I'd been stitched up. Eventually Green Gully paid $4000 for me and I swore that I would never trust a club again.

I was coming up to my twenty-second birthday and from day one, Green Gully was fun. It was one of those seasons when, win, lose or draw, there was always something to laugh about. For instance, when we played Heidelberg United at Green Gully Reserve, Charlie Yankos, who was a Socceroo defender, was lining up a free kick about 30 metres from goal. Charlie had the hardest shot I've ever seen and, with just my luck, his free kick was coming at me at a million miles an hour. I had to try to head it away and it was like being hit by a semi-trailer. I was staggering around in a daze and my team mates couldn't help laughing. Later in the game an attempted clearance spun off my boot and flew past our goalkeeper Lou Denys for an own goal. To this day I blame Charlie Yankos for my misfortune, as I was still in a daze. The match finished 1–1 after Ken Smart had scored for us.

In every game for the next three or four weeks I kept getting in the way of thunderballs. At Preston one of our players blasted the ball out of the goalmouth and I tried to get out of the way, but it hit me in the back and went over Lou Denys and into the back of the net for another own goal. Once again it cost us points because the game finished 1–1. I had cancelled out Les Carter's goal and this time the guys weren't laughing. My mate from Croydon, Ian Dobson, had joined Preston and he gave me heaps. Dobbo would always ring on a Monday and ask, 'Any OGs this week, Wadey?'

Most of the time I was very happy with my form; in fact, I was having an absolute blinder of a year. I caught the attention of the Socceroo coach, Frank Arok, thanks to some very flattering media coverage. Two days before we were to play Melbourne Croatia there was a newspaper story saying Arok was coming to watch me. That made me so nervous. The match was at home at Green Gully Reserve and I kept imagining Frank with a big notepad, writing down everything I did. As it turned out, Frank wouldn't have had to make many notes. Croatia was buzzing and it was one of those days when I couldn't get near the ball. No matter how much I chased it, ran it down and tried to get close, I hardly got a touch. Croatia beat us 1–0 with a goal from Joe Biskic. I didn't see Frank Arok, but the Green Gully officials told me he left without saying a word. I heard no more until the end of the season, in October. Frank included me in a Socceroo trial match against Tasmania in Hobart. An overseas tour was coming up for the Socceroos, but my name wasn't on the list. That was the first time I'd ever thought about playing for the national team.

I reckon Green Gully got their money's worth that season. I won the *Soccer Action* NSL player of the year award, with a tiny bit of help from Ken Kontra, a soccer coach who was also a journalist. Everyone at Green Gully called him 'Wadey's uncle'. Ken kept giving me votes in the award. He had coached Slavia, but I don't know if that's why he took such a shine to me. He just liked the way I played and I suspect I got votes when sometimes I didn't really deserve them. Going into the final round of the season, John Bradley of APIA Leichhardt was five votes ahead of me. The maximum votes per game was six, so I had to be judged the man of the match and hope Bradley didn't get any votes. We beat Footscray JUST 3–1 and I came off the ground thinking I'd done reasonably well. Ken Smart of Green Gully was the best on the ground in my opinion and deserved the six votes. In Sydney, APIA Leichardt was thumped 4–1 by Marconi, which helped my cause. Even so, I was sure I'd finish second, but on the Wednesday I picked up *Soccer Action* and there was a big picture of me on the front page. I was the Boral Bricks Player of the Year, thanks to Ken Kontra and the six votes he awarded me in the final game. Bradley didn't get one vote. The honour was great, but mostly it was a year of learning.

Jimmy Rooney taught me so many little things about being a footballer. I'd now allow myself only a few light beers — with Jimmy there to keep an eye on things I wasn't going to let alcohol ruin my career. One night at training I was walking from my car to the dressingroom in bare feet across the gravel car park. Jimmy slapped me around the back of the head. 'Don't you ever, ever let me see you walking around with no shoes on again!' He was angry. 'Your feet are the tools of your trade, you lose them or injure them and that's it. You've got to look after yourself.' Jimmy rammed home the message about becoming more professional, treating soccer like your job rather than just a sport.

It was a brilliant year for me. Even though Green Gully was always in the bottom half of the table (we finished ninth in the 12-team league), we had a great time anyway. Les Carter and Bobby McGuinness are two mates I still keep in touch with. All the wives and girlfriends got on well together and that made for a terrific social life. After the game the players would go back to the club rooms and ask the girls, 'What did you think of the game today?' All we'd get was hiccups and giggles. They wouldn't have a clue. They'd just sit in the VIP box and drink complimentary wine! I was driving from Hallam to Green Gully three times a week for training, a round trip of about two hours, but I was having such a good time on the park and the girls were having fun off the park, so I didn't mind the miles.

After such a good season my biggest fear was complacency. In my first year in the National Soccer League I had won a player of the year award. I needed a new challenge and maybe Green Gully was too sociable. It was a tough decision to leave that comfort zone, but since Frank Arok had shown a bit of interest, it seemed to be a decision I had to make.

When I told Green Gully I wanted to leave they didn't stitch me up the way Croydon had. They paid a $4000 transfer fee and got $8000 when they sold me (to Brunswick Juventus), as stipulated in my contract. I have great memories from Green Gully. Because Green Gully weren't a British club the pressure was also off my Pommy accent, so there were no more accent games. I didn't have the same need to fit in; I could relax and start talking like my brothers, who sounded like Aussies.

Brunswick Juventus had joined the NSL at the same time as Green Gully, but had more money and had assembled a good squad. Goalkeeper Yakka Banovic had come back to Melbourne from Derby County in England and Richard Miranda was a very tough and mobile midfielder from South Africa. We had a hard core of Scottish-born players. John Dowie was a tough nut who'd been a pro with Fulham in Britain, Peter Lewis was a hard-as-nails full-back, Brian Brown was a solid centre half with professional experience, Robbie Cullen was a very skilful wide midfielder, Joe Sweeney was a typical British centre forward and Eddie Campbell was a skilful left back who always used to fake a pass off the left foot. Nobody picked it and he used it dozens of times every game and dozens of players bought the dummy.

I was one of the younger players, along with Andrew Zinni and Fab Incantalupo, who'd come through the Juventus junior ranks. A few games into the season the club bought Micky Petersen from Heidelberg. That would turn out to be one of the most significant events of my career. Micky P, as he is affectionately known, was a huge talent, one of the most skilful players ever to come out of the Victorian junior ranks. He had a great first touch, but it was his passing that made him stand out. He was the classic playmaker, able to change the game with a single pass. I didn't think it at the time, but Micky Petersen and I were made for each other. Over the next 10 years we were midfield partners and best mates, both at club and international level. Micky provided the skill and I supplied the hard graft, and that midfield combination helped two clubs win national titles.

John Margaritis, the coach, was one of the great characters of Australian soccer. I'm told he was a top player when he came to Australia from Greece in the 1960s, but I knew him as a coach who worked in mysterious ways. He would scribble on the lockers with a piece of chalk, because we didn't have a blackboard, and expect us to make sense of it all. He was very superstitious and if we had a string of good results he would pick something, such as an overcoat he was wearing, or a pair of boots, and treat them as if they were a good luck charm. It meant he would wear the same coat or make sure the player wore the same boots, until the end of the winning streak. Then it would start all over again. He'd have us in stitches because of his broken English. One of the classics was his pronunciation of Jimmy Cant, the Sydney City midfielder. When John said 'Cant', it sounded like the swearword that has a similar spelling. We'd be cracking up laughing in the middle of John's very serious team talk, when he would get to 'when dis C...t gets da ball' or 'who will be chasing C...t in the midfield'. It was the first time I've seen players pay attention in team talks — but for all the wrong reasons!

We trained at the Gillon Oval in Brunswick and shared the facilities with the Brunswick VFA footy team. They had signed big Mark Jackson, of the Eveready battery commercials, and in the middle of John's team talks Jacko would sometimes stomp through and say, 'Evening gentlemen', with as much arrogance as Maradona.

After a shaky start to the season, we finished second in the 1985 Southern Division behind South Melbourne, who were the reigning national champions. We played South in the Major Semi Final at Olympic Park. It was 0–0, with not long to go, and Joe Sweeney passed the ball square to me, about 35 metres from goal. I was on the right and as I received the ball Bobby Russell was closing me down. I touched the ball with my right foot, inside Bobby, and with my left foot just whacked it as hard as I could. It shot off like a guided missile right into the top left-hand corner of the goal, and goalkeeper Peter Laumets was left standing there, with no chance of getting it. It was one of the best goals I've ever scored and I love slowing down the video to watch it sail in. There is definitely no better feeling in soccer than scoring goals, especially if they're spectacular.

The celebrations were almost as good, though, with eight players piled on top of me. My goal gave us a 1–0 win and a place in the Southern Division Grand Final. Preston Makedonia were our Grand Final opponents after they beat South Melbourne in the preliminary final. They slaughtered us in the first half. It was one of those days when nothing was going to go right and even today when we watch the video we can't believe how we weren't three or four goals behind at half-time. Instead, it was only 1–0 to Preston, thanks to a Steve Smith goal after 31 minutes. The best thing about that Juventus team was the attitude of hanging tough. We went in at half-time and sorted a few things out and were a lot better in the second half, but couldn't find an equaliser. With ten minutes to go we were still losing, so John Margaritis started throwing the team around. Only he knows why he did it. Micky Petersen was having a blinder as the sweeper and had cleared two shots off the goal line. He was thrown back into midfield. I went from midfield to centre forward and Joe Sweeney went the other way to full-back.

All I could think of was missing out on our bonus. Tony Schiavello, the club president, had promised the team a trip to Italy if we won the national title, but it looked as though we were going to bomb out in the Southern Division. We were finishing all over the top of Preston, who could only defend desperately and try to hang on. We won a corner and it fell to Micky Petersen, who accidentally handled the ball before smashing it into the net. We all looked at the referee, thinking, 'He must have seen that', but instead he pointed to the centre spot and awarded the goal. It was 1–1 in the 84th minute, six minutes from full-time. The equaliser was a huge blow to Preston, but gave us new legs.

A minute later Rino Minichiello set off with the ball, dribbling past several tackles, and found Robbie Cullen out wide. My legs were really tired from the heavy ground, but I kept running towards the penalty area. There was a buzz of excitement from the crowd, as though they could sense something was about to happen. Cullen whipped in his cross, but the ball was cut out by a Preston defender and bobbled into the clear. Sean Lane mistimed his clearance and it fell right in front of me. I was dead in front, on the edge of the six-yard box. Goalkeeper Phil Trianedes was caught out of position because he'd gone to the near post, anticipating Cullen's cross. All I had to do was smash the ball as hard as I could. George McMillan was on the line, trying to defend the open goal, so I took a mental picture of the ball, closed my eyes and swung as hard as I could. The doubt was whether the ball would hit McMillan, or Trianedes, who was trying to get back across the goal. In the mud it seemed like a big effort, but I made solid contact and opened my eyes to see the ball coming down off the top of the net, safely over the line.

I was off to celebrate. I took off to the far side of the ground at Olympic Park and then realised that all the Brunswick supporters were in the main stand. As I was running past the goalpost I stuck out my hand to swing back the other way and I nearly ripped my arm out of its socket. I did my usual celebration jig, arms pumping up and down in time with my legs. It's amazing how you can find energy so quickly. I then collapsed on the ground and everybody piled on top of me again. On successive Sundays I'd scored the most unbelievable goal of my career to beat South Melbourne, the best team in the country at that stage, and scored the winner in a Grand Final. It was the best week of my life! The whistle went with the score 2–1 in our favour and within minutes there was champagne everywhere. You couldn't move in the dressingrooms, it was bedlam.

We didn't party too hard because we had to play Sydney City, the Northern Division winners, in the national Grand Final. They had some big names — John Kosmina, Joe Watson and Steve O'Connor all played for the Socceroos, Frank Farina was the best young striker in the country and Tony Pezzano was rated as one of the best goalkeepers around. They also had the unforgettable Jimmy Cant. To be honest, I was not very confident when we went to Sydney for the first leg of the Grand Final at St George Stadium. Neither Sydney City nor Brunswick had a big supporter base and, in fact, there were probably more of our fans there that night. Sydney City had their usual couple of hundred diehards, but the Juventus fans made all the noise after Fab Incantalupo smashed the ball from 25 metres and it bobbled right in front of Pezzano and bounced into the back of the net. We hung on to win 1–0.

Eddie Thomson, the Sydney City coach (and Socceroo assistant coach at that time), told the media that no matter how hard he tried to motivate his players, they did not respond. Sydney City was probably overconfident because the final was a real David and Goliath battle. Sydney City had won three national championships and were foundation members of the NSL in 1977. Brunswick had only been in the NSL for two seasons.

The return game the following Sunday was back at Olympic Park in Melbourne. We only needed to draw to become the national champions and get our trip to Italy. John Margaritis was very superstitious and because we'd stayed in a hotel in Sydney before the first leg we had to do the same in Melbourne. So on the eve of the game we spent the night in a hotel. Most of us hadn't had a shave during the finals because when we won our first game five or six of the players hadn't shaved and John believed our winning run would disappear with our whiskers. Who says soccer is a simple game? It was the biggest game of my career to that point, and I tossed and turned all night. In the middle of the night I went for a walk to try to relax, but no matter what I did I couldn't get to sleep. I must have dozed off just before sunrise and woke up feeling terrible. I had about an hour's sleep.

My Grand Final was an absolute shocker. I didn't get a touch. I felt exhausted and the entire day was an anticlimax. Incantalupo scored again and we won comfortably, 2–0 on aggregate, but I could hardly get excited. I'll never forget the feeling of disappointment; it spoiled, a bit, a successful season. Nerves had made me a different person and it was such a bad experience I vowed never to let it happen again.

In any case, Tony Schiavello kept his word about the trip to Italy. Team manager Joe Caruso made sure we had everything we required as a football team and Schiavello made sure that Caruso was provided with the money to make it happen. AS Roma, the Italian champions in 1983 and European Cup finalists in '84, agreed to play us, but our best eleven couldn't travel: Joe Sweeney, Peter Lewis and Yakka Banovic had work commitments. All of a sudden our champion team was being pulled apart. We were worried about embarrassing the club and Australian soccer.

We played at a stadium in Rome that could hold 40,000 fans and all Roma's stars were playing. I think they got fed up after scoring their seventh goal. That's right, 7–0. One of their goals was a shot that hit our goalkeeper Sean Keogh smack on the chest and put him and the ball in the back of the net. I managed to score, but the goal was disallowed for offside.

We were totally outclassed. And to cap off a miserable day, I hurt my ankle, the first of many ankle injuries that would plague me during my career. Roma's full-back dived into a tackle and connected with my standing leg. Oh boy, my ankle went over and I had to come off straight away. I couldn't walk on it for days. I was going to see my grandparents in England and arrived on crutches.

Even so, 1985 was another great year. In September Frank Arok had picked me for the Australia 'B' team. I had a national championship medal, I'd scored the winning goal in a Grand Final and had been on a tour to Italy. My soccer career was one high after another.

South Melbourne and Brunswick Juventus swapped coaches for the 1986 season. John Margaritis had won the '85 championship for Brunswick, but negotiations over a new contract broke down and Brunswick showed him the door. Money seemed to be the problem. Margaritis was a real favourite at Middle Park so he headed back to South Melbourne. Len McKendry had won the Southern Division minor premiership, the Grand Final and the national championship with South Melbourne in 1984 and had taken the club to the top of the Southern Division in '85, before being destroyed by a Paul Wade goal in the finals. Lennie was out of the South Melbourne job and came to Brunswick.

Like Jimmy Rooney, Len McKendry would have a major influence on my career. I know that Jimmy and Len don't get on well, but in Paul Wade they have something in common. Having said that, it makes me laugh to think how different they are. For example, Jimmy Rooney was a gifted ball-player and always said that good balanced players never needed to wear long studs in their boots. No matter what the conditions were, Jimmy recommended rubber-studded boots because they were more flexible and allowed a better feel for the ball. Len was at the other end of the debate. He had a rule. 'If I ever see anybody, especially guys in the back line, wearing rubber-studded boots, they will be kicked out of my team.' Len said all it needed was for one player to slip and it could cost a goal.

Their attitudes were poles apart. Jimmy Rooney was all for entertaining the crowd. He regarded players as entertainers, employed by a soccer club to entertain supporters who paid good money to watch. Jimmy believed he had a responsibility to entertain for 90 minutes and that meant individuals had to show off their skills in dribbling, shooting, passing or whatever. Jimmy Rooney didn't believe in playing it safe. Len McKendry, on the other hand, regarded the people on the terraces as ignorant. To him, soccer was a game for players and if people wanted to pay to watch, that was fine, but it wasn't something for him to worry about. He had a very low opinion of soccer fans: 'All they do is watch the ball for 90 minutes and they wouldn't have a clue whether you played well or not.'

In McKendry's team every player had a specific job to do and specific instructions about how to do it. Whether you touched the ball or not didn't matter, as long as you did the job. He'd say, 'As long as I'm happy, you will stay employed with the club that I am coaching. Don't worry about what the idiots on the terraces are saying.' Jimmy Rooney taught me about having a professional attitude, looking after your health, and about the individual skills of the game. Len McKendry taught me how to get the best out of my ability and apply it for the good of the team. When we had the ball in the midfield, all Lennie wanted me to do was knock it into the feet of the forwards, then support them from midfield. Len would work for hours on where and when to pass the ball and where to make position in support. When we didn't have the ball I had to do the hard work of closing down and pressuring. Again, Lennie would go through things in detail — how to close down, how to support other defenders. He gave me jobs that I could understand and carry out.

It was during 1986, when I was playing under McKendry, that Frank Arok decided I had a role to play for the Socceroos and for that I have to give a lot of credit to Len. He gave me confidence in my ability, and used me in a way that suited my strengths. Knowing how to pressure and close down players, and how to play simple balls forward made me an influential player, even though I wasn't as skilful as others around me. That got me into the national team, I'm sure. I was never going to make it for my dribbling, or flair, or ability to hit bending, 50-metre passes. Len made me focus on how simple the game can be if you have a plan. Get it and knock forward into feet, instead of playing two balls square and trying to dribble. One good forward pass can put three or four opposition players out of the game. It was simple and direct and I knew exactly what I was going to do and so did every other player in any of Len McKendry's teams.

Yet when you look back at how many people went to watch South Melbourne when they were winning the championship, the crowds were very ordinary. I remember Bobby Russell complaining, 'It's boring for a defender at training with Len McKendry because all you do is defend and if you win the ball he stops it.' A lot of players couldn't cope with McKendry's tactical discipline. There was a feeling that he 'cloned' players so that everyone would be the same, with no individuals standing out. Players would go to Len and say, 'I'm not scoring enough goals.' Len would wave them away. 'Don't worry about it. The guy next to you is scoring enough goals for the team.' It was always the team, never the individual, and I guess that's why I played so well under Len McKendry. My game was all about hard work for the team. Lennie has sort of disappeared from the NSL and it's become fashionable to criticise his way of coaching, but I will always have respect for his work.

Our opponents learned to respect us in 1986. We were in the top three all season in a very even Southern Division. Going into the final round, Footscray JUST was on top with 27 points, with us on 26. Footscray had to play away to Brisbane Lions, which is always a tough trip. Juventus had to play South Melbourne at Middle Park, and they don't come any tougher than that. We really had the harder task because, while the Lions had no chance of making the final five, South Melbourne had to beat us to qualify for the final five. It was a day of tension, when Len's method was shown to be rock solid. The final scores: Brunswick Juventus 3, South Melbourne 0, and Brisbane Lions 1, Footscray 1. We both finished with 28 points, but we won the minor premiership on goal difference. For the third time in a row, a team coached by Len McKendry had won the minor premiership.

Maybe that made us overconfident — the finals were a disaster. In the Major Semi Final, Adelaide City beat us 2–0. We were still shell-shocked the next Sunday for the preliminary final, and Footscray JUST beat us 2–1. That was that for '86.

THROUGHOUT THESE YEARS VALERIE Pegg had been my No. 1 supporter and my harshest critic. We'd been going out for five years and I was quite happy to have it go along that way. I was happy living at home and seeing her after training or on the weekend. For me it was no big deal, yet everybody else seemed to think I was dragging my feet to avoid getting married. I took it as a joke until Val got fed up and said she was thinking about a holiday in Europe with a girlfriend. 'I will go if you tell me that you're not going to marry me or you don't want to play any part in my life.' I was wondering, 'Is she fair dinkum? She might go to Europe and come back with some Frenchman on her arm who's got a villa in the south of France!' All these things were going through my mind.

I didn't want to lose her. I made a plan. Usually when I picked up Val I was late. If we were going to a function I'd never remember to bring drinks so we'd have to detour via a pub. I rarely took her flowers. This night was to be different. I made a booking at Dimitrio's in Canterbury Road, Bayswater. I arrived at her place on time, with the drinks and a big red rose. At dinner I laid it on thick, telling her how gorgeous she looked, what a wonderful person she was and how much she'd changed my life. Eventually I said, 'Will you do me the honour of being my wife?'

I thought she might have guessed what was happening, but my proposal seemed to be a complete shock to her. She said 'yes', then excused herself and headed to the ladies' room. I sat waiting. And waiting. A few minutes later she returned and I later found out the delay was caused because she couldn't believe I'd proposed and was asking herself if I really had popped the question. So a nervous game of squash finished love all.

That was in October, 1986, and five months later we were married. The wedding was fine, except for the 'telegrams' read by my best man, Ian Dobson. His advice was, well ... simple. 'Val, just imagine that your wedding night is like a football cup final. Try Paul in all 11 positions and if he doesn't score, pull him off.' Everyone was having a good laugh, except my mum and dad. Thanks, Dobbo, a nice way to be sent out into the big, bad world.

CALL OF THE
GREEN AND GOLD

THE PRIDE AND PRESTIGE of being part of the Socceroos was something I'd never experienced until one warm December night in 1985. Normally I'm a bad spectator, but on this night I was watching a Socceroo game for the first time. Three months earlier I'd played for Australia 'B' in a friendly against China in Canberra, in front of a few hundred spectators, but it wasn't until I paid my money to stand on the terraces and watch the Socceroos that I really appreciated just what it meant. Pulling on the green and gold was one thing, but it wasn't until I heard the chant, 'Australia, Australia', go around Olympic Park that the whole Socceroo experience hit me.

On this night it was Australia versus Scotland, the second leg of a World Cup qualification play-off. Scotland had won the first leg 2–0 in Glasgow two weeks earlier and I was now standing on the terraces with thousands of other Aussie fans, willing the Socceroos to score three. Olympic Park was packed. The official capacity was 35,000 or so, but it felt as if 100,000 people were there. I had a personal interest, of course, because if we beat Scotland the Socceroos would be off to Mexico for the 1986 World Cup finals and, even though I was very much a fringe player at that stage, it was an exciting prospect. I wasn't thinking about that on the terraces, though. I was like any other fan, screaming, 'Go on Mitch, get in there Kossie!' Of course plenty of expatriate Scots were there, and whenever they started to shout, we'd come back with 'Australia, Australia' and drown them out. I was enjoying myself so much I wondered why I'd never wanted to go to Socceroo games as a kid. It felt brilliant to be an Aussie that night.

The Socceroos took the game to Scotland and in the opening few minutes the Scottish keeper Jim Leighton made a superb save from a John Kosmina header.

We had to win, but it just wasn't going to be our night. Zarko Odzarkhov, our replacement midfielder, hit one from 35 metres and it just went over. I thought the team really battled hard and you felt proud to be there supporting them. The game finished 0–0 and Scotland went to the World Cup finals, but I'm sure most people left feeling, as I did, that Frank Arok and the Socceroos had done us proud to go so close.

THE FIRST TIME I was in the same room as Frank Arok, I couldn't believe how big he looked. He filled the room with his presence. I daren't move an inch for fear that he would look at me. I was sitting in a draughty dressingroom at Olympic Park No. 2 in Melbourne with about 20 players from Melbourne and Adelaide. Some were Socceroo regulars, but most were just hopefuls like me. I hadn't played in many representative teams before, so it was a whole new experience getting ready with players I hardly knew. Frank gave us a lecture on the way we should be preparing ourselves and what it meant to play for your country. He was getting louder and louder and waving his arms around. He was speaking with so much passion and was sweating, even though it was freezing cold. It was pouring off his brow. He was so worked up about what he wanted to say. He always had his watch in his hand and every now and then would look at the watch and then launch into some other topic. I swear I didn't understand half of what he was saying. He was rambling on so much. I could make out the individual words, but put them all together and it was a total mess. I didn't have a clue.

Frank finished his rave and sent us out onto the training ground. I had to ask Micky Petersen what he was on about. That season, 1985, I was playing with Micky at Brunswick Juventus and he had been in Frank's squad for a while. He explained in plain English what Frank had said. John Margaritis, the Brunswick coach, was there as one of Frank's assistant coaches so I was hoping that Micky and John would help me get through that first session. I couldn't understand exactly what Frank wanted and I wasn't the only player having trouble. Frank had to actually grab players and move them into position because he wasn't getting his message across.

Frank screams and shouts at training, especially when the media are there. If a camera turns up, the sound of his voice and how he speaks to players rises to another level and becomes even more confusing. We started with a game of 'keepings off', a circle of players with three in the middle trying to get the ball. Frank would always say silly things, like 'Kill the bastard' or 'What to do with that one, son?' If you made a poor pass and it didn't make the distance or it was a difficult ball, he'd let you have it.

That first training session was an absolute nightmare. We all knew Frank was assessing our strengths and weaknesses for future Socceroo selection. Some players weren't invited back, but I was called up for two or three of the camps in Melbourne. Eventually I went to a training camp in Sydney and I got the feeling I was doing something right. Frank is an expert at keeping players on their toes, never letting them get comfortable. He'd throw you into what was called the 'Cage' at St George Stadium. It was an area surrounded by a huge cyclone fence about five metres high. Once you went in there was no way of escaping. You couldn't walk out and rest on the side. There were two small goals and the pitch was only 15 by 20 metres. Frank would make you work in there for 10 or 15 minutes and you would really work yourself to a standstill, while he was screaming and demanding excellence. 'Lift yourself to a higher level!'

My first international game, as I said, was at the Bruce Stadium in Canberra against China, on September 23, 1985. We were the 'B' team, players on the fringe of the Socceroo squad. I was 23 years old and made a perfect start. Garry McDowall whacked the ball out of defence and I just chased it. The Chinese defenders were out of position and I took the ball around the goalkeeper and with my left foot slotted it in from an acute angle. We won 2–0. China wasn't exactly a world soccer power and a deserted Bruce Stadium wasn't the biggest stage, so it was a very unceremonious start for my international career. Two days later we played China again, this time in Newcastle, and won 1–0. I wasn't picked in Frank's World Cup squad later that year. My 'A' international debut was another year away.

By August, 1986, Frank Arok was starting to rebuild the Socceroo team, but quite a few of the players from the World Cup campaign were still around. I had made it through the training camps to the squad itself for a three-game series against Czechoslovakia. I figured I was in the squad for experience and had little chance of playing. The first game was in Melbourne and I was really nervous, even though I was only sitting on the bench. The Czechs looked so fit and professional. After about 10 minutes Kenny Murphy wrecked his knee in a 50/50 block tackle and all of a sudden Frank screamed, 'Wadey, get warmed up!'

Hang on a minute! I was supposed to sit on the bench and enjoy the experience, get nervous, but just learn a bit about international soccer. Before I knew it I was out there with the ball at my feet. I played a pass to Marshal Soper, but he didn't move, and made me look really stupid. That season at Brunswick Juventus I was playing under Len McKendry and his coaching was all about playing balls into feet. I got the ball again and played it forward once more to Soper, with the same result. He didn't anticipate the pass and the Czechs won possession. Soper just stood there glaring at me. I was thinking, 'What the hell's going on here?' Your first reaction is to think you can't cut it at the highest level, but I'm not one to feel sorry for myself so I got on with the job.

The Czechs were winning 1–0. Towards the end I was involved in a move: I made a challenge, got a touch to the ball and Graham Arnold was on the spot for an equaliser. We held on for a 1–1 draw and when I looked at the TV news the last words of the commentary before the ball hit the back of the net were 'and it's Wade'. It made it sound as though I had scored the equaliser or, at the very least, set it up. I don't score too many goals so I was happy to take the credit!

We went to Adelaide for the next game and I was picked in the starting line-up. Ken Murphy was the engine room in Frank's midfield, but his knee was a mess, so I took over in a wide midfield role. We lost the game 1–0, but I was happy with my performance. The Socceroos were in transition. Players such as Charlie Yankos, Graham Jennings, Oscar Crino and John Kosmina were still regulars, but guys like goalkeeper Jeff Olver, defender Robbie Dunn and me were trying to nail down a permanent spot. We went to Sydney for the third game and I was still in the starting eleven, but trouble was heading my way. The biggest Czech I've ever seen in my life went over the top of the ball in a tackle and wrecked my ankle. I had to come off early in the match and we were hammered 3–0. Back at the Camperdown Travelodge I was hobbling around and remember thinking, 'We've let Frank down.' He put in so much effort and wanted us to lift to that extra level, but we'd gone backwards against the Czechs. I felt Frank might look for someone else in the wide midfield role, but I must have done enough.

Once I recovered from the ankle injury I was back in the squad and over the next year I went on two Socceroo tours to Asia: to China, and to South Korea for the President's Cup. By the end of 1987 I felt I was very much part of Frank's plans, and what plans we had! The Bicentennial year, 1988, was shaping up as the biggest challenge for the Socceroos since the 1974 World Cup finals. We had Olympic Games qualification games at the start of the year, the Bicentennial Gold Cup with Argentina, Brazil and Saudi Arabia in the middle, then the Olympic Games in September, if we qualified.

Frank Arok was like a general planning for a war. In December, 1987, he mapped out the hardest pre-season training schedule I'd ever seen. There were Socceroo squads all over the country following the same routine. Ahead of us was a month of commando training — six days a week, twice a day — but nobody refused. We all knew 1988 was a once-in-a-lifetime chance.

In Melbourne there were a dozen players training under John Margaritis. My alarm was going off at 5.45 am so I could get ready and drive to Olympic Park for a 7 am training session. On the first day we had to do a 12-minute run on a course through the parkland and it wasn't a casual jog. There must have been 30 trees on a full lap and we had to sprint from every second tree. That meant 15 sprints per lap and we were doing four laps in the 12 minutes. After the running we would work on ball skills. The next day it would be a 15-minute run doing the same thing and then it went up to an 18-minute run. On the seventh day we did a 30-minute run with over 100 sprints! After an hour of training I'd have a quick shower and drive to work at A.E. Smith in North Clayton, about 40 minutes away, for a 9 am start. Then at 5 pm it was back into the city for another session! The evening sessions were solely ball work, but by the time I got home at 8 pm I was exhausted. The workload was incredible. This went on six days a week and the running got harder by the day.

After a week of stamina work the load changed. We moved from the parkland to Olympic Park No. 2, which had a running track. We had to do six 1500-metre runs in the one training session, all against the clock, with the results recorded for Frank Arok to scrutinise. Soon the distance was shorter, but there were more repetitions. It was twenty 400-metre runs, fifty 100-metre runs and finally a hundred 50-metre runs. You can imagine how the boys felt at seven in the morning when we had just done twenty-five 100-metre sprints and had twenty-five to go. Just thinking about the kilometres we sprinted was enough to break some guys and at the end of each session most of us were off to work!

John Margaritis had to make a note of all the times and distances so Frank Arok could compare each group. Frank couldn't believe the times coming in from the Melbourne group and he came down to check for himself. 'I can't believe you guys. You are killing the Sydney group as far as fitness goes. This is brilliant. This is the sort of commitment I'm looking for.' He reckoned if we didn't qualify for the Olympic soccer tournament we'd surely get picked for the track and field team. Ernie Tapai was in our group and I have never seen a guy run so fast over 400 metres. He was flying, and Frank reckoned he was right on the pace that an Olympic 400-metre runner would be doing in training.

One morning we had to do twenty 400-metre runs and thanks to Micky Petersen, who kept a copy of the times, I've been able to check the record. Ernie did the first one in 58 seconds and more or less stayed on that pace. On the 12th run he clocked 56 seconds and on the last 400, when your legs and lungs are screaming at you, Tapai went around in 60 seconds. I was averaging about 65 seconds, which put me in the middle of the pack with Micky Petersen, Oscar Crino and Alan Davidson. My first 400 was 60 seconds, but after that I never got near Tapai. Andrew Zinni, who was also at Brunswick Juventus, was the second-quickest, averaging 63 seconds. Bringing up the rear were the goalkeepers Jeff Olver and Phil Trianedes.

Frank was delighted with our efforts, but there were a few little details Frank didn't know. The track at Olympic Park No. 2 wasn't actually 400 metres, it was about 360! No wonder Tapai's times were quick! The other little detail was our running style. After so many laps you'd run inside the bends just a bit and then Micky Petersen would run on my inside and pretty soon each lap was about 300 metres. It was the same with our 50-metre sprints. John Margaritis asked me to stride out the 50 paces. I got to 42 paces and thought, 'That looks far enough.' We were on Olympic times, but not Olympic distances.

Later we caught up with some of the Sydney players and they all wanted to know about our super running. While we were running around a short track, those poor bastards were running around the outside of St George Stadium on uneven grass and through car parks, with Frank screaming at them the whole time. All these things were in our favour, so no wonder there were so many Victorians in Frank's team. Even though we were running a tiny bit less than we should have, the training was still gruelling and I was as fit as I'd ever been. By the time the Olympic Games qualifiers came around, the Socceroos were ready for anything.

For various political reasons Israel and Chinese Taipei weren't given home games, so the four-team group would play in Australia and New Zealand. On March 6, 1988, we had to play Israel in Melbourne. Frank picked a very strong team. Jeff Olver had made a brilliant start to his Socceroo career when he came on as a substitute goalkeeper in a World Cup game in Israel in 1985 and was now the No. 1 choice. We had a good, strong back line. Charlie Yankos could kick the ball from one end of the park to the other and usually did. Garry McDowall was the type of defender who would kick his own sister and Wally Savor was a tenacious full-back. Graham Jennings used to be a winger and still attacked like one from left back. In the middle, Oscar Crino, Micky Petersen and I were all good at different things, so we made a good blend. Crino had the typical South American ball skills, Micky had excellent distribution and I could run and tackle all day. Up front we had Graham Arnold, a real workhorse with a nose for goal, Frank Farina, who was lightning quick, and John Kosmina, who was very strong and great at holding the ball up. The team had speed, aggression, height, endurance — it had absolutely everything.

Our biggest test was going to be the Israelis because they had Avi Cohen of Glasgow Rangers (and formerly of Liverpool) and Ronnie Rosenthal, a quick striker who later played for Liverpool and Spurs. Against New Zealand it was going to be different — a contest decided by who could kick whom the hardest — but we knew we were up against a football team when we played Israel. The match was tight. It was 0–0 at half-time. In the second half Yankos scored from the penalty spot and then, late in the game, I had the ball on the right and dinked it over the back four for Farina to go one-on-one with the last defender. Frankie slotted it at the near post to make the score 2–0. It was exactly what we'd been working towards for months. This had been my best game for my country yet. Absolutely everything I tried worked out. I always said my job was to cover every inch of the park and people were saying I was starting to actually do it. When I look at replays now I can't believe the number of times I hit both penalty areas, one after the other in quick succession.

We nearly blew it, though, in the next game, against Chinese Taipei in Adelaide. It was one of those brave moves by Frank to rest half the team. I was sitting on the bench, watching the Socceroos play uninspiring soccer. In the end we escaped with a 3–2 win and went to Sydney to play New Zealand. Frank was playing games in the media to wind up the New Zealand coach Kevin Fallon, who had said some unpleasant things about us. As a result, we hated everything about him: his look, the way he spoke, everything. Frank would sell him dummies, telling the media the wrong team, and they'd print it, knowing full well we were going to do something else completely. We took great delight in walloping New Zealand 3–1 and with three wins from three games we were sitting pretty.

We had to go to New Zealand for the three return games and again Israel was the biggest danger. The first game, in Melbourne, was a game of top-class soccer, but the second game, in Auckland, was a kicking match. It was very spiteful and involved the infamous stomping incident. I was wearing Diadora boots at that stage and so was Garry McDowall. Things got out of control and there was a big melee in the Israeli penalty area. The camera was focused on the head of an Israeli player who'd gone down and you could see a Diadora boot stomp on the guy. I was doing my usual wimpish thing, trying to separate everybody, and because I was in the melee and wore Diadora boots, some people thought I was the stomper.

Garry McDowall was sent off for the stomping incident, so Frank switched me to centre back in his place. It was 0–0, we were down to 10 men and I feared one mistake could cost us a place at the Olympics. I'd never played the offside trap before so I was running with my opponent and stuffing up the plan. Somehow we held on for a draw and afterwards Frank said, 'I'll never ever play you as centre back again. You were an absolute nightmare.' The trouble was, McDowall was automatically suspended from the next game, the match with New Zealand, and Frank decided to play me at centre back again.

He then shocked everyone by leaving Frank Farina on the bench. Farina had a blood blister on his foot, but both he and the physio said he'd be okay to play. Frank Arok decided otherwise and it caused a bit of friction, which we didn't need, because it was a crunch game. If we avoided defeat we'd be pretty certain of qualifying for the Seoul Olympics, so there was plenty of pressure. Frank should have stuck to his original vow never to play me in defence again. I was marking Mike McGarry and he was giving me some trouble. A ball was played into the penalty area, I committed myself to a slide tackle, but McGarry was a fraction of a second quicker to the ball and went tumbling over my leg. The referee awarded a penalty! I had a sickening feeling my mistake would cost us a place in the Olympics. New Zealand took the lead from the penalty and we had to chase the game, with the Kiwis hammering us in every 50/50 tackle. Time was running out.

Then Farina came on as a sub. As he did, Kevin Fallon, the despised Kiwi coach, tried to wind him up. 'Come on, Frankie, give us a kiss, you big poofter.'

Frankie ignored him. We were still losing 1–0 and Farina's job was to rescue us with a goal. Charlie Yankos got the ball at the back. I was trying to get him to pass the ball to me, but he whacked it and I was about to say, 'Charlie, you idiot, we've got to play the ball, play to feet', but Frank Farina took off chasing Charlie's long ball. It bounced into space and Frank ran on to it. Without breaking his stride he smashed a volley right in the corner from 25 metres out. Unbelievable! We were destined to go to the Olympics. After scoring, Farina went back towards the Kiwi bench and gave it to Fallon. 'When this is finished I'll give you your kiss, with my tongue right down your throat!' For a change, Fallon was speechless.

We held on to a priceless 1–1 draw. All we had to do on the last day of competition was to beat Chinese Taipei, which should have been a formality, but the nerves got to Micky Petersen, Graham Arnold and I. We kept thinking, 'What if ...' and we couldn't sleep for thinking about what could go wrong. At 1 am we woke Dr Brian Corrigan and asked for a 'Moggie', a Mogadon sleeping pill. I'd never taken a sleeping pill before, but I wanted to get a good night's sleep. I slept all right, so well that I could hardly wake up the next morning! I was dizzy and feeling lethargic. I had to go and do a training session to try and work the sleeping tablet out of my system. The best tonic was an early goal from Arnold. We cruised to a 3–0 win after Farina and I also scored. Seoul Olympics, here we come!

That night we celebrated for the whole night. I remember walking back to the hotel at five in the morning with Jeff Olver, singing all the way. It was to be the first of many Socceroo celebrations in 1988. The wise words of Jimmy Rooney, warning me about drink, were still with me, but I'd allow myself a few at the end of a tournament.

THE BICENTENNIAL GOLD CUP was billed as a tournament of champions. Argentina were the reigning world champions, having won the World Cup in Mexico in 1986. Brazil were three-times World Cup winners and the people's champions. The Saudis were the Asian champions and Australia were the Oceania champions. Our first game was at Olympic Park in Melbourne against Brazil. We played really well that night, but were beaten by the toe of their outstanding young striker, Romario. He just stuck out a toe and it was in the back of the net, 1–0 to Brazil. The ground was soaking wet, but the Socceroos were very proud of ourselves. Unfortunately, Romario, 'that little bastard' as Frank Arok referred to him, turned out to be our jinx in 1988.

We then went to Sydney and beat Saudi Arabia 3–0 on an absolutely disgraceful pitch at Parramatta Stadium. That paved the way for the big night at the Sydney Football Stadium, Australia v Argentina, Thursday, July 14. A draw was enough for us to qualify for the Gold Cup final against Brazil, but

Argentina needed to win to get through. The pitch was again a bit of a mess because of the combination of a wet winter and Rugby League.

It was a superb night for the Socceroos, in front of 19,000 fans. Absolutely everything went right for us. Four minutes in we attacked down the right. I had run into the box in an offside position, so for a second I stood off the pitch. The ball was bobbling around and Aussie midfielder Vlado Bozinoski challenged and it took a ricochet and spilled free. The goalkeeper was going to dive on it, but one of his defenders pushed the ball away from his hands, out wide in my direction. The ball came to me slowly and I could see the open goal. As I ran towards the ball the gap between the two posts was getting narrower and narrower as the ball trickled towards the by-line. I thought, 'All I've got to do is hit this straight.' It's amazing how many things flit through your mind in a split second. I put it right in the middle. A goal against the world champions after four minutes of play!

I took off to the crowd behind the goals. I'd kicked a souvenir ball to those guys before the game and they were great Socceroo supporters, just like those at the Kop at Anfield. Team-mate Scott Ollerenshaw raced over and a couple of fans jumped the fence to help celebrate — they got dragged out by the police, for which I felt partly to blame. I finally turned around and the rest of the Socceroos were almost at the half line. None of them had bothered to come and celebrate with me. That goal stirred up the Argentinians and they really came at us. Their captain, Oscar Ruggeri, equalised after 33 minutes and we were under heaps of pressure. Then three minutes before half-time Charlie Yankos scored a famous goal — I still don't know how it could swerve so much over the 35 metres it travelled. It was 2–1 at half-time.

In the 67th minute Frank Farina did the biggest dive I've seen in my life for a penalty and Charlie scored our third. Everyone in the stadium was going crazy. I had a hand in the fourth goal when I got the ball on the right-hand side and I turned inside onto my left foot. Eddie Thomson, Frank Arok's assistant, said afterwards, 'When you turned onto your left foot, Wadey, I knew that ball was going to go either into the grandstand or over the crossbar for a goal kick, but you shocked me.' It was a perfect cross. I hit it flat and hard and it went straight to the far post. Bozinoski tried to head it, but ended up shouldering it over the keeper's head to make it 4–1. It was a dream night.

Back at our hotel, the Camperdown Travelodge, two hundred fans with green and gold scarves, and a big media contingent, were waiting for us. It was the best feeling. We signed autographs for almost an hour. That night the Socceroos made inroads into the Australian public's consciousness. From then on, fans were coming to watch and support Australia, rather than treating the visitors as the attraction. It had been that way for too long: playing on home soil, but feeling as if we were playing a million miles from Australia. At the

Sydney Football Stadium that night we were the heroes. It was heady stuff. That night was the party to end all parties. There was no way anybody could stop us drinking. The record for the most money spent behind the bar on alcohol at the Camperdown Travelodge had been set by a Rugby Union team, but we smashed that. We guzzled over $3000 worth of booze.

A photographer woke Bozinoski at 5 am to get a photo for the early edition of the afternoon newspaper. Bozinoski was sitting up in bed with a smile on his face, looking as if he was still under the influence. Paul Trimboli and I had to get up early to go to a coaching clinic with some kids, organised by Terry Greedy, the former Socceroo goalkeeper. We had to do a juggling demonstration, but after gallons of booze and three hours sleep we couldn't speak, let alone juggle the ball. By some fluke, we bluffed our way through. Most of the day was spent doing interviews. Charlie Yankos did most of them because he was the skipper, but we all felt like celebrities. Then we tried to get back on track for the final.

In hindsight, the Thursday night drinking binge was the most stupid thing we did in 1988. Pedro Ruz, the Socceroo physio, says it can take seven days for the body to fully recover from heavy drinking. We had two days rest before playing a world-class team. Look at some of the names. Romario, Jorginho, Taffarel. They all went on to play in the Brazil side that won the World Cup in the USA in 1994. A year after we played them in Sydney the very same Brazilian squad won the 1989 South American championship. We just couldn't compete with them. They were world-class players. Muller, their brilliant striker, completely tore us apart, even though Jorginho was sent off. Brazil won 2–0 and it was a real anticlimax.

We were a shadow of the team that had beaten Argentina. It was good that we reached the final, but disappointing that we couldn't play to our potential once we got there. It was the biggest moment in Australian soccer to date, next to making the 1974 World Cup finals; the best result on home soil ever, but it could have been even bigger.

THE GOLD CUP WAS one of many peaks for the Socceroos in 1988. Thanks to all the publicity, our self-esteem was pretty good when we headed for the Olympic Games in Seoul. There was a big send-off for all the Olympic athletes and we went together on a Qantas jumbo. On that flight the Socceroos earned themselves a reputation as the party boys of the Olympic team. It started when we ran into the guy who does the NEC ads on television as Mr Okimura. Anyway, he's also a Qantas steward and we recognised him. The boys had a good laugh and a chat and it went from there. 'Listen, is there any chance you could get us a beer?' He said, 'Sorry, this is a dry flight.' We should have guessed. On board were the elite of Australian sport, heading for the Olympics. The Socceroos didn't fit the mould.

Anyway, Mr Okimura disappeared for a while and came back with a couple of beers. Pretty soon all the boys were calling for beers. Even Frank Arok enjoyed a red wine. There were all our great athletes, many of whom never let one drop of alchohol pass their lips, and they were absolutely disgusted that the Australian Olympic soccer team was drinking on the way to Seoul.

We got a bad reputation, and it stuck. It was as though we'd done our job by qualifying for the Olympics and there was very little chance we were going to win a medal. Yet for most of the Olympians on that plane, the really hard work was only just starting. When we got to the Olympic Village, silly things were happening. Condoms were left in the lift and water was thrown out of the upper floors. The Socceroos were blamed for everything, even when we didn't do it. Guys were making paper planes and throwing them from the upper floors to see how far they could fly them. Whoever was throwing them was starting to set them alight, and they were landing on top of these marquees made of plastic and melting holes in them. Boys will be boys.

In our group we were playing Brazil, with 'that little bastard' Romario, Yugoslavia (as it was then) and Nigeria. It was a tough draw. Yugoslavia, one of the medal favourites, was our first opponent. Frank had spent weeks working out a way to beat them. We had elaborate plans for that game, not the others, because if we didn't get a good result first up, we would be in trouble. Frank even went to Switzerland to watch Yugoslavia play. Also, Frank came from Yugoslavia, so I guess he had extra motivation to beat them. All he wanted me to do as a wide midfielder was to stay in the channel on one side of the ground, even if the ball was on the other side. Frank had worked out Yugoslavia's tactics of playing short passes on one side and then quickly switching the ball to the other side to catch teams out.

I spent 90 minutes against Yugoslavia waiting in this channel, waiting for the cross-field balls. In the 90 minutes maybe it happened twice, so my involvement in that game was next to zero. It was probably the worst game that I've been involved in as far as my participation was concerned, but it was for the good of the team. Frank's tactics worked perfectly and Frank Farina scored the solitary goal. We hung on for dear life against these full-time professionals and scored a massive, upset victory. To this day it's probably the best victory for the Socceroos because it was a fair dinkum game: Yugoslavia had their full squad and they were being tipped for the gold medal.

Our next game was against Brazil, who had beaten us twice in the Gold Cup. In his team talk, Frank Arok was really getting some passion into his words. He said, 'We've played these guys twice now and this little bastard has stuffed us up twice. Now we know what we have to do.' A great theory! We lost 3–0 and Romario scored a hat-trick. Far from us working out Brazil, it seemed they had worked us out. Frank admitted defeat with Romario. 'He's the best player

I've ever seen.' Romario could score goals from nothing and he did it with a little toe poke. Nothing spectacular, just a little bit of magic and that was it. We were still in the hunt for the quarter-finals, though, and thanks to a great goal from John Kosmina we beat Nigeria 1–0 and qualified for the next round.

We were drawn to play the Soviet Union, another medal favourite. They were like machines and ran for 90 minutes. We had David Mitchell sent off, which didn't help, but we just weren't in the game anyway. The Soviet Union played the ball and ran, and we were chasing shadows. The final score was 3–0 and my direct opponent, Alexei Mikhailichenko, scored two and set up the other one. I walked away from that game feeling totally inadequate. All that we'd done against Argentina, all that we'd done in the Olympic Games qualifiers, was just a dream, and that's all it would be. I was a footballer with very limited ability and was never going to play as a professional. I felt like a pretender. The only consolation was that Brazil and the Soviet Union played in the final and the Soviets won, so at least we had played and lost to the best.

The group games and the quarter-finals were played in the first week of the Olympics, so we had another week before going home. That meant one week of partying. We'd arrive back at the Olympic Village at 5 am, when other athletes would be getting up for training runs. We weren't the quietest footballers in the world and we would get officials lecturing us. 'A little bit of respect. This is the Olympic Games, these athletes have spent four years getting ready for this.' We were the ugly Aussies. We did not have one bit of respect for other people.

One morning we staggered back to the Olympic Village and saw 'Spike' Cheney, the boxer, who was fighting for the gold medal later that morning. At 5 am he was having breakfast because he couldn't sleep. The Olympic gold medal bout was the biggest fight of his career. We sat down half tanked and tried to rev him up. 'Come on, Spike, you have got nothing to worry about, buddy. You are guaranteed a silver medal anyway. Just go out there and bash the living daylights out of that rotten Russian.' He really didn't need the advice of a couple of soccer players, but that was us at the 1988 Olympics.

At least we spent some of the week supporting other Aussie athletes. If we saw another Aussie in the Olympic Village we'd say 'G'day'. The response was usually cold, especially from the swimmers. We couldn't believe how arrogant they appeared at times. Then again, our reputation had spread, and maybe we'd woken them up with our noise. We sneaked into a semi-final for the Australian women's basketball team and you could have mistaken it for a soccer final. We were shouting and singing as the girls battled Yugoslavia for a place in the final. By the end of the game, which the Aussie girls lost by only one point, a couple of us had lost our voices from singing.

During the game we'd seen two beautiful blondes with an Aussie flag so we called them over. They sat with Micky Petersen and me. There wasn't a huge crowd there and the cameras would often focus on these nutcase Aussies. Of course the pictures were going back home and when I rang my wife the next day the first thing she asked was, 'Who was that blonde with you?' Oops.

The Olympic Games were great fun for us, but we still had plenty to do in 1988. A month after the Olympics we had to play New Zealand home and away in the Trans-Tasman Cup. We did it comfortably, 2–1 and 2–0. The second of those games was our 13th full international game for the year. I had played every one, and my body was starting to show the strain. Our final assignment for 1988 was a World Cup preliminary tie against Fiji, but I couldn't travel to Fiji because of a pelvic injury. I wasn't the only one missing from the team that had done so well in the Gold Cup and the Olympics. Kosmina and Dunn had retired, Bozinoski and Farina had transferred overseas and, like Mitchell, were unavailable. In any case, it was only Fiji. Or so we thought.

The Socceroos lost 1–0. It was a disaster. I missed the return game as well, but we won 5–1, much to everyone's relief. The warning signs were there, but it was hard to read them. We were on such a high. The Gold Cup, the Olympics and, to cap off a great year, I was named the NSL player of the year. I didn't know it, but I had reached a peak of success and was about slide down the other side.

RUNNING IS the basic part of my game, but the 1988 workload was too much. On top of Frank Arok's commando pre-season training there were 40 league, cup and practice matches for South Melbourne, 13 Socceroo games and four or five Socceroo training camps. I was getting a lot of discomfort in my pelvis whenever I was running. Trying to get out of bed in the morning was sheer agony. I had this excruciating pain behind my balls and it was diagnosed as ostitis pubis, a condition that involves the ligament between the pubic bone stretching through over-use. Because of the amount of running soccer players do, and partly because of the kicking style when you pass the ball with the inside of your foot, there's a lot of pressure on that part of the pelvis.

Dr Brian Corrigan took a great interest in this complaint because he found a lot of soccer players were suffering from it. The cure was rest, with intensive physiotherapy and rehabilitation to strengthen the pubic region. The problem became unbearable in November, 1988, and it lingered into the pre-season for 1989. It badly affected my preparation for the World Cup qualifiers coming up in March and April. Not only was I struggling to reach the same peak of fitness, it was hard to come up in the same frame of mind and have the same level of enthusiasm.

It was going to be twice as hard because of our recent successes in the Gold Cup and the Olympics. Somehow, the World Cup qualifiers didn't have the same glamour, even though we knew the World Cup finals, not the Olympic

Games, were the pinnacle. What made things even harder was the break-up of the team. We had spent lots of time together in 1988, but our success meant that guys were noticed by European clubs. Charlie Yankos in defence and Frank Farina up front were two key players for the Socceroos, but they were both playing overseas, Charlie in Greece with POAK Salonika and Frank in Belgium with Club Brugge. We no longer had the camaraderie that we'd had in '88, when we were virtually living with each other.

One other departure was permanent. Eddie Thomson quit as assistant coach. Thommo was definitely a steadying influence. You always had the feeling that Frank Arok was a genius, always leaps and bounds ahead and full of ideas, but Thommo was needed to get hold of the reins and slow Frank up so he didn't get too far ahead, especially when it came to tactics. But when it came to motivation, nobody could touch Frank Arok. Thommo always had a big influence on tactics, although I'm sure Frank would never admit that. They didn't get on, but it was like the Hawke/Keating relationship: behind closed doors they had very little respect for each other, but on the surface it was a great team and a successful combination.

Despite all these changes, the year started well enough. The Swedish club team Malmo toured in February and we beat them 3–2 and 3–0. The World Cup qualifiers were a three-team competition with our old enemies, Israel and New Zealand, with the winner going into a play-off with a South American country for a place in Italia '90.

Our opening game was against New Zealand in Sydney on March 12, 1989. Because of club commitments in Europe, Farina, Bozinoski and Mitchell were absent, but Charlie Yankos came back from Greece. The Kiwis had already lost to Israel away a week earlier and came to Sydney complaining about the scheduling that called for them to play two games in eight days on two sides of the planet. We gave them heaps, winning 4–1. Graham Arnold got two, Yankos scored from the penalty spot and I set up one for Oscar Crino with a header at the near post.

Then it was our turn to play in Israel, but this time Farina was available. Frank Arok caused a stir when he announced that Eddie Krncevic would be playing in Israel. Eddie was a Melbourne boy who had played in the 1982 World Cup campaign and then made it big overseas. He was playing in Belgium with Anderlecht and there was no doubt he was a class striker, but he hadn't played for the Socceroos for seven years and I had never met the guy. He joined the squad in Greece, where we played a warm-up game en route to Tel Aviv. That gave us just 90 minutes to get to know his style of play and that was difficult. Eddie was very mobile and great in the air, but it was hard to get used to where he wanted the ball played. However, he scored a goal with a header and we drew 1–1, so the signs were promising.

Playing Israel on their home soil is a daunting task, and this game was especially hard. The Israelis scored from the penalty spot through their Belgium-based striker Eli Ohana, and then we had Wally Savor sent off for a tackle on Ronnie Rosenthal. We were really looking down the barrel, but Charlie Yankos came to the rescue. From 30 metres out, he bent a free kick past the wall for an equaliser. I've never experienced total silence in a stadium packed with 50,000 fans. All you could hear were the Aussies jumping up and down, congratulating Charlie. The Israelis were stunned. We escaped with a 1–1 draw, which was a great result under the circumstances.

There was plenty of discussion about Frank's decision on Krncevic. We were thinking, 'Is it better to have guys who've got reputations in Europe thrown together as a team or to have a bunch of players with lesser ability and lesser experience, but who know how to play together?' You couldn't deny the European-based players a spot in the team, but at what expense? We were about to learn a hard lesson.

Two weeks later we travelled to Auckland, with a very different team, for the return game against New Zealand. Our Tel Aviv strikers, Farina and Krncevic, were unavailable. In defence, Wally Savor was suspended and Graham Jennings was injured. The Socceroo line-up was a little bit shaky — Olver, Davidson, Yankos, Calderon, Van Egmond, Wade, Petersen, Crino, Ollerenshaw, Arnold and Spink. There were three or four guys in that line-up who were fringe players at best. Even so, we were red-hot favourites for the game in Auckland on April 2, 1989. New Zealand soccer was going absolutely nowhere, and people were convinced it was just a matter of how many goals the Socceroos would score.

The All Whites had a new coach, John Adshead, who'd taken over from the unpopular Kevin Fallon, but we'd beaten the Kiwis comfortably in our previous three meetings so we certainly knew we had their measure. The lesson, of course, is never to underestimate the Kiwis when they're taking on the Aussies. They were fired up in a way we had not seen for years. Robert Ironside, Fred De Jong and Malcolm Dunford had a fighting spirit that was incredible. From the first minute, they started crunching us with some ferocious tackling. They used what we call 'Wimbledon' tactics, where you tackle like crazy and just whack the ball into the penalty area as many times as possible. The Socceroos, as a ball-playing side, just could not string together any passes. We couldn't keep possession under the relentless physical pressure. New Zealand scored from a corner: Malcolm Dunford rose above the pack inside the six-yard box to score.

From then we were chasing the game, having to commit players forward and risk being caught on the break. That's exactly what happened for the second goal. The ball broke to me and my first touch was what I call the usual Paul Wade first touch and it went a metre or two further than I wanted. I chased it and I was going to have a shot from about 25 metres, but Robert Ironside hit

Australia 1, South Africa 0. Sydney Football Stadium, June 1994.

CALL OF
THE GREEN
AND GOLD

Above: Confronted by Preston's Gary Cole during Brunswick Juventus' extra-time victory in the 1985 NSL Southern Division Grand Final.

Right: In my eight and a half seasons at South Melbourne, I always enjoyed a close relationship with the club's magnificent supporters. This photo is from 1987, my first year with the club.

My first full Australian cap came on August 3, 1986, against Czechoslovakia at Olympic Park. The other Socceroo in the photo is defender Robbie Dunn. The game ended in a 1–1 draw.

Coach Frank Arok (far right) outlines his battle plan to the Socceroo squad before the 1986 series against Czechoslovakia. The long-haired youngster in the middle of the group (between former Socceroo Atti Abonyi, standing at the back, and fellow tyro Graham Arnold), looking just a little overawed, is me.

CALL OF
THE GREEN
AND GOLD

Right: Do something stupid while the Australian team is in camp and you might end up wearing this ugly green T-shirt.

Opposite page: On the attack against Brazil in the opening match of the 1988 Bicentennial Gold Cup, at Melbourne's Olympic Park.

Above: With four other members of the 1988 Australian squad which travelled to Seoul for the Olympic football tournament, outside our Sydney hotel before we set off for South Korea. Left to right: Alan Davidson, Micky Petersen, David Mitchell and Oscar Crino.

Above: The 1988 Olympic squad. Back row (left to right): Paul Wade, John Kosmina, Robbie Slater, Oscar Crino, Alan Hunter, Jeff Olver, Mike Gibson, Alex Tobin, Andy Koczka, Micky Petersen, Gary Van Egmond, Vlado Bozinoski. Front row: Scott Ollerenshaw, Graham Arnold, Robbie Dunn, Eddie Thomson (assistant coach), Charlie Yankos (captain), Frank Arok (coach), Alan Davidson, Frank Farina, Graham Jennings. (Absent: David Mitchell)

Left: Micky P. and I chair goalscorer Frank Farina from the field after the Socceroos' stunning 1–0 victory over Yugoslavia in Seoul.

The future of the game in Australia depends on the next generation of Socceroos, and the way the current generation looks after them. Youngsters never forget promotions such as an impromptu training session on a bitumen playground (top), or a school visit by the Australian captain (middle). The little bloke in the bottom shot is Sinan Aydogan, who broke his leg in 1992 but fought back from his misfortune in a way I'll always remember.

A congratulatory kiss from my wife Valerie after being named the 1988 NSL Player of the Year.

With the other major award winners from that night — South Melbourne coach Brian Garvey (left), who was named NSL Coach of the Year, and team-mate Paul Trimboli, the Under-21 Player of the Year.

me with a block tackle. I reckon my knee nearly shattered. It was a fair tackle, but Ironside was like a ton of bricks. From that tackle the ball broke to Billy Wright, who went up the left-hand side, cut in to within 25 metres of goal and chipped his shot perfectly over Jeff Olver, who was standing no more than three metres off his line. It wasn't as if he was on the edge of the penalty area out of position, but Wright's effort, whether it was a deliberate shot or mistimed, sealed the game for New Zealand.

No matter how hard we tried to motivate ourselves, nothing went right. It was all New Zealand. Ironside dominated the midfield with his crunching tackles. They destroyed us. There were no big hearts in the Socceroo colours to stand up and be counted. We laid down and died, we had nothing left to give. In the end we were a rabble, nothing like the team that had beaten Yugoslavia just over six months earlier. I mean, Charlie Yankos was known for how far he could kick a soccer ball, but against New Zealand in Auckland I have never seen Charlie take a divot so many times. He could not kick a ball 30 metres, never mind the 300 he normally does. Quite possibly, all the travel was getting to him: he had flown from Greece to Sydney, back to Greece, to Tel Aviv, back to Greece again and then finally to Auckland, all in the space of three weeks.

No matter how many times we got the ball into the Kiwi penalty area that day, we couldn't score. Over the 90 minutes we were in possession for at least 70 per cent of the time, but did nothing with it. Graham Arnold had a great chance in the second half where he took the ball inside the full-back and was one-on-one with the goalkeeper, Clint Gosling. At the time it was 'Goal-a game' Arnie, but Gosling threw out his hand and somehow the ball looped over the bar. We sank, 2–0. Jeff Olver, our goalkeeper, got the biggest slagging of his career from the media because of the two goals, but I don't think he could be singled out. As a team we were terrible, both in our commitment and our performance. Our passing was the worst I'd ever seen. Frank Arok was disgusted. He was going off his head in the usual way, making lots of noise without actually pointing the finger at anybody. The guys were in a bit of a daze. We couldn't believe we'd made such a mess of things.

The final qualifier against Israel was two weeks away so we went out to drown our sorrows. That was the Socceroos' custom, win or lose. Gary Cole passed on the message from Frank that the curfew was 11 pm, but the boys didn't fancy an early night. At 11 pm we went back to the hotel for the head count, then nicked back for a few more beers. The few beers turned into an all-night session. At five in the morning we were crawling back to the hotel. Graham Arnold was up to one of his pranks and was banging on the door of Robbie Slater's room to wake him up. The trouble was, Arnie had the wrong room. When the door opened it was Ian Brusasco, the then ASF Chairman!

Frank was wild. Not only had we played terribly, but we'd broken the curfew. He called a meeting the next morning and we were dragged over the coals again. He was screaming that we were a disgrace, not only to ourselves, but to 17 million people on the other side of the Tasman.

OUR WORLD CUP DREAMS were dented, but not destroyed. We had one more chance — we had to beat Israel in Sydney to win the group. Thankfully, Israel was held to a 2–2 draw in New Zealand, which gave them four points from three games. We had three points from three games: we had to win, while a draw would do for Israel. I was happy going into a game needing to win to qualify, that was no big deal. If you can't win at home when it matters, you don't deserve to go any further. At that stage I didn't feel that the loss against the Kiwis was going to cost us a World Cup campaign.

For the showdown with Israel, Frank called up all the European-based players: Eddie Krncevic, Frank Farina and even David Mitchell, who hadn't played with us since the Olympics. There was plenty of debate in the media. Mitchell, Krncevic and Farina had never played up front together so it was a gamble to do it in a World Cup elimination game. Then again, we had to win. In the end, Frank named the following line-up. Olver, Davidson, Yankos, Savor, Van Egmond, Crino, Wade, Arnold, Farina, Mitchell, Krncevic. That meant four changes from the Auckland game a fortnight earlier and, on paper, our strongest line-up.

The build-up to the game was very tense. The European-based players didn't arrive until two or three days before the match, so we had to cram our preparations. Over the previous two years, Frank had always been on about our diet. A lot of guys would have a little bit of soup, a bit of pasta and then fill up on cakes and trifle. We didn't have a dietitian to look after us, just Frank nagging away. In Adelaide, during the Olympic Games qualifiers, Alan Hunter (or 'Blockhead', as he was known) copped a blast from Frank. 'You should be looking after your diet more than anybody.' Big Al carried a bit of weight. The next day we went to the training ground and 'Blockhead' was starving, so he raided a vending machine for a packet of chips and was caught stuffing his face by Frank. Looking back on it now, our diet, with the alcohol and sweets, was pretty poor.

Anyway, the night before the Israel game, my room mate Micky Petersen was hungry. We'd had pasta for dinner, but Micky wasn't a big fan of pasta, so he ordered a steak on room service. He also ordered two milkshakes, one of them for me. Micky polished off his steak and we were sitting there, both with our straws in our mouths, when Frank walked past and looked into our room. He just shook his head and muttered, 'I can't believe you bastards', before walking off. Micky and I didn't finish our milkshakes.

THERE WAS A NEW attendance record on the day the Socceroos played Israel. The Sydney Football Stadium has an official capacity of 42,000, but that day thousands of extra fans packed in. It was a fantastic atmosphere and the crowd really got behind the Socceroos. We knocked the ball around well at the start and created a few half-chances. The boys were really pumped up, and Eddie Krncevic was looking good. Things were going to plan until five minutes before half-time. Charlie Yankos cleared the ball into midfield and an Israeli won it in the air and knocked it back into our half. It was such a harmless ball and we seemed to have things under control. Charlie Yankos had it covered, but he left it for Gary Van Egmond, who left it for Charlie! In that moment of hesitation, Eli Ohana ran past both of them and collected the ball. Suddenly, Ohana was one-one-one with Jeff Olver. He sold a dummy to Jeff and left him helpless on the deck. Van Egmond was trying to get back to cover the goal, but Ohana kept his head. It was the coolest goal I'd seen in a high-pressure situation. What a disaster! Now we needed two goals to win.

I was reasonably happy with my own performance as we trooped off at the interval. I'd done my job defensively, won headers in the Israeli box and played a few good passes, even though I got caught in possession a couple of times. I was sitting catching my breath in the rooms when I saw Frank Arok and John Margaritis, Frank's assistant coach, point towards me in the middle of their discussion. 'Wadey, you're coming off.' Micky Petersen was told to warm up as my replacement. We were losing 1–0 and Frank wanted Micky because he can create more with his passing. I was gutted; any player would be in those circumstances. I sat motionless as Frank gave his half-time talk. The lads went out for the second half and I was feeling lousy. I didn't shower, just put on my tracksuit top and sat on the bench. I started to get cold, sitting there wanting us to win and feeling absolutely helpless.

At this point I have to mention the match referee, an Italian, Carlo Longhi. In his pre-game comments, Les Murray of SBS TV had described Longhi as one of the finest referees in Europe, and said that Australia couldn't be happier to have him here to referee such an important game. This was the same Carlo Longhi who had given Israel a penalty in Tel Aviv when the ball accidentally struck Alan Davidson on the arm. In the first half, Frank Farina was brought down in the penalty area and I reckon everyone in the stadium, except Longhi and the Israelis, thought it was a penalty. There was worse to come. In the second half Paul Trimboli came on as a sub and crossed the ball into the box. I'm not kidding, but the Israeli full-back Tikva threw his arm at the ball and stopped the cross. Longhi waved play on! Our players ran from all angles to protest to the referee. David Mitchell was right up to the referee's nose, appealing for a penalty, to no avail. You could sense it wasn't our day.

Micky Petersen played well when he came on and had a shot that went past the post by six inches. Mitchell had a couple of near misses and Krncevic had a few good chances in the air. From one Trimboli cross all Eddie had to do was hit it with his forehead and it would have been in the back of the net, but he got pushed in the back at the crucial moment by Nir Olon and completely missed his header. The ball came off his shoulder and went over the crossbar. One disastrous attempt on goal after another was the story of the day. Finally we scored, when Mitchell flicked on a long clearance from Olver and it fell to Trimboli, who smacked a volley under the goalkeeper. There were three or four minutes left, so that gave us a glimmer of hope.

But no sooner had play restarted when Longhi blew his whistle for full-time. He played only 30 seconds of injury time, when clearly three or four minutes had been lost treating injuries. Most of our guys exploded but, of course, it was no use. I was watching the chaos from the bench. I was numb from the cold and emotionally drained from being taken off at half-time. I did feel happy for Paul Trimboli because he scored the goal. The incredible thing was that Trimmers had been with his girlfriend, Samantha, until 5 am, as he was expecting not to play. I remember thinking, 'I can't believe that I go to bed at 10 o'clock before every game and Trimmers stays up until five in the morning and scores a goal in a major World Cup qualifier!' Otherwise, it was one of the saddest days of my life. We were out of the World Cup. Whenever I look at a video of that game Les Murray's words of praise for the referee Carlo Longhi rub salt into the wounds. Those words will haunt Les for a long, long time.

THE 1989 WORLD CUP qualifying games showed exactly what preparation means. If you don't prepare properly and get your squad settled, you are going nowhere. If you throw players together and somehow win, it's like winning the lottery, but World Cup campaigns shouldn't rely on luck. In 1988, we spent months preparing for the Olympic qualifiers, the Gold Cup and the Olympic Games. By comparison, our build-up for the 1989 World Cup qualifiers was amateurish. In the end we threw our best players on the park and expected them to perform as a team. In '88 the Socceroos were a cohesive unit, but by March and April '89 the squad was fragmented. Players were coming and going, and Krncevic bobbed up from nowhere. Frank Arok put the same amount of passion into his team talks, but it felt as though it was going in one ear and out the other.

In hindsight, the success we had in '88 was the reason we failed in '89. The Bicentennial year left us physically and emotionally tired, and saw some of our best players go overseas. We simply peaked too soon. Even so, Frank Arok deserves the respect of the nation for his achievements. The Socceroos under Arok put soccer in Australia on the map. Under Arok the Socceroos earned respect by beating Argentina and Yugoslavia. Australian players went out believing they could win games, instead of feeling inferior. It was no longer good enough to take the attitude, 'If we keep it down to 1–0 we've done well.' Frank instilled self-confidence in Australian soccer, both on and off the park. He was ahead of his time in many ways. The Socceroos used to laugh at some of the things Frank Arok got up to. We knew when the media had turned up without even looking because all of a sudden Frank would go berserk, screaming and shouting, pulling players by the shirt to get them in position. He really played to the media like an actor, but at the end of the day Australian soccer got the benefit. Frank would always use the media to wind up opposition coaches and he knew exactly what he was doing with the media. I think Australian soccer owes him a huge debt of gratitude.

I personally owe Frank an enormous amount, for giving me the chance to represent my country and play at the Olympics. He didn't get too much thanks at the time. Frank wasn't reappointed as Socceroo coach in 1990 and that saved my international career. He had made it clear that no player over the age of 26 would be selected if he stayed in the job. He was thinking towards the 1994 World Cup when his 26-year-olds would be 30. In January, 1990, when Frank picked his squad to play the visiting Torpedo Moscow, I was two months shy of my 28th birthday. I was selected in the squad and played in the first game, which was something of a pleasant surprise. In the second game I was on the bench and there were plenty of signs that I wasn't a part of Frank's long-term plans. The new Socceroo squad was full of ball players, and I didn't fit that category, so I was on the way out. Too old and not enough skill. I could hardly complain. Under Frank Arok I played for my country 43 times, travelled around the world and had many great memories. Those years were dreams come true. So to hear that the ASF had invited Frank Arok to apply for his own job was a blessing for me. I knew there was no way in the world Frank would do that. He's got too much pride. Now I just had to hope the new national coach needed someone in midfield who could run all day, compete for every ball and maybe bob up for the occasional goal. If he did, I was the man.

CAPTAIN OF
MY COUNTRY

CAPTAINS CARRY GREAT EXPECTATIONS. The captain of any Australian national sporting team is meant to be a great leader, a great player and a great inspiration to his or her team. If the team wins, the captain is there to take the cup and the glory. If the team loses, the captain has to face the media and take the rap. Charlie Yankos was the Socceroo captain for most of my first 40 games for Australia and he fitted the bill. He was a tough defender, a street-wise guy from Melbourne's western suburbs who was built like the Incredible Hulk. Charlie had an air of authority, as if he was always in command. Few players dared to tangle with Charlie Yankos, but I once made the mistake. I recall one hectic Socceroo game where we were under the hammer and I was trying to organise a few things in midfield. I was shouting directions and in the middle of the chaos Charlie told me to shut up. I was too fired up and went on with it. I'm never short of a word on the soccer pitch. Alan Davidson, who played in three World Cup campaigns for Australia, turned around and said, 'Wadey, who the hell do you think you're talking to? He's the captain of this team so you bloody well listen to him.' With that, I shut my mouth, and fortunately Charlie didn't make anything more of it.

When it came to talking on the field, my attitude was that we had eleven captains. Every player had a job to do and if they thought something was going wrong in their area they had to try to sort it out. I had never believed that the captain was the only player allowed to shout instructions on the park, but after that I made sure Charlie Yankos had the last word! In many ways Charlie was a great leader. When things got tough, he was there with the last-ditch tackles in defence. He took responsibility for all the penalty kicks and free kicks. A couple of times he rescued games with his incredible kicking ability. I'll never forget the 1989 World Cup qualifer in Tel Aviv when we were down to 10 men and losing 1–0. Charlie placed the ball and the Israelis knew he was going to have a shot, but he hit it so hard and with so much swerve that the goalkeeper didn't get near it. We left with a precious 1–1 draw. In a vital Olympic Games qualifier in Auckland in 1988 he whacked a 60-metre pass that Frank Farina vollied for a late equaliser. Of course, no one could forget the Yankos special against Argentina in the Bicentennial Gold Cup, a 35-metre rocket that swerved in every direction before thumping into the back of the net.

Charlie was a good speaker and comfortable with the media, so he was really a good captain, on the field and off. He was a key player in two World Cup campaigns, but after that terrible day at the Sydney Football Stadium in April, 1989, when we were eliminated from the Italia '90 World Cup race, Charlie knew his time was up. He played a few more times for the Socceroos, but in June, 1990, he retired from international soccer. Alan Davidson had quit after the World Cup game against Israel in April, 1989, but there was a lot of speculation that Davo would be back and the captaincy might just be the lure. Eddie Thomson was appointed to replace Frank Arok as Socceroo coach in May, 1990, and I remember seeing a newspaper cartoon showing Thommo holding a fishing rod with the captaincy dangling on the end of the line. The idea was that Davo would eventually bite, come out of retirement and take the captaincy.

No one could argue with Davo's credentials. He was one of the first Australian players to get a contract in Europe, even though his time at Nottingham Forest was ruined by injury. He had the international experience and was a brilliant and confident player, ideal as a captain. I think captains are picked partly because of their experience and partly because the coach sees some leadership qualities on and off the park. The trouble was that Davo had made up his mind. He had started a family and didn't want to spend months away from home every year touring with the Socceroos.

While all this going on in the middle of 1990 the captaincy was the furthest thing from my mind. I was just happy to still be a part of the Socceroos under Eddie Thomson. If Frank Arok had stayed I would have been finished, but Thommo kept me in the squad and that was enough. When Eddie Thomson named Graham Arnold as the new Socceroo captain to replace Yankos it didn't even occur to me that I'd been overlooked. As far as I was concerned I wasn't even in the running and I certainly didn't have a desire to be captain. Arnie was popular among the players, although if captains were selected for their attitude on the training track he never would have got the job. We used to call him 'Statue' or 'Seagull': at the cricket, seagulls settle in the outfield and scatter only when the ball comes near them. Arnie was the same at Socceroo training. Well, we never did find out what sort of captain he was, because Arnie accepted a contract in Holland and took off without ever leading the Socceroos onto the park as captain. Once again the captaincy was vacant.

In August, 1990, the Socceroos were heading to Indonesia for the Independence Cup. The squad was picked and had a training camp at the Australian Institute of Sport (AIS) in Canberra. After the last training session, Thommo called a meeting to tell us what he expected from the tour. He wasn't travelling to Indonesia because the Australian Olympic squad had a European tour that coincided with the Independence Cup, and with the Barcelona Olympic qualifiers coming up the Olympic team had priority. Thommo ran through a few things and casually mentioned at the end of the meeting that I would be the captain for the tour. There was no applause or speeches because I, along with everyone else, figured it was a stop-gap measure. Davidson or Arnold would be Socceroo captain in the long term, I thought, so there was no need to get too excited. Even so it wasn't a bad feeling. The more I thought about it, the better I felt. So what if it was only a second-string tournament in Jakarta? I was the captain of Australia, at least for a few games.

My FIRST GAME AS Socceroo captain was August 20, 1990, in Jakarta. The Socceroos played the Malaysian Olympic team in the opening round of the Independence Cup, and won 3–0. Ernie Tapai scored the first goal and Kimon Taliadoros scored twice after coming on as a substitute. It was a game we were expected to win easily and we did. It was a low-key game, but at least we had won. Immediately I felt the extra responsibility that comes with captaincy. Every player is responsible for the team's performance, but at the end of the day it is the coach and the captain who have to face the music.

Thommo had said that one of the reasons he picked me as captain was because of my infectious attitude at training, but I soon discovered that the captaincy is a whole lot more than geeing the guys up at training and tossing the coin before the game. Les Scheinflug was in charge in Jakarta and my role off the park was to be the go-between: to pass on instructions to players and give feedback from the players on how they were feeling. If the guys needed geeing up or were moaning about something, I could pick up the underlying tones. I could let the coach know what was going on and help the overall preparation by smoothing out a few bumps. In the same way, if players were unsure about what Les wanted, I could check things with him. That was my role for that tournament in Jakarta. Les Scheinflug is also the Young Socceroo coach, and a lot of guys who'd played under him in youth teams were wary. He made them call him 'Boss'. To me he was always just Les, and he was easy to talk to.

Things went really well in Jakarta. In the next match we beat Indonesia 'B' 7–0 with Andrew Zinni scoring a hat trick. We defeated the Thai Olympic team 2–0 and were in the final of the Independence Cup against Indonesia's full national team. I'd grown up watching English FA Cup finals and I have always dreamed about standing at the top of those steps at Wembley and accepting the

FA Cup from one of the Royal family and then turning round to the fans to hoist the cup up in the air. In reality, I had next to no chance of ever captaining a team in the FA Cup final, so I was going to make the most of the Independence Cup at the Semanyan Stadium in Jakarta. For all I knew, it might be the first and last time I would be captain of Australia!

The boys did the right thing and we won the final 3–0. I scored two goals, which capped it all off. Now came the moment I'd been waiting for, the cup presentation. I accepted the trophy from an Indonesian official. There were 40,000 fans watching the game and I was ready to do the big Wembley-style FA Cup salute, even though there were only about half a dozen Aussie supporters there. At least thousands of Indonesian fans would see Paul Wade's first triumph as Socceroo captain, or so I thought.

As I turned around I couldn't believe my eyes — it was as though they'd taken the side of the stadium away or the whole side of the stadium had become a gate. Indonesia had lost and somehow 40,000 people had left that stadium in about five minutes, straight after the final whistle. I sheepishly held up the cup to about four people sitting in the stand on the other side who hadn't bothered to leave. I could picture Wembley with 100,000 people and millions watching on television. Instead, I had my moment of glory in front of four spectators.

The Indonesian official then gave me an envelope and told me to look after it very carefully. I thought it was probably full of tickets to the next year's final or something like that. I held on to the envelope in one hand and the cup in the other and called for the other players to come over and take the cup. I didn't win it on my own, they won it, too. I handed over the cup then took a look inside the envelope.

I peeled back the top and all I could see were US$100 bills. It must have been the prize money. I panicked. I thought, 'It could be a set up. Someone's going to knock it off and I'll cop the blame.' I took another look — there were thousands of dollars there. It turned out I had US$25,000 in the envelope. There were people milling around everywhere and not much security. I went looking for the tour leader to get rid of the money so that I didn't have the responsibility any more.

Vito Cilauro, the Victorian Soccer Federation chairman at the time, was the tour leader. I gave him the money. He didn't even know there was prize money for the tournament. He stuck the fat envelope in his pocket. As the lads returned to the dressingroom I told them the incredible story about the US$25,000. Pretty soon I was copping all sorts of abuse. The lads gave me heaps. They wanted a cut of the money and wanted to know why I hadn't just stuck it down my shorts, walked off to the dressingroom and said nothing. I'd never even contemplated doing that. Too honest for my own good, was the general assessment from my team mates. I was suddenly feeling as though I'd let them

89

down in some way. I asked Vito about a bonus for winning the cup and he said he'd pass on the request to the ASF. We didn't see one cent of the US$25,000. Given another chance I wouldn't have done anything differently, because the cash wasn't mine to dole out, but as national team players should we have to beg for a bonus? I think not.

W HEN WE RETURNED HOME after the Independence Cup, people kept asking, 'How does it feel to be the captain of the Socceroos?' To be honest, I didn't feel like the captain. I'd say, 'I was the captain for the Independence Cup, but Thommo hasn't officially appointed me as captain.' I got the nod for Indonesia in a casual one-line sentence in a team meeting, so I wasn't about to parade around telling the world I was Socceroo captain. A month after the Jakarta trip we went to South Korea and again there was no fanfare. In fact, Thommo said nothing about the captaincy so I assumed I was the caretaker captain until further notice.

I still hadn't captained the Socceroos at home, so when a tour by Czechoslovakia was announced for January, 1991, I was hoping to get the chance to lead out my country in front of our fans. Around the same time, Alan Davidson announced he was making a comeback. Thommo had been working on him. I was ready to kiss the captaincy goodbye. We went into a training camp to prepare for the first game in Melbourne and there was no mention of the captaincy. I wasn't about to bring it up. A couple of days before the first game in Melbourne I figured I still had the job, but thought it was only a matter of time before Davo took it. Even so, it was a great feeling to lead out Australia on home soil. My mum and dad were there to see the game and before the kick-off I was presented with a trophy to mark my 50th Socceroo appearance, which had come against South Korea in the previous September. Davo played both games against the Czechs, but we lost both, 1–0 in Melbourne and 2–0 in Sydney. A few weeks later Davo retired again. He had his eyes on a fat contract overseas and eventually made a move to Malaysia, family and all.

It wasn't until England came to Sydney for a one-off game in June, 1991, that I was confirmed as Captain Socceroo. A few days before the game, Eddie and I were doing some TV interviews with Channel 9's 'Wide World of Sports'. Before the cameras were rolling the reporter asked a few background questions. The topic of the captaincy came up and I answered, 'I'm captain now, but for how long, who knows?' The reporter asked Thommo about this, and he said, 'Of course he's the captain of Socceroos. It's his job.' That was the first time Thommo had indicated it was a permanent appointment. That's when I finally felt like Captain Socceroo.

I realised that I was no longer just a club footballer, or one of dozens of players lucky enough to represent Australia. I was the captain. It's no guarantee of stardom or wealth, but without the title of Socceroo captain I was plain Paul Wade, an ordinary lad from the suburbs earning a quid as a draftsman. Being the Socceroo captain made you a public figure, the leader and spokesman of the Australian national team, an ambassador for the game. I had not been a captain since my days at St Mary's as a 10-year-old.

On the other hand, the captaincy didn't change my playing style. My job in the Socceroo midfield was to cover every blade of grass on the park, win as many tackles and as many headers as possible and get the ball to players who could do the damage. Throughout my career I had been a talker, always encouraging team mates and giving instructions, so nothing changed. My first tour under Les Scheinflug had set the guidelines and I developed an excellent working relationship with Eddie Thomson. If players were unsure of their positioning or their specific job I had such a good understanding with Eddie that I could quite confidently ask him what certain players should be doing without feeling I was sticking my nose into his business. I would go back and tell the player, but I would never say to Thommo, 'Hey, guess what, so and so is confused', or 'He wasn't listening when you explained the tactics'.

As I saw it, my job was to liaise between the players and the coach, because quite often, especially for guys in the squad for the first time, the prospect of having to front the national coach is daunting, as I had discovered when I first met Frank Arok. I had to know everything about the team tactics and make sure we stuck to them. I was the go-between, but I still wanted to be one of the boys. Thommo likes to keep things informal and that suited me fine. He never sat down and said the captain should do this or that. I figured if Thommo didn't like what was happening he would say something. He would let me know what he was thinking about the tactics or the team selection: he wasn't asking my opinion, but I felt he was sharing privileged information. I enjoyed the responsibility and I felt there was a mutual trust in the relationship.

Of course, Eddie Thomson was a very different coach from Frank Arok. Frank was always looking at the big picture, with big dreams and a big mouth to go with it. Thommo was closer to the players and paid attention to detail. That made it easier for the captain. When Thommo was Frank's assistant, he hated the way Frank played up to the media, but when I look at Thommo today, he sometimes carries on as much as Frank did. The one place you don't want to be when Thommo is sitting on the bench during a game is next to him or playing on the wing in front of him. For the whole 90 minutes he never shuts up. He's swearing, cursing and screaming at his own players, the referee and the opposition. Maybe it's the way he handles the pressure, but in any case it makes good TV, just like Frank Arok did. Coaches are always strong characters; they wouldn't be coaches if they weren't. Having to deal with them is part of a player's education.

As captain of the Socceroos, my education has gone further, because I became a public figure. I know it's lifted my self-confidence. My mum and dad often say, 'Whose son is he? He's not ours.' They are basically reserved people, but I've had to learn to be big and bold. When my parents see me with sports commentator Bruce McAvaney on Channel 7 talking just the way I talk to the guy next door, they ask, 'Where did it come from?' Well, it came from the old 'sink or swim' survival instinct, but I hope I've retained the values of modesty and honesty, things Mum and Dad hold dear.

The captaincy didn't affect my game at all, except to make me work harder. I knew the public and the media treated the captain differently, and I wanted to set the best example for my team and the fans. The biggest shock to my system was the workload for the captain off the park. There are some dirty jobs that have to be done, and I found out the hard way.

When the Socceroos played England at the Sydney Football Stadium in June, 1991, there was talk that it would be the first million-dollar gate for Australian soccer. Naturally, the Socceroo players wanted to be paid accordingly because we were the main part of the show. Thommo had said that we were going to get $1000 per player, win, lose or draw, and if we didn't get it from the Australian Soccer Federation then he would pay it out of his own pocket. Of course, being a Scotsman, he was saying it in jest, but he was confident the ASF would pay the bonus. Our normal match payments were $300 a win, $200 a draw and $100 a loss, before tax.

Well, we lost against England and were paid a miserable $100. By the time we paid tax we pocketed $70 each for playing in front of 40,000 fans and a million people on TV. It really was a farce. When Croatia toured Australia a year later, in July, 1992, things had come to a head. The players were sick of being ripped off. We were getting paid more to play club football than to play for the Socceroos, in some cases twice as much. Four days before we were supposed to play Croatia in Melbourne, the boys decided to take a stand. Players were telling me, 'Wadey, you're the captain of this team so go and tell the ASF that if we don't get what we want we're not going to play.' In other words, they were threatening to go on strike unless the ASF agreed to increase our pay to $500 a win, $300 a draw and $200 a loss. Just what I needed. I was saying, 'Lads, just settle down. You can't very well hold a gun to the ASF's head a few days before the game, when the team we are playing is already here. It's too late for this.' I didn't have too many supporters.

I went to see Les Scheinflug. I didn't want to bother Thommo a few days before the game, but I had a responsibility to speak on behalf of the players, even though I didn't like the idea of threatening a strike. Les listened and said, 'Wadey, understand one thing. There are a lot of players standing behind you now, but when it comes to the crunch they will run a million miles away and you'll be left all alone. Don't ever be sucked in like that.' Both Eddie and Les agreed we should be paid more money, but they themselves couldn't give us a pay rise. My next stop was Ian Holmes, the ASF Chief Executive at the time. He went through all the figures about how much it costs to run the Socceroos, the daily wages, the cost of bringing out the Croatian team and all sorts of stuff. 'We can't pay you any more money' was the bottom line. Paul 'Gullible' Wade swallowed it. I wasn't sure what to do. The players wanted more money and I agreed. So did the coaches. The ASF claimed they were broke and I had to go back and tell my team they deserved more money, but weren't going to get any, and tell them that a few days before a game wasn't the right time to solve the problem.

I called a players' meeting at the team hotel in Melbourne, the Southern Cross. 'I know we should be getting more, but it's wrong that we put a gun to their heads and say, "Pay us or we are not playing." After this tournament we'll get it sorted out.' They didn't want to listen. Micky Petersen, Warren Spink and Zeljko Kalac were the hardliners, I suppose, and they had most of the squad behind them. 'We're sick of being taken for a ride', was the general view. Over the next couple of days I went back and forth between the players and the ASF. I was getting nowhere. I'd had enough and decided to take a stand. In the end I said to the players, 'Alright, I'm playing against Croatia and I want you to put your hand up now if you're not going to play. If you're willing to walk away and never play for your country again put your hand up.' There was silence. Not one of them put his hand up. I knew then Les Scheinflug was dead right. In the privacy of a hotel room there was tough talk, but no one wanted to stand up and be counted.

In the end I was the one who suffered the most. The players thought I hadn't gone to bat for them and the ASF probably thought I was a troublemaker. I did not believe threatening a strike was the right way to go, so eventually I had to back my own judgment and go against some of my team mates. It wasn't the last time Socceroo wages made my life a misery. The joke is that I don't have a clue about money. I don't even look after the money in my own house. My wife Valerie handles all that. I wasn't even doing the household finances, but I was expected to negotiate deals worth thousands of dollars between 20 players and a national sporting body. No wonder it caused me grief. It's not in my make-up to be a domineering captain. I would rather be a quiet achiever who does his own job well and might just inspire others. I never wanted to be seen shooting my mouth off or giving orders, but with the talk of a strike I had to act, to give the stamp of authority to my captaincy.

There weren't too many tests of my leadership, but there is one case I'll always remember. In August, 1992, Eddie Thomson and Les Scheinflug were with the Olympic team at the Barcelona Games while the Socceroos went back to Indonesia again for the Independence Cup. Vic Fernandez was in charge of what was a very ordinary-looking Socceroo team for a very ordinary tournament. Our attitude was lousy. Without Thommo and Les to crack the whip the tour became a farce. We just beat the Thai youth team in the first game and then had to play Malaysia, who were being coached by Kenny Worden.

Kenny had taken Melbourne Croatia to the 1990–91 NSL Grand Final so he knew most of the Socceroos. It was a nightmare. Malaysia beat us 1–0 and two days later the South Korean under-19 team did the same thing. Kenny Worden gave us a serve in the media, describing us as 'the disgrace of Asian soccer' because we hadn't taken the tournament seriously. Players were spending as much time in the nightclubs of Jakarta as they were on the training ground.

Our final game was against Indonesia and we had to salvage something from the mess. There was a fairly big crowd and we couldn't afford to lose three in a row. I didn't fancy trying to explain that to the media when we got home. I was determined to put in a big game. As I put on my boots before the game something felt odd. My foot was slipping all over the place, so I checked the boots, only to find Vaseline smeared inside. I found out Micky Petersen was the culprit so I grabbed a handful of Vaseline and rubbed it in his hair. I was fed up with all the mucking around. I was wearing a training shirt for the pre-game warm-up because it was so hot in Indonesia. As I was about to go I saw Micky and Ernie Tapai stuffing around with a tube of Dencorub, the heat liniment. I was still furious about the Vaseline. I warned Micky, 'If you touch anything of mine while I'm out there warming up I'm going to belt you.' I meant it. I came back into the dressingroom to get my playing strip and by that time Micky and Ernie had made their way up into the grandstand. They were both injured. We lined up for the national anthems and I was thinking, 'Gee, my armpits are burning and my balls are warm.' I thought, 'Petersen, you bastard!' I knew exactly what had happened, the old Dencorub trick. For the first 20 minutes of the game I couldn't concentrate, I couldn't pass a ball, I couldn't run. My mind was preoccupied by the burning sensation and the desire to belt the crap out of Micky Petersen. My skin was on fire. Gradually, the discomfort passed and I got on with the game. We were two goals up and were awarded a penalty. A few other guys were debating who would take the spot kick and I thought, 'Hang on a minute! I'm the captain. I'm taking the penalties. I'm going to take them in the World Cup campaign so I'm going to take them now.' I grabbed the ball and scored. I knew then from that show of authority that I was going to finish what Micky Petersen had started. We won the game 3–0.

I went straight into the dressingroom after the game and found Micky sitting on the physio's table. I walked up and said, 'What did I tell you before I walked out of here?' and he played dumb. 'I told you I was going to belt you if you stuffed around with my gear ...' and with that I let fly with a big left, a clenched fist right on the end of his jaw. I'm left-handed and made sure I gave him a good thump. Then it was on for young and old. Ian Gray was trying to separate us. I landed one on Micky, but he landed about five or six on me because I'm not a fighter. A dozen punches were exchanged before we were separated and then it was 'F..k you, Wadey', and insults flying back and forwards. It must have made an impression, because I discovered later that Ernie Tapai had locked himself in the toilet, thinking he was next! Things were pretty hostile until we got to the bar that night and had a good laugh about it. At least the jokers would think twice before they messed with me again.

WHEN THE QUALIFICATION MATCHES for the USA '94 World Cup began in September, 1992, I was ready for the challenge of being the captain for such an important campaign. Over the previous two years I'd captained Australia in 28 internationals. In fact, I hadn't missed a game. In March, 1992, I'd quit my job as a mechancial draftsman to work as a development officer for the Victorian Soccer Federation. I really was a full-time Socceroo captain and I was committed to the job of being a roving ambassador. If I was asked to get out of bed early to do an interview for breakfast radio, no problem. If fans wanted autographs, I wouldn't let anyone leave disappointed. If there was a shopping centre promotion, I'd give it all my energy. My working day was filled with coaching clinics at primary schools around Victoria.

You soon realise that all youngsters have dreams, and that some of them want to be Socceroos. My dreams of being a full-time footballer had more or less come true. Standing in front of these wide-eyed kids I'd think, 'I am where they want to be.' It was a daily reminder of what it meant to be Socceroo captain and I realised the importance of the right image for the game. I found it very easy to say all the right things because I really do believe the message. You have to work hard, love the game and, most of all, hang on to your dreams. Spending so much time at the grassroots really does change your outlook. As much as we play the game for our own satisfaction, at the end of the day the Socceroos are there for the people. The kids in the schools who kick a ball around at lunchtime and their parents who take them to a Socceroo match are the people I play for. I can relate to them. I don't earn $13,000 a week like the best-paid Australian player in Europe. I know what it's like to struggle to pay the mortgage. I know that $50 or $60 to take a family to a Socceroo match is a big financial commitment. That's why the people on the terraces are as much a motivating factor as your own will to win. When you're the captain of Australia that is the ultimate responsibility.

Going into the '94 World Cup campaign, I desperately wanted success for myself, the team and all those people who support us. And I wanted all Australians behind us. Every time I did an interview, signed an autograph or talked to fans at a shopping centre, at the back of my mind was the thought that all these little things added up to something big. If you talk to a hundred people and only one goes away with a better view about soccer, it's worth it. Time and time again I hear about the 1974 World Cup and how Socceroos making it was meant to be the start of a new era for soccer in Australia. We all know it didn't happen. The Socceroos went to the World Cup, it was big news for a while and then it died.

I had to believe we could do it in 1994 and this time get it right. For that reason I never turned down a request for an interview. I owe it to the fans of soccer to be accessible and to promote the game whenever I can. When we are touring overseas I always get phone calls in the middle of the night from the media. It's tempting to tell the hotel operator to block the calls, but I wouldn't be doing my job. And when I've got twenty soccer balls in my hotel room, each one needing to be signed by 20 players, I do the slog and make sure it happens. I drag myself to shopping centres and schools when my team mates are resting. I sign autographs until my hand is cramping. I do it all because it's important and it's enjoyable and it's what the Socceroo captain should do.

THE WORLD CUP CAMPAIGN began with a bit of a scare when we travelled to the Solomon Islands in September, 1992. Only a late goal by Tommy McCulloch of Marconi secured a 2–1 win in a game we were expected to win easily. The return game was more like it, a 6–1 win, and a couple of victories over Tahiti had us over the first hurdle in the Oceania qualifying group. Sadly, the second game against Tahiti, in Brisbane, was the end of Micky P's Socceroo career. For seven years we had been partners in the Socceroo midfield, but he was sent off for foul language and never again selected.

Those games were played without any of the European-based Socceroos. By May, 1993, the European season was over and all our expats were available for the next World Cup qualifiers, against New Zealand.

Money was again the cause of irritation. The threatened strike against Croatia in July, 1992, was something I didn't want to go through again. In the months leading up to the New Zealand World Cup games I sat down with John Constantine, the ASF Chairman, and Ian Holmes, the Chief Executive, and worked out a deal to cover the entire World Cup campaign. I didn't want to get caught again. We looked at the likely games and settled on the following formula. To beat the Kiwis was $500 a win, $300 a draw and $200 a loss per game. If we got past New Zealand, our next opponent would be a team from CONCACAF, the Central and North American group. There the match fees would be $750, $500 and $250. The final qualifying matches would be against a South American nation and a win would earn qualification for the USA '94 World Cup. We settled on payments of $2000 a win, $1000 a draw and $500 a loss. That meant we could collect $6500 if we won all the qualifying games and secured a place at the World Cup finals. On top of that we would be paid at the $500, $300 and $200 rate for any friendly internationals during the campaign. It was the end of the hassles, or so I thought.

When all the European-based players joined the home-based Socceroos in Melbourne for a training camp before going to Auckland, I broke the good news. Graham Arnold, who was playing for F.C. Liege in Belgium, burst out laughing. 'I get $5000 a week to play club football and somebody wants me to win a game that gets us to the World Cup for two grand! You've got to be joking!' My heart sank. I'd stuffed up badly. I was so naive. I had no idea how much money these guys were earning in Europe. It was the biggest mistake I have made as the Socceroo captain and it was to haunt me for months. You can imagine how popular I was when Arnie told the other expats.

The squad assembled in Melbourne had been dubbed the 'Dream Team'. It was an impressive list. Mark Bosnich of Aston Villa, Ned Zelic of Borussia Dortmund, Robbie Slater of Lens in France, Frank Farina of Strasbourg, Aurelio Vidmar of Waregem in Belgium, Jason Van Blerk of Go Ahead Eagles in Holland, Vlado Bozinoski from Ipswich Town in England, Milan Blagojevic, from Ekeren in Belgium, Ernie Tapai from Stoke City, Dominic Longo from Cercle Brugge and, of course, the ever-faithful Arnie. They thought 'Wadey's deal' had sold them down the creek. Arnie said, 'Wadey, we are not going to put up with this crap, we're not playing for that. You'll have to renegotiate.' I was so embarrassed by the whole thing. We decided it was too late to do anything before the New Zealand games. We just couldn't afford any distractions, so Graham Arnold, Alex Tobin and I were going to sit down after the two games to work out the next move.

The squad was neatly split into the 'haves' and 'have nots', with a contract in Europe the thing that separated us. There was bound to be a little bit of friction, and there was. Zelic and Aurelio Vidmar would spend a lot of time together and you got the feeling they had something in common, as European footballers, that quite a lot of us couldn't understand or relate to. It was a kind of barrier; nothing major, but when you are living together 24 hours a day, little things can become irritating. It wasn't long before I'd had enough of Mark Bosnich's attitude. I felt he was quite happy to let everyone know he was at the top of the tree in the English Premier League. Quite possibly there was also a generation gap between those guys — Bosnich, Zelic and Vidmar — and me. Under Frank Arok we were a rowdy lot who didn't mind a beer and a laugh, but this younger generation had to look after themselves because soccer was big money to them. Their outlook was different, which is why so many have gone to Europe.

My blunder over the World Cup bonuses undermined my position. I think I was respected as the captain, but not as a footballer. I know that the traces of my Pommy accent bugged a few people and that's the last thing I wanted to be judged on. At the end of the day, I felt something wasn't quite right. The camaraderie was slow to take off. The Adelaide City players, Carl Veart, Alex Tobin, Milan Ivanovic and Tony Vidmar, were a pretty quiet lot. It was left to guys from the Arok days, like Arnold and Slater, to stir things up. They would slaughter anybody, take the mickey all day long. After a while you'd just want them to shut up, but it was all good fun. In any case, being captain of what was a new team made things tricky.

The trimmed-down squad left Melbourne for Auckland, worried about our first game together. Four years earlier the Kiwis had stuffed us 2–0 and we couldn't afford a repeat on May 30, 1993. It was a two-legged tie, so at the very least we wanted a draw from the away game. And as usual, it was a battle. Ironside, Dunford and Wright, who'd destroyed us in '89, were back for more, but this time we were ready for them. Graham Arnold scored the winner, but really we should have had at least two more. It was a big test for the 'new' Socceroos, and I was very happy with the way we'd played. Personally, I felt like I'd squared things up for the disaster in '89 by playing a solid game in the middle of the park.

We celebrated in the old Socceroo style and I could feel that the team spirit was slowly coming together. We flew back to Melbourne for the return game a week later. The last training session was at Olympic Park and it was a fun session of a small-sided game, mainly to keep the legs ticking over and to get a feel for the pitch. Those sessions before a game are never very long, so I usually like to go flat out. It's a confidence booster to have a good, sharp session 24 hours ahead of the game. On that day, though, I was feeling terrible. I couldn't move, and there were comments about 'Paul Wade's a seagull'. I knew I was sick, but there had been other times when I'd been crook the day before and recovered to play. It's not too often you go onto the field feeling 100 per cent right. There are always little knocks or some fatigue to overcome. You get a big adrenalin rush before a game and that usually is enough to get over any niggling problems. Besides, the Socceroo doctor, Brian Corrigan, always had a bag of tricks to fix things up.

There was no way in the world I was going to put my hand up and tell Thommo I was ill, but he was smart enough to know something was wrong. Seven weeks earlier I'd suffered a bout of pneumonia after a Socceroo trip. In April, towards the end of the NSL regular season, the Socceroos went to Singapore for two friendly internationals against Kuwait. We won the first game 1–0, but lost the second 3–1. The World Cup qualifiers were coming up, so I was doing extra training with assistant coach Raul Blanco. I wanted to make up for any loss of sharpness because I'd played most of the club season in defence, not in midfield, where you do heaps of running. I don't know whether or not I pushed too hard in the humid conditions of Hong Kong, but I picked up a bug.

I flew back to Melbourne feeling a bit off-colour, and ended up missing the first two games of that season's NSL play-offs.

On the eve of the New Zealand game in Melbourne, there was a suggestion that I was having a bit of a relapse of the pneumonia. That night Doc Corrigan was pumping me full of medicine, careful not to give me something on the banned list. As far as I was concerned, it was just a 24-hour thing and I'd be okay to play. On Sunday morning Thommo was doing a live interview with Channel 7 from the foyer of the Southern Cross. He called me in my room and asked me to come down. He said, 'I've been told you're not feeling the best. How do you feel now?' I replied, 'I didn't feel well yesterday, but I feel really good now.' I declared myself fit to play. With that I left, thinking I still had my place in the starting eleven. I went back to my room to sort out some chores. We had a youngster who'd won a 'Socceroo for a Day' competition and I was keeping him busy, sorting out soccer balls to be signed.

I got a message to go to Thommo's room. I walked in to face Eddie Thomson, Les Scheinflug and Raul Blanco, the entire Socceroo coaching staff. I sensed trouble. Thommo asked, 'Are you sure you're feeling okay?' I said, 'Yep, I'm fine.' He told me to go to the mirror and check the colour of my eyes. I went to the bathroom, knowing what I was going to see. I didn't look too bad. 'You're not right, are you?' I didn't feel 100 per cent, but compared with the day before I felt good. 'You're looking tired and drained, and yesterday you didn't train the way you normally do. You're not right at all, are you? I think what we're going to do is leave you out for this game.' Damn. There was no use arguing because I knew I wasn't 100 per cent right. I trooped back to tell Doc Corrigan that his bag of tricks wasn't working. He said, 'I told them that you were fine.' I replied, 'They have just ruled me out because of the colour of my eyes.' He laughed, and to this day whenever I bump into him he bungs on a serious doctor's face and says, 'Wadey, I want to have a look at the colour of your eyes', just as a wind-up.

In any case, I was now a spectator instead of the Socceroo captain for the game against New Zealand. Graham Arnold took the captain's armband for the first time, three years after he was first appointed. It's always a rotten feeling to miss out. Jason Polak took my place in midfield and we won 3–0. It was a game full of highlights. Carl Veart scored a great early goal, Aurelio Vidmar got the second with a powerful header from a cross by Robbie Slater, who was burning. I was hardly missed because Polak put in a solid performance in my position. I was feeling sorry for myself as I sat and watched. I didn't know it, but the worst months in my career as Captain Socceroo were about to engulf me.

THE MONEY TROUBLES HUNG around, like a ball and chain around my ankle. Ten days after we beat New Zealand in Melbourne, the Italian champions AC Milan, one of the biggest clubs in the world, were brought to Australia by a private promoter. Milan was being paid US$800,000 for two games and the tickets were $42 a head. There was money rolling around everywhere, except for the Socceroos. We were still on $100 a day expenses plus match fees of $500 a win, $300 a draw and $200 a loss. The ASF said the private promotor was making the money, not them. They told us to negotiate with the promoter. We were stitched up, once again.

The money issue was still red-hot when the Socceroos regrouped for the next phase of the qualifiers against Canada. They were the runners-up in the CONCACAF group, behind Mexico. We played the first leg in Edmonton on July 31, 1993, and the mood was pretty sour when we picked up the Canadian newspapers on the morning of the match to discover the Canadian squad had threatened a strike and won a pay deal to get around $10,000 per player if they beat us over two games. Under 'Wadey's deal' we would get $1500 to beat the Canadians. To cap off a really crappy experience, I was dropped from the team and we lost 2–1, but more on that in Chapter Five.

The lid blew off the payment troubles back in Sydney, before the second game against Canada on August 15. The players went to John Constantine and things went from bad to worse for me. 'Renegotiate? What do you mean, renegotiate? We have a signed document from your captain, agreeing to those payments!' My attitude had become cynical — I was being crucified by my team mates and I had been dropped by my coach in Edmonton. I was getting really fed up and I felt like an idiot, so I stood up and told John Constantine, 'You haven't even honoured the previous deal.' We had played a number of friendly games in Europe, en route to Canada, against Borussia Dortmund and Duisburg, two German clubs, and the Dutch team, Go Ahead Eagles. 'You haven't paid us for any of them. You owe the team $5000 in wages.' Tony Labbozzetta, who was the Head of Delegation for the World Cup campaign, stepped in. 'Hang on a minute! When we negotiated this I didn't say anything about friendlies. You only get paid when we get some income from the gate at home.' That wasn't what I understood. We had a heated discussion. 'Don't talk to me about reneging on a deal because you haven't paid us half of what you owe.'

I was no longer trying to be the voice of reason. I thought back to the troubles we'd had before we played Croatia; at that time Micky Petersen, a cynical bastard, figured the ASF officials were there to rip us off as many times as they could, to let us play for next to nothing. I was starting to think he was dead right. Nothing was resolved so the players decided that Graham Arnold, David Mitchell, Frank Farina and I would keep negotiating with the ASF.

By this stage the European guys were coming to my defence. Arnie gave the ASF officials a serve. 'You have taken the mickey out of Wadey, knowing full well how much money you are going to get from the World Cup games.' At the time no one knew that we would end up playing Argentina (with Maradona) and that the ASF would make millions of dollars on TV rights, ground advertising and ticket sales. Even so, Arnie, Mitch and Frankie made a very strong case that a World Cup play-off game would bring in loads of money, even if it was against Colombia, Paraguay or Peru who, with Argentina, were playing group elimination games. We sat down with Ian Holmes and John Constantine and told them the original deal wasn't good enough and to tear it up. They knew we were serious, so the haggling started. There were all sorts of offers and counter-offers. David Mitchell told them the Socceroos back in 1985 had a better deal than was being offered in '94.

The players were resolute. We had a players' meeting and the feeling was, we've got to make a stand or we'll get rolled for ever more. Someone suggested that to let the ASF know we were serious, we should refuse to train that afternoon. The tension was enormous. We were packed into a room, threatening to go on strike. I was nervous. I wanted to play for my country, but the problem was too big. It wasn't just the money any more, it was the principle: the Socceroos, with a dozen highly paid European professionals, couldn't be treated like part-timers. Then again, I was aware that the average guy in the street, earning $600 a week or less, wouldn't have much sympathy for us. We were getting $100 a day expenses, all our meals and accommodation were covered, and the ASF had agreed to pay up to $2000 for 90 minutes of soccer. On the surface it sounded good, but we wanted an increase to $5000 to beat Canada and $10,000 for the final qualifying games.

I'm forever thinking about our image among those fans on the terraces, and I was scared that all our good work for the game as a whole would go down the drain and we'd look money-hungry. What are people going to think of me? That was my greatest concern. I was earning less than $500 a game for South Melbourne, so $2000 was a lot of money for me. I guess that's why I struck the deal in the first place. Now all the school kids who'd listened to my advice about hanging on to your dreams would hear the stories that the Socceroos wanted more money or they wouldn't play. So much for national pride. It was a terrible dilemma. I could sense that quite a few other players had the same feelings, so we decided on a secret ballot before we went any further. After a few arguments we held the vote. I voted 'yes' to take a hard line. That meant we wouldn't train until the ASF agreed to a better deal.

Unlike the Croatia episode, this time I was with the majority. I'd become Mr Cynical. We'd been ripped off too many times. Another example: when we played AC Milan, the tickets for the players' friends and families turned out to be behind the corner flag, not on the halfway line as we'd expected. We were told the ASF had to look after sponsors, which is fair enough, but what about looking after the players? I was a completely changed man. Les Scheinflug had warned me about being the front man and being deserted, but this time I had

Arnie, Mitch and Frankie right beside me. After the secret ballot, Arnie, who really was the leader in this case, laid down the law. 'No matter what happens, don't anyone say a word outside this room, not one word about what's going on here. We know we're right, but we'll always be looked on as troublemakers if this gets out.'

Within an hour, two Sydney newspaper reporters, Mike Cockerill and John Taylor, were in the hotel asking, 'What's happening with the strike? What are you guys asking for?' Hell, how did it get out so fast? It was too late to turn back so we didn't go to training. All the media knew something was up. Thommo was sympathetic to the players. He wanted us to be looked after, but even more importantly, he wanted the whole thing sorted out before it totally stuffed up our preparation for the Canada game. He said, 'I don't want this to blow up in the media. We've got to sit down and sort this out. I'll say training was optional so it doesn't look like you lot are pulling a stunt.' That didn't work, either. The 'Socceroo strike' was front-page and back-page news. There was a pre-arranged publicity event in Martin Plaza in Sydney and instead of signing autographs for kids, we spent the whole time trying to duck questions about the 'strike'.

That night, Graham Arnold and I sat down with John Constantine and Ian Holmes at the Novotel Hotel. We put our case and asked for $5000 if we beat Canada. We settled for $4000, with a promise of a bonus if the crowd was big. We negotiated a fee of $10,000 for two games against whatever South American team we faced, win, lose or draw. The bonus for qualifying for the World Cup was $20,000 per player. The numbers were mind-boggling. I'd done a deal for $6500, but now we stood to earn over $35,000! The ASF approved the deal. It wasn't as though we were going to bankrupt them: the ASF announced a profit of $1 million in 1994, thanks to the World Cup campaign and the games against Argentina.

The $5000 match fee was the most I've ever been paid for a game. Nowadays it's something I tell the kids about with some pride. I use it to show that there are rewards for all the hard work and the sacrifices.

OVER FIVE YEARS I've made a career of being captain of the Socceroos. In 1992, when I left my job as a mechanical draftsman to become a development officer with the Victorian Soccer Federation, it was like turning professional. In 1994 I left the VSF to work in the promotions field for Mars Confectionery and Blades football boots. I worked in the media for Channel 7 and Melbourne radio station 3AW. I have been a full-time soccer player, thanks to the opportunities that came from being captain of the Socceroos. Am I lucky? You bet!

Better still, I get to pick whatever number I want. Nobody has ever dared to ask for No. 6 because that's my number. It goes back to my devotion to

Liverpool. Emlyn Hughes, the Liverpool captain in the '70s, was No. 6 and that was good enough for me. Am I a good captain? It's not for me to say.

I would never claim to be a great player or a great leader. My best attributes as a player are that I never give up and I hope that, over the years, I've inspired other players to put in that little bit extra. I wouldn't say I usually inspire a team with a 50-metre pass or a brilliant goal. The inspiration is more likely to come from winning a desperate tackle or chasing an opponent down. I always play that way, but I know that when a captain does something like that it can affect the team. There's something about the captain's armband that lifts the expectations. I never shut up on the park and I guess that's something I'd do whether I was captain or not. When the shouting and encouragement come from the captain, at least it sets the right attitude for the team. Keeping players' legs and minds going for 90 minutes has never been a problem for me and my big mouth.

Having said that, you can't treat all players the same way. I always use the example of Micky Petersen. We've played together for the best part of 10 years, at club level with Brunswick Juventus and South Melbourne, and at international level for the Socceroos, but people have said, 'I can't believe that you two are still friends and combine so well, because all you do on the ground is slag each other.' It's true, but we do it because we know each other so well. That's why it works: it makes us go harder. But I would never slag another player the way I slag Micky. Some players go to pieces if you have a go at them, or they forget about the game and put their energy into answering back. As Socceroo captain I think that more often than not I've picked the best way to treat guys. I don't think I'm a difficult person to get along with and I've done my best to make sure the Socceroos were a team in the true sense of the word. Does that make me a successful captain? You will decide.

I'd like to finish with the words I spoke at the River Plate, minutes after we'd lost 1–0 to Argentina in the World Cup play-off. It was live on SBS TV and I was fighting back the tears. After saying a few words of congratulations to Argentina, who really were a world-class team, I turned to the camera so I could address the Australian viewers. 'It just shows, when we pull on that green and gold, what we can do. To the people of Australia, I sincerely thank you, from all the players, for all the faxes and the well wishes. We went out and did it for you as well as for ourselves and we just hope we haven't let you down. We'll be coming home with big green and gold hearts. We love you.'

Maybe not a great speech, and maybe you don't think I'm a great captain, but I'll tell you what, every time I lead out the Socceroos I feel great to be an Australian.

CRISIS IN CANADA

TWICE IN THE MONTHS before my duel with Diego Maradona, I thought my international career was finished. Twice I had an absolutely sickening feeling that it was all over. No more captaincy. No more Socceroo games. No more World Cup dreams. One occasion will be easily recalled by any Australian soccer fan. It came in the Canadian city of Edmonton in July, 1993. I was dropped from the Socceroo team for a World Cup qualifier, gaining the dubious honour of being the first Socceroo captain to be dumped to the bench. At the time, the ASF would fax the newspaper coverage from home to our hotel in Edmonton. You can imagine how delighted I was to see 'Socceroo Captain Axed' in big headlines. Coming back from that very public setback was one thing, but there was an even bigger crisis away from the cameras and the public eye.

On Monday June 14, 1993, two days before the Socceroos played the visiting Italian club AC Milan in Sydney, Eddie Thomson summoned me to his hotel room. I was the Australian captain and he was the Australian coach, so there was always plenty to talk about and plenty of things to organise. On this day I had no idea what was on Thommo's mind. I took a seat and was ready for a bit of chit-chat. Instead, I copped the biggest serve of my career. Eddie Thomson slaughtered me. He was fired up in a way I'd never seen him before. 'What the hell's wrong with you?' he demanded to know.

He started by slagging my fitness. I had arrived in Sydney on the previous morning, a Sunday, after an early flight with my then South Melbourne and Socceroo team mates Paul Trimboli and Mehmet Durakovic. We were all a wreck after the South Melbourne presentation dinner on the Saturday night, which had gone on until one or two in the morning. We were tired and all we wanted to do was sleep when we arrived at the Novotel Hotel on Botany Bay, where the Socceroo squad was staying. After resting in the afternoon, we trained on the Sunday night at the nearby St George Stadium. As I soon found out, that training session had upset Thommo.

As I sat in his room, he let fly. 'You're breathing out your arse', he said, which is a crude way of saying a player is unfit and struggling to get his breath back. The attack went on. 'You're taking five minutes to get up from a tackle.' I was sitting there, stunned. I tried to defend myself, but Thommo just bulldozed over the top of me. 'You're obviously struggling for fitness and I'm not happy about your attitude. I've heard you've been whingeing about arriving early yesterday morning and not training until the evening.' I couldn't believe what I was hearing. I was stuck in my chair in front of the national coach, someone whom I respected, getting torn apart. I thought to myself, 'You've got to be kidding.' Not only had I not complained about the scheduling of the Sunday evening training session, I was glad about the timing. I remember saying to the lads, 'Beauty, at least we can sleep before training.'

I was sitting there in Thommo's hotel room, speechless. I don't know how or why it had happened, but something had suddenly changed drastically in our relationship. I had a horrible sinking feeling it was to be the beginning of the end for Paul Wade's international career. I thought, 'He's had enough of me.' Either that or he was trying to wind me up to get more out of me. In any case it was right out of the blue.

He attacked everything I stood for. I've never pretended to be a ballplayer, but one thing I pride myself on is fitness and commitment. I will always try my hardest, whether I'm in good form or not. In football, some days everything goes right and other days everything goes wrong, no matter how hard you try. I can live with that, it's the essence of sport. Sport is about doing your best. As far as I was concerned I was doing absolutely everything right at that training session. The trouble was that the man who picks the team thought differently.

I was shaking. Here were the Socceroo coach and captain in a room in the Novotel on Botany Bay, in the middle of a World Cup qualifying campaign. The middle for the Socceroos, but maybe the end for Paul Wade. I'm not usually stuck for a word, but now I didn't know what to say. I was in shock.

Just when I thought it couldn't get any worse, it did. 'I saw you get off the bus like an 80-year-old man' was a line I'll never forget. It was a reference to how I arrived at that Sunday evening training session at St George Stadium. I remember as clear as day that Thommo and the Socceroo assistant coach Les Scheinflug had got off the bus first. How could he have even seen me? It's funny how you remember things, how you take a photo in your mind. They were walking well ahead. There was no way in the world they could have seen me. Either someone was informing him, a gear steward or someone the coaches had planted to keep an eye on players, or he was trying to get me mad, to see how much I had left in the tank.

The crazy thing was that only four months before, the Socceroos had been away in Europe playing top teams — Borussia Dortmund in Germany and Go Ahead Eagles in Holland. Raul Blanco, one of Thommo's assistants, had told me on that European tour, 'Wadey, you must be happy with your game.' Raul is a serious football man and doesn't give out praise lightly. My game is all about hard work, fitness and aggression towards the ball, but with daily training and regular matches in Europe I was getting a good first touch, improving my skills and confidence on the ball. I was very happy with my fitness and my form. That's why Eddie Thomson's attack left me bewildered and worried about my playing future.

It went on. 'You're believing all the crap people are writing about you. Listening to everyone and forgetting about your job. You should be alive and bubbly and motivating the rest of the team.' I thought I was! Again I tried to have my say. I tried to get a word in, but Thommo was too fired up. I was on the ropes, reeling. Then came the knock-out punch: 'If you weren't Socceroo captain I would have dropped you six months ago.'

That was it. I fired back, 'I don't believe the shit you're talking. I can't believe this crap.' For me that reply was like getting up off the canvas. Thommo had floored me with all these cheap shots, but I wasn't going to lie down and take that sort of criticism. I stood up and was heading for the door. I didn't want to hear any more. The whole attack came out of nowhere. I started for the door and Thommo shouted, 'Come here. Sit down and shut up.' I paused for a second. My head was spinning. The whole thing was so unexpected and the things he was saying, I thought, were so untrue. If I had continued out of the door, maybe it would have been the end of my international career there and then. Thommo would have had a ready-made excuse to axe me if I had disobeyed him and left the room. I was frozen there at the door. I had no breath in my lungs. He had knocked the stuffing out of me. I was white. Even thinking about it now sends my nerves on end.

I had walked into this battering totally unprepared. I turned away from the door. I did what I was told. No sooner had I sat down than Thommo was back into me, going over the same things again: looking unfit, having a poor attitude towards the previous night's training session, getting off the bus like an old man and the stuff about listening to what people were saying about me. I couldn't believe it. I was frantically trying to work out what was going on. Did he want me to explode and tell him to get stuffed? Did he expect me to sit there and take it? Either way, I figured I was on my way out of the Socceroo team.

Finally, there was a pause. I was still in a state of shock. It was hard to think in a rational way, but I began to reply. I was almost pleading as I put my case, like a man about to be sentenced in court. I began to defend myself, trying to explain everything, without ever saying, 'You're a liar.' To this day I maintain he did not, and could not, have seen me get off the bus at St George Stadium. Why he thought I got off the bus 'like an 80-year-old man', I'll never know. As for the Sunday night training session, I explained that I was working my bum off. We had been playing a small-sided game, an eight-against-eight. There were no rest periods, I'd had a late night, an interstate flight and all the carry-on. I was going flat out, the way I try to do at all training sessions. As for supposedly complaining about having to train in the evening, nothing could be further from the truth. I was glad to have a snooze in the afternoon. His line about me listening to what other people were saying about me topped it all off.

This was the turning point in my relationship with Eddie Thomson. It would never be the same again.

IN JUNE, 1993, THE Socceroos were in the middle of the USA '94 World Cup qualifying campaign. We had beaten New Zealand 1–0 in Auckland on May 30, and 3–0 in Melbourne a week later, with expatriate Aussies Mark Bosnich, Frank Farina, Ned Zelic, Robbie Slater, Graham Arnold and Aurelio Vidmar back on international duty. There was lots of media talk about the Socceroo 'Dream Team', filled with European-based professionals. I told the media over and over that no one was guaranteed a place and that the best players, be they based locally or in Europe, would get the nod.

Each year I'd do hundreds of interviews as Socceroo captain and I'd learnt how to deal with the media in a professional way. Part of that learning means never taking things to heart: journalists have a job to do and writing stories about the Socceroo captain being finished makes for sensational reading. Not that I ever like reading that kind of stuff, mind you. I didn't have any doubts about my ability or value to the Socceroos. I still don't. I want to play international football as long as possible and after the pain of two unsuccessful World Cup qualifying campaigns (Italia '90 and USA '94), I've got to keep going. I'm desperate to play in the World Cup finals.

On June 14, 1993, I was kicked in the guts by the man who controls my destiny. Perhaps Thommo assumed that my comments about no one in the Socceroo team being guaranteed a place were a sign of my own insecurity, or meant that local players would struggle for a place in the 'Dream Team'. Quite a few of those who'd played in the first part of the qualifying campaign against the Oceania nations were no longer a part of things. I thought I had my place as long as I performed, not just because I was captain. That's why I was using the media to ram the message home to my team mates that no one should get too smug about being a Socceroo. We couldn't afford any complacency if we were going to qualify for the World Cup.

Maybe Thommo didn't see that my public comments were designed to fire up the boys. He may have thought it was the wrong thing for the captain to be saying. I had missed the second leg of the World Cup qualifier against New

107

Zealand in Melbourne ten days earlier because of illness. Jason Polak came in and did quite well. Then there were media reports that Paul Okon would be available for the forthcoming qualifiers against Canada, and if you put one and one together it was reasonable to assume Okon would be challenging for my spot in centre midfield, even though he was playing as a sweeper for Club Brugge in Belgium. The Socceroos already had two class sweepers in the squad in Ned Zelic, then playing for Borussia Dortmund, and Milan Ivanovic, from Adelaide City. Okon was new to the squad, so it was odds-on he wouldn't go straight in as the sweeper.

I explained all this to Thommo as clearly as I could, but I got the feeling he didn't really want to listen. I was almost pleading. I needed to know what was next. It's weird how silly things flash into your mind when you're under pressure. I recalled ringing Thommo one time and briefly speaking to his wife Pauline. Thommo would always joke that if he couldn't make up his mind on the line-up, Pauline would pick the team. I remember joking with Pauline about who would be selected. Now this was not so much of a joke.

I tried again to explain, to make him see my point of view. I felt I was down on my knees, but I wasn't getting anywhere. He'd thrown the KO punch about dropping me if I wasn't captain and was waiting to see how I'd react. I was trying to collect my thoughts. My blood pressure was still sky-high. It was hard to think rationally. 'What do I have to do?' I asked. I was half expecting Thommo to say, 'It's too late, you're finished.' Instead, he said, 'Just be yourself. Just be Paul Wade. Just be the enthusiastic guy that I picked in the first place.' It didn't really make sense. I paused for a moment. Why was I criticsed so much if all Thommo wanted to say was, 'Be yourself'?

I think that was the last thing said at that meeting. It was the only thing Thommo said the whole time that gave me a ray of hope. It hardly put me at ease, but at least I now felt I'd got something out of him about what he wanted. Until then he'd never played any mind games with me.

Later that afternoon we went back to St George Stadium for training. I hadn't told anyone about the Thommo blast. I was still upset. I couldn't stop thinking about it and what it meant for my international career. Would this training session be one of my last? I tried to get on with it, but the more I tried to put it out of my mind, the worse it got. I've never been one to keep things to myself, and I needed to spill the beans. So, back at the hotel after training I told my two team mates from South Melbourne, Trimmers (Paul Trimboli) and Yuggsy (Mehmet Durakovic, called 'Yuggsy' because he is from the former Yugoslavia), in confidence, about the way Eddie Thomson had slaughtered me. I told Trimmers I wanted to go for a walk. It was getting dark as we set off. We walked for ages.

I was waiting to see how Trimmers would react. He's a cool character. What I wanted to hear was, 'The guy's an idiot. How dare he say that to you?' Trimmers will never say it when you want to hear it, though. He's too laidback. But he's a great listener. He made a few comments, but I didn't get the reassuring words I wanted. I felt I was on the verge of getting booted out of the national team midway through a World Cup qualifying campaign, and I needed some reassurance. Trimmers made no real judgment. I never knew if he thought Thommo was right or wrong. He was asking questions as a reporter would, investigating. Occasionally, in the darkness, we'd stop, in silence. Lost in thought. Then Trimmers would ask another question. And so it went on. But he never said, 'The bastard.' That's how Trimmers is.

But Paul does have a sense of humour, and he used it to lift a huge weight off my shoulders the next day. We returned to St George Stadium for another training session. As the bus pulled up, Trimmers said, 'Let me show you how to get off the bus without looking like an 80-year-old.' He skipped and danced and bounced, smiling like an idiot, as he jumped off the bus. Then he jogged back onto the bus and did it again. Then he said, 'I want you to show me.' I was in fits of laughter. I couldn't do it. It relieved a great deal of my stress. I played the two games against AC Milan, trying my hardest to be myself.

Until the day of that bollocking, I had no hesitation in saying that Eddie Thomson and I got on well. Looking back now, I think maybe as coach and captain we got on too well. We were almost too close, and maybe that's my fault. Possibly I was losing sight of the fact that he was the coach and I was the captain. I wasn't an assistant coach and maybe that's what I was starting to think. There's no rule book for the Socceroo captaincy so I had no way of knowing whether I was doing the right or wrong thing. It all stopped on June 14, 1993, though. Getting ripped apart was one thing, but when it comes so unexpectedly, from someone you thought was a close associate, it's devastating. I still can't work out why I got slagged so badly if all he wanted to say was, 'Be yourself.'

I wasn't convinced that everything was sweet when I finally left the room after that showdown. From then on I was treading a real tightrope — the wind could blow and I could fall off at any minute. I just kept hanging on to that comment, 'Just be yourself.' It's as if Thommo was saying, 'I am going to kick you out, Wadey, unless you go back to being the Paul Wade that I picked three years ago.' On the other hand, the line about being dropped six months earlier if I wasn't captain was a huge negative. If Thommo was trying to set things straight, he had not succeeded. He had only succeeded in filling me with doubts. I'd been captain for almost three years and I came out of that confrontation thinking to myself, 'Okay, I'm obviously not the person he picked ages ago, and maybe I've lost sight of what my role really is.'

I'd always been able to talk openly with Thommo until that confrontation at the Novotel. It hurt. It had never happened to me before. No coach has ever slaughtered me like that. The most trouble I ever got into with a coach was at Croydon City in 1983, when my mate Des Shannon and I arrived late and were dropped to the bench. The team beat Ringwood City 7–0 and I had to sit on the bench and watch it. That was the biggest kick up the backside I'd had until now, and I certainly didn't need a kick up the bum from Eddie Thomson. I took the blast as a warning that I had somehow gone off the track, as far as he was concerned, and he was dragging me back onto the straight and narrow in a shocking way. He had given me the serve, but he had not actually said to the media that he wasn't happy with me or that he wanted to give me a serve to wake me up. I wondered what it all meant. One thing was sure, I no longer felt secure as Socceroo captain.

A MONTH LATER THE home-based Socceroos were together again, heading to Holland to meet the Europe-based players before heading to Canada for the first leg of the World Cup qualifiers. Slater, Arnold, Zelic, Okon, Bosnich, Aurelio Vidmar, Van Blerk, Farina, Longo and Mitchell were all doing pre-season training for their European clubs and it was an important time for them. The clubs wouldn't release them for training camps in Australia, so we had to go to them. Instead of flying direct to Canada, the home-based players would end up flying halfway around the world.

We began our training sessions in Holland, but there was trouble from the start. Most of the Europe-based players couldn't get away from their clubs. Graham Arnold, as usual, would do anything for the Socceroo colours. After his club training session he would drive five hours from Liège in Belgium to Holland to train with us. Robbie Slater had the same problem, but when he arrived from Lens in northern France he made a typical Slater entrance in his shiny black Porsche! We were only a little bit jealous. We had a week in Holland with the European players coming and going. Some didn't make it at all. Mark Bosnich didn't arrive from Aston Villa and Paul Okon was busy at Club Brugge in Belgium.

We ended up training without them, and there was talk that they might not make the trip to Canada. Eddie Thomson and Tony Labbozzetta, the tour leader, were spending heaps of time on the phone trying to sort things out. It wasn't looking good. Word spread that Mark Bosnich had told Thommo he couldn't play. We figured Aston Villa had put the pressure on Bosnich because the Canada game clashed with the start of the English season. When the media picked up the story there was a huge fight between the Australian Soccer Federation and Aston Villa. We left Holland without Bosnich or Okon. Once we arrived in Edmonton things got worse for Bosnich. The ASF took a hard line and demanded that Bosnich be released for the international, in accordance with FIFA rules. The penalty for clubs refusing to release players was suspension of the player concerned. Bosnich responded by announcing he was quitting the Socceroos — at 21 years of age! It didn't do much for our preparation.

In Edmonton I was rooming with Milan Blagojevic. Paul Okon and Milan are good mates. I just happened to answer the phone when Paul rang to talk to Milan and I got a surprise. 'The bastards are going to make me play', Paul Okon told me, the 'bastards' being the ASF officials. 'I want to play for my country, Wadey, but I have worked so hard to be where I am right now and if I go to Canada it might all go down the drain.' Okon had joined Club Brugge two years earlier, but injuries had cost him dearly. He'd spent months out of the game and once he was fit again, had to start from scratch in youth and reserve teams. 'Wadey, I'm fed up with playing in front of 200 or 300 people.' By this time, Okon had finally won a place in the first team and was desperate to retain his position. 'I know as soon as I leave to go to Canada this coach will find somebody else and I'll be in the reserves for another six months.' That's the sort of pressure Australian players in Europe were under. 'Wadey, I'm not willing to make that sacrifice at this stage for my country. I don't want to play and I have told Labbo and Thommo.'

As captain, I was worried about having a player in the squad who didn't want to be there. No coach is going to get the best out of a disgruntled player. Okon made a very good point. 'I would be better off establishing myself here in Belgium, playing a full season with the first team, then if Australia gets to the World Cup finals I'll be available and I'll be a better player by then. In Belgium I'll obviously be playing in top company and if I'm still playing well for Club Brugge I'll be good enough to play with you guys in the World Cup finals. If I leave now to play one game against Canada then go back, my club might give me the flick. I won't have a club. This is my profession, my living. There's no point making me play in Canada. We all lose, so why should I do it?' I had a lot of sympathy for Paul. Unfortunately for him, the ASF took a stand. He knew that if he didn't come, he'd get suspended by FIFA. Two days later Paul Okon arrived in Edmonton.

Our first training session was at a school ground and we had on our King Roo training gear, which nobody liked. The horrible green training top rubbed on your nipples and made them sore. I used to wear a windcheater under it. After warming up, Thommo started handing out the bibs for game, the first eleven versus the rest. I didn't get one. Thommo didn't say anything. There was no warning at all. I thought, 'Hang on a minute. Is he testing me? Is he just working out his options?' I was with 'the stiffs'. There are never quite enough players on tour to have two teams of 11, so usually the team physio or the assistant coach makes up the numbers. It means the stiffs have to work twice as hard to impress the coach. I remember thinking then that I had never before fully appreciated what the stiffs had to go through — I'd never been in the stiffs before. I got the feeling the coach wasn't looking at the stiffs. I was thinking, 'How can I let him know that I'm still good enough?' I was going flat out to win tackles and use the ball, but when you have two or three players to mark, it's very, very difficult. I kept this all to myself.

Lots of little things flashed through my mind. Is Thommo trying to motivate the rest of the players? Is he trying to motivate me? Am I going to get the chop? Back at the hotel a few guys asked, 'Wadey, you were in the stiffs today. What's going on?' I told them I didn't know. I still didn't relate the spray Thommo had given me at the Novotel back in June and getting left out of the first eleven at training.

The next day I was in my room when Thommo phoned. He asked to see me in the foyer. I went down and we grabbed a seat in a coffee lounge just off the foyer. After a bit of chit chat, Thommo said, 'Look, let's get one thing straight. You're the last person I want to drop, but what I have decided to do tactically is to go for Okon, Vidmar and Slater in the midfield.' I said nothing. Thommo went on to explain that it was purely a tactical move. 'There's nothing wrong with your attitude or the way you're playing.' I could accept that. Maybe I should have blown my top, but I didn't feel angry with Thommo. I was upset, of course. I'd been in the Socceroo team for seven years and had never missed a big game, but the way Thommo explained it, the decision made sense. The coach had decided tactically to go with a ball-playing midfield that was quick out wide. I couldn't argue that I was a better ball-player or faster than Okon, Vidmar or Slater. In any case, the coach is the one who picks the team and decides the tactics. So I wasn't immediately angry with Eddie Thomson.

I went back to my room and it began sinking in. I was thinking about Okon. He didn't even want to be there and he was picked ahead of me. I couldn't get angry with Paul either, but the whole thing made me think. Who's to say Okon is going to perform the way he can when he's worrying about his contract with Club Brugge? I could see Thommo's point — he was hoping Okon would be professional about it. Most of the team had sussed out what was going on from that very first training session. The only thing that seemed to surprise them was my reaction, or lack of it. Arnie and Slater were saying, 'I can't believe the way you have taken this, Wadey.' They were expecting me to spit the dummy and go berserk. They said they would be kicking the walls in if Thommo dropped them. I told them, 'How can I argue with him? If he was dumping me for poor form I might get upset, because I know I've been doing the job he wants.' 'So what?' was the reply.

I guess it shows that the one thing players dread is getting dropped. The reasons don't matter. We're players and we want to play. After the big blast from

Thommo in June I had been as focused and as enthusiastic as could be. I desperately wanted to play, and spitting the dummy wouldn't help my cause. What hurt more than anything else about the incident was hearing stupid comments a month or so later. People were telling me they knew I was going to get dropped, knew that Thommo was going to use me only until the crunch came in the World Cup games. As much as you try to ignore those comments they still sit there in your stomach, churning away. I was probably being naive to not see any links between what happened at the Novotel on June 14 and the decision to axe me in the last week of July. Maybe the swing of the axe started at that meeting on Botany Bay, maybe not.

BEING THE FIRST Socceroo captain to be dumped to the bench made me big news. Not the sort of 'first' I really needed. I was getting calls at all hours from radio and newspaper reporters in Australia. There were four or five journos travelling with the team and they were chasing me. Some were obviously baiting me. What do you think of Eddie Thomson? Maybe it was because I was experienced in dealing with the media that I didn't bite. If I had been, say, 22, I might have blown up but, as I've stated, I could understand tactically what the coach wanted. I had accepted what he had done, but I had to field dozens of questions, asking the same thing. 'Come on, you must be upset. You must be angry. What do you think of him? Why did he do it to you?'

Since early March, 1989, at the end of the previous World Cup campaign, I'd been building up to this campaign. Three years into a four-year plan and suddenly, I was out of the team. But I wasn't going to bite, even though I was hurt. I had been around too long for that. They all expected me to bag Eddie Thomson and could hardly believe what I said. I must have said these words over and over: 'Eddie Thomson's the coach and I'll abide by his decision. I'm going to work twice as hard to get back into the Socceroos. As long as we're in this World Cup campaign, I've got a chance of getting my place back.'

I said that, but deep down I didn't think there was much chance of regaining my place in the short term unless things went wrong in the first game against Canada. I was prepared to wait and take my chances, but one thing I wasn't going to do was bag Thommo and jeopardise my position. I hadn't come this far and put in so much work for nothing. I kept thinking of the World Cup finals. That was my aim and I'm not one to give up. Of course, it really hit me on match day. To wake up and see Milan Blagojevic getting ready brought it all home. He was in the starting eleven and I wasn't. Instead of the usual match-day nerves, I felt flat as a pancake. I had to work hard not to show my disappointment. Graham Arnold was now the on-field captain, but I still had a responsibility as an off-field leader. I had to be positive and help the lads.

We had a good side. Robert Zabica was in goal in place of Bosnich. Blagojevic and Jason Van Blerk were the full-backs, with Durakovic and Tobin the markers. Zelic was the sweeper. Slater, Okon and Vidmar were across the middle, with Frank Farina in the hole behind Graham Arnold up front. We knew the Canadian team was fairly physical. Reports had come back that they were a tough outfit. Their centre midfield player was a tough, stocky Scottish-born character called Colin Miller, and he wasn't in the team for his ball skills. It was going to be Canada's very British style against our more skilful European style.

When we arrived at the stadium the conditions were against us. It was very windy. It took the Socceroos a long time to settle. After 20 minutes Robby Zabica was sent off. The Canadian centre forward got through our defence and Zabbie rushed out of the penalty area and brought him down. The referee was a Mexican who flashed the red card. There was chaos on the bench. The reserve keeper, Mark Schwarzer, had to come on and Milan Blagojevic was substituted. Being down to 10 men made things even more difficult. Watching from the bench gave me a terrible, empty feeling. Even though we took the lead, thanks to an own goal, Canada came back at us. I thought I was going to go on: I was doing a warm-up behind the goal with Jason Polak and we were both called around to the bench, but Polak went on. I sat down. The final score was 2–1 to Canada. I remember Randy Samuel, the big Canadian centre back, waving to the crowd and they went absolutely berserk. Canada didn't outplay us, they just out-battled us.

I can remember feeling glad that things hadn't gone well, and then feeling guilty for that. It was the survival instinct. If the team had done well, my chances of a recall were slim. As it was, I figured I was a chance to get back into the team. I certainly wasn't devastated about the result, but I didn't let that get out to the other players. It was just a natural feeling of, 'I wonder what would have happened if I had been out there?' For a few self-indulgent minutes I felt that way.

After such a miserable day I had no hesitation whatsoever in going out on the town that night. At five in the morning, a few of us climbed into a taxi to get back to the hotel. Mehmet Durakovic was in the front seat. We'd only travelled a hundred metres when he turned to the cab driver and said, 'If you don't turn that meter off I am going to break your nose.' The cab driver was stunned. Mehmet was raving on. 'Look, you haven't turned the meter off from the last cab fare and we're not going to pay.' The lads broke up laughing. Mehmet was looking at a digital clock that told the rest of us it was 5.35 in the morning. Mehmet thought he was getting ripped off! At least we finished the night laughing. A few beers and a few laughs. It cheered me up. All the pain seemed to fade into the background.

THE RETURN GAME IN Sydney was two weeks away. I decided not to return home to Melbourne, but to stay in Sydney so I could concentrate on the job. I set myself up in the Novotel and did plenty of training. I also spent a fair bit of time on the golf driving range. It's good relaxation, and controlling a golf swing gets you in tune with your body.

It was an interesting time. Paul Okon had picked up an injury in the Edmonton game and decided to leave the squad and return to Belgium before the game. His involvement was unhappy from start to finish, but at least he was back in the Club Brugge first team soon after. The pay dispute covered in Chapter Four was about to blow up and there was tension on the training ground. Robbie Slater and Frank Farina had a huge punch-up. Not a push and shove, but a proper fight with a dozen of the best punches I've ever seen thrown. In the middle of it, Graham Arnold grabbed Farina and pinned his arms to try and separate them. Slater took the chance to throw another punch and whacked Farina, who couldn't get free of Arnie to defend himself. So Frank was wild at Arnie because he thought he was helping Slater. It took a while to sort things out. Thommo said nothing at the time, but later, on the team bus, he laid down the law. Luckily, there were no media cameras to see the fight, but word spread quickly. It meant our preparation was hardly ideal.

Thommo made changes after the disappointing result in Edmonton, but I still failed to make the first eleven. With Okon missing, Ned Zelic moved from defence to midfield. Milan Ivanovic came in as sweeper in Zelic's place. I was a spectator again. At the Sydney Football Stadium there's a sectioned-off area for players and other staff. The coaches — Thomson, Scheinflug and Blanco — usually sit on chairs on the sideline, with the team doctor and the physio. I sat in the sectioned-off area.

Right from the opening kick-off, we missed chance after chance. Frank Farina missed an open goal. We only needed a 1–0 win to go through. That would have made the aggregate score 2–2, but we would have progressed under the away goals rule. Getting that solitary goal was a nightmare but finally, just before half-time, Farina did the trick with an overhead kick. It was brilliant and I was pumped up. I was getting emotionally involved, like all the other spectators. I may as well have been up in the stand having paid my $25 to get in — I wasn't the cool, relaxed professional sitting on the bench! At half-time everyone was confident we'd finish Canada off, but not long into the second half they scored again. That made the score 3–2 to Canada. I'd been looking towards the coaches, looking for a sign that I might be needed. Les Scheinflug usually handles the subsitutions for Thommo, so I was keeping an eye on Les. Inside I was pleading, 'Come on, give me a go at this mob. Let me have a chance.'

When Canada had equalised, I was given the signal from Les to warm up. That didn't mean I was going on. Coaches always get subs warming up like that.

When a team concedes a goal or a player goes down injured, the coach automatically turns around and gets players warming up. In this case my appearance was aimed at geeing up the players on the field. Fortunately, I've spent very few games on the bench in my career, but I had picked up a few tips from players who were forever on the subs' bench. Rule number one was warm up close to the bench so the coach can see you. Coaches are so involved in what they are doing they can forget about who they have told to warm up and why. I have seen players warm up for half a game and not get a run. On this night I did my warm-up right behind their seats, close enough so they wouldn't forget. On the field, the team weren't playing any better. In fact, we were getting worse.

I started to think back to March, 1989, when we were knocked out of the World Cup qualifiers on the same ground. I got sick of warming up, and then I didn't really want to go on any more. I'll never forget that sickening feeling of '89 and I could see it all happening again. I could sense that it just wasn't going to be our day. I continued warming up down towards the corner flag, away from the bench, out of the coaches' view. I didn't think that they would put me on anyway, because at that stage we needed a goal and there were other attacking players on the bench. There were some youngsters asking for autographs so I signed a few, which wasn't really the thing to do. I should have been concentrating on the game, just in case I was called on, but I felt really flat. It was looking like yet another all-time low in my football career. I was signing away and every time there was a roar from the crowd I would have to ask someone in the crowd what happened. We were attacking the goals at the other end and finally there was a huge roar. Mehmet Durakovic had equalised with a miracle goal, with about 12 minutes to go.

That changed my afternoon. The crowd was going crazy. I didn't sign any more autographs and I started doing my warm-up again. I did a few sprints behind the goals, a few more stretches. The Aussie cheer squad always gathers behind that goal. They are always singing and dancing and jumping with the Socceroo colours. When I scored against Argentina in the 1988 Bicentennial Gold Cup I went to those guys to celebrate. They're all superb supporters and I could hear their encouragement as we tried to overcome Canada. 'Come on, Wadey', all positive stuff. 'Come on, get out there. We need you.' They didn't know it, but I needed them more than ever. I started to sprint that little bit faster. I was flicking my legs up at the back and kicking up my knees at the front. I was buzzing. The adrenalin was pumping. I was mentally back into the game. I made my way back to the bench because I wanted to get on. The final whistle went with the aggregate score tied at 3–3. The lads were sitting down near the halfway line, resting before extra time started.

I jumped up off the chair and walked out to gee up the team. Coaches can say so much, but I think it means a little bit more if you hear it from your team mates. I went around to Arnie, Farina and Robbie Slater. I was saying anything I could think of to fire them up. Extra time started and I kept looking at the bench. Every time there was a close miss I would look at the bench. Finally, Les Scheinflug turned around and shouted in his big German accent, 'Wadey!' It was about five minutes into extra time and I jumped up like a schoolboy. I didn't even have a chance to do any stretches. I just had time to get my tracksuit off when the game stopped and I was being dragged over to the touchline by Les. He told me to sit in the middle of the park. Ned Zelic was obviously tired — he was playing sweeper for Borussia Dortmund, and playing in midfield for the 90 minutes, then extra time, was too much. I had to make sure that there was some depth in midfield. We were chasing a winner, but we couldn't allow Canada to catch us on the break. For the last 25 minutes of extra time I won every tackle, every header, made every pass count and did a really good job, I thought. But the aggregate score stayed at 3–3.

My biggest test came in the penalty shoot-out. Our World Cup campaign was on the line. When Thommo asked, 'Who's taking the first penalty?' I immediately took the job. There was not one second of hesitation. I wasn't trying to be a smart-arse. I had been captain for three years. Just because of a tactical change that saw Okon replace me, I wasn't going to shy away from my responsibilities. After that, Thommo said, 'Who else?' Silence. He repeated it with a little more urgency. I wasn't looking at Thommo. I was looking at all the legs and feet, sprawled out. The lads had played 120 minutes of intense football. The pressure was huge.

I recalled the 1990–91 National Soccer League Grand Final. The pecking order for the penalty shoot-out was settled very quickly and efficiently. 'Who's first? Wadey. Who's second? Trimmers', and so on. We sorted things out and and we could see the Melbourne Knights players sitting down. Their body language was tired as though they were beaten. They were arguing about who was taking the spot kicks. Sure, it's a scary thing when there are 25,000 people and your spot kick will decide the game, the championship and the happiness or sadness of thousands. I could see that the Knights didn't have a lot of volunteers. We were on a high, we'd fought back in the final minutes of normal time, we'd equalised and dominated extra time. They were on the way down and the signals were, 'It's only a matter of time before we lose this game.'

I tried to get the same purpose in the Socceroos but, to be honest, the Socceroos looked more like the Knights: tired and not very confident. We had all the 11 players plus the subs, the doctors, the physio, the gear steward and officials. There were dozens of people and that added to the pressure. Finally we had some order. I was saying, 'Come on, lads.' I still had wind in my lungs, trying to lift everyone, trying to be positive to get a good mood going. I took the first one. It wasn't a particularly good penalty. If Craig Forrest, in the

Canada goal, had gone the right way, he would have saved it. I side-footed the ball low and right. He went left. I wheeled away to get the crowd revved up. I put a finger in the air to signal, 'That's No. 1.' Unfortunately, some people read it as a gesture to Eddie Thomson, saying, in effect, 'I'm No. 1 so don't you dare drop me again.' It wasn't that at all. The No. 1 was goal No. 1 in the shoot-out, and I was just trying to get the crowd fired up. It just shows how the Socceroo captain has to be careful with everything he does.

We kept our nerve with the spot kicks and our goalkeeper, Mark Schwarzer, made a couple of brilliant saves. We won the shoot-out and I felt I had made an important contribution. I knew I'd done a good job, but it was great to have Les Scheinflug and Raul Blanco after the game put their arms around me and say, 'See, just keep your mouth shut and do your job. You never know what might happen.' It was comforting to have their support, because when you're the captain and you're watching your team from the bench, it feels like the wilderness.

If you had talked to me before that game in Sydney I would have told you my career was coming to an end. The 25 minutes and the shoot-out were as important as that: I'd shown leadership qualities and played well under pressure. If I hadn't played those 25 minutes against Canada I would have had every right to feel insecure and unstable, and to lose confidence. But against Canada I proved to myself once again that I could lead the Socceroos. I felt as if I'd played the whole game, not just a fraction at the end.

What's more, I'd come through two very harrowing experiences: the showdown with Eddie Thomson at the Novotel in Sydney and his decision to drop me in Canada. Those dramas were in the months before Australia played Argentina in those famous World Cup games. Thinking back now, I realise how close I came to missing my duel with Diego — a scary feeling.

ALL THE BEST

A LEXEI MIKHAILICHENKO IS NOT as famous as Diego Maradona, but from my close encounters he's every bit as brilliant as Diego. Alexei who? Alexei Mikhailichenko is a Ukrainian midfielder who made his name with the Soviet Union at the European championships in 1988 and at the Seoul Olympics later the same year. He went on to play with Sampdoria in Italy and Glasgow Rangers in Scotland, but that was all ahead of him when he crossed my tracks.

In the Olympic Games quarter-final Australia was drawn to play the Soviet Union, the eventual gold medal winner. It was always going to be a David and Goliath battle and we were forced to be cautious. Frank Arok gave me the job of marking Mikhailichenko. He only touched the ball four or five times and ended up scoring two goals and setting up one. Final score: Soviet Union 3, Australia 0. In other words, Alexei won the game and gave me a lesson. I took my eye off him for a split second, to check where the ball was on the far side of the ground, and that was enough time for him to sprint to the far post. A cross came in, Alexei nodded it in and Paul Wade was left looking like a dill. I still can't believe that a player I was marking scored two goals and made one. I stuck like glue and yet he still did the damage. I was marking him so tightly and he knew I was trying to stop him, so that every time he scored or made one he'd walk past me, smile and give me a wink just to rub it in even more.

He was all class, and I wanted his shirt. I went to his room in the Olympic Village and knocked on his door. There were half a dozen Soviet Union team members playing cards. I saw him at the end of the table — how could I forget him? A tall guy with blonde hair. We had no common language so I tried to get my message across the best way possible. 'Could we swap shirts?' He just shrugged his shoulders, grabbed his shirt and threw it at me. I offered mine in return and he shook his head. I was shocked. What arrogance! He destroyed me on the park and now he was destroying me off the park by refusing to take my shirt! Well, I couldn't really blame him. Our strip wasn't too flash. It was the tightest T-shirt you've ever seen, not even a proper soccer strip, just T-shirts with a collar, three stripes on the shoulder to the bottom of the arm. The shorts were a nightmare because they were Rugby League shorts. It's no wonder Alexei turned me down. It was the best destruction of Paul Wade ever seen! Nevertheless, I walked away down a long corridor thinking, 'That's one of the best players in the world and I've got his shirt.'

I'm often asked, 'Who's the best player you've played against? Which was the best team you played against?' Now, I'll stick my neck out and name the 'best'. Alexei Mikhailichenko gets the nod as the best I've played against in a single game because he absolutely destroyed me, whereas I reckon I did a good job of containing Maradona. Alexei was at his peak in 1988 and maybe if I'd played against Maradona in 1986, when he won the World Cup, I'd have a very different view.

The best player I've played with would have to be Paul Trimboli, my long-time team mate at South Melbourne and the Socceroos. I can't think of another player who can do the things that Trimmers does. He's not a role model as far as his physique or how he looks after himself, quite the contrary, but as for his football brain you won't find a better player in Australia. You'll find players who can run faster, jump higher, tackle harder or score more goals, but as far as being able to dance with the ball, nobody does it better than Trimmers. That's why I admire him.

He can change his mind in a split second. He'll have something in his mind, but at the last possible moment he'll change it and do something completely different, all the while staying in control, still balanced and still aware of all the options. In that split second he can open gaps that didn't exist and make tight defences look loose. With a flick of his boot he can change the game. Coaches can't teach that skill, you're born with it, like Maradona. I'm not saying that Paul Trimboli is in the same class as Diego Maradona, but they have the same uncanny ability to find time when a game is going at 100 miles an hour.

Yet if you scan the record books, you'll see that Paul Wade has played over 100 times for the Socceroos and Paul Trimboli has just over 10 appearances. You might be thinking, 'Well, Trimmers can't be that good, then.' All I can say is that I'm very disappointed that Paul Trimboli hasn't played more times for Australia. I think most soccer supporters would agree. Every time he played for the Socceroos he scored a goal, or at least performed up to expectations. When we played the Croatian club Hajduk Split in Melbourne in June, 1990, he scored the winner on the volley, catching the goalkeeper off the line. It was sheer brilliance.

Unfortunately for Paul Trimboli, he doesn't suit Eddie Thomson's plan. Thommo wants a centre forward up front on his own, a player who's very mobile and strong enough to hold the ball up. Trimmers just doesn't fit those requirements. If Thommo played two up front all the time he could have somebody like Graham Arnold working off Trimmers, as long as you played balls into Trimmers' feet. I'm not saying he's not mobile, but he can do more damage when he's got the ball at his feet with a defender at his back. Under Thommo's style, Trimmers has to compete with guys like Aurelio Vidmar and Robbie Slater for the attacking midfield roles, and he is just not that sort of player.

It was a twist of fate that Trimboli came onto the international scene just as Frank Arok was departing. Frank described Trimmers as 'my little genius', and if Arok had been reappointed as Socceroo coach in 1990, his new team would have been built around Trimboli and I would have been on the outer. Even though we are very different as soccer players, Trimmers and I are good mates. I admire him as a footballer and as a person. I love the way he doesn't care about anything, as long as he's happy. I've told him dozens of times to go to Europe, find a club and earn some money, to get the rewards for all his talent. He says, 'Come on, I'm happy living in Melbourne, I like going to the tennis, I like going to watch North Melbourne, I like to see 'Plugger' (Sydney Swans full-forward Tony Lockett) taking superb marks, I want to go to the Boxing Day cricket Test at the MCG, I want to go to the beach when it suits me. Why should I leave Melbourne?' As long as he is happy, who can argue?

T HE BEST TEAM I'VE played against is AC Milan of Italy. In terms of pure professionalism, Milan is in a class of its own. The team came to Australia in June, 1993, after winning the Italian championship and narrowly losing the European Cup final to Marseilles of France, for a gruelling two games in two days. People thought that Milan, like so many other club teams that visit Australia, might be jaded after a long season, and would only go through the motions. No way. Milan did bring most of their stars: Baresi, Boban, Costacurta and Albertini, for a start.

In Sydney I was marking Roberto Donadoni, and he was magic. In fact, he was working so hard, I was getting tired tracking him around the midfield. There was never any suggestion that it was a friendly international. Milan had come to play and win, and you could only admire their dedication. Tickets that night were over $40, but the fans had their money's worth, even though the Milan winner was a bizarre own goal by Tony Vidmar.

He claims he's always said he was naturally right-footed, even though he plays left back for Adelaide City, and after that own goal we believed him. All he had to do was dink the ball out for a corner with his left foot. Instead, the ball mustn't have come onto him as quickly as he thought, because as his foot was swinging across the ball it hit his toe and went like a rocket past Mark Bosnich into the net. Milan won 1–0.

We went to Melbourne for the second game the following night and again Milan's professionalism was there for all to see. The game was at Optus Oval, an AFL ground. Both teams went for a stroll to check out the pitch and the AC Milan players were quite astounded. They were asking in broken English about the huge, rock-hard square in the middle of the ground. There was no point trying to explain what a turf cricket pitch was all about. It was a disgrace. The cricket wickets covered probably a third of the soccer pitch and were rock hard, but the rest of the grass was quite lush. That meant players needed long studs in their boots, but once you hit the hard stuff it was like skating on ice.

As if that wasn't bad enough, there weren't proper floodlights at Optus Oval, so temporary lights on trucks were brought in. The light towers were so low that when you were waiting for a corner kick the ball got lost in the light. You couldn't see a thing! It was a farce, a total embarrassment for Australian soccer. My mum and dad paid their own way, as they always do when I'm playing: $40 each for seats in the front row on the fence. The trouble was, the advertising boards were very close to the touchline, which meant that those spectators close to the boundary fence, who'd paid top dollar to be close to the action, couldn't see the ball on the near side of the ground. On top of all this, after the start of the game, the fans who had paid $15 for standing room tickets jumped into the $40 seats. And to add insult to injury, the first half was ended after about 36 minutes, instead of the regulation 45, because of a mistake by the referee John Fraser. Or so we were told. There was a story going around that the game had to be cut short so Milan could catch their flight back to Italy that night.

But here was a team worth $200 million playing a friendly game, under conditions that were an absolute joke, and they still applied themselves to the job like true professionals. Jean-Pierre Papin, Milan's French striker, was being closely marked by Mehmet Durakovic and got really angry. He was throwing his elbows around at Mem in frustration and really battling for the ball. Papin was eventually substituted and stormed off the ground. He wouldn't even shake hands with Durakovic, and instead of swapping his shirt after the game he threw it into the crowd. There was a big pushing and shoving contest as the fans fought over it. It showed that Papin wasn't there to just cruise around and pick up his pay cheque. (Or maybe it had something to do with the way Mem kept shouting, 'Hey, Frog, you still haven't scored', every five minutes!)

Milan won 2–0, but not before Tony Vidmar suffered another nightmare. He split the defence with a run that beat the offside trap and was heading towards goal with only the keeper to beat. He skipped around the keeper and all he had to do was tap it into the net. He obviously wanted to make sure and take that extra touch and set up the shot with his right foot. Well, this 'natural right-footer' had the touch of a baby elephant this night, because his next touch was like a clearance and went out for a goal kick. He'd missed an absolute sitter and, boy, did we give him heaps after the game. What a point to have on your résumé, a goal against AC Milan, but he blew it.

T HE BEST CLUB TEAM I've been part of is the 1990–91 South Melbourne team. We had a truly champion team. We had so many different blends of players, it was the perfect cocktail. It was thrown together in 1988 by Brian Garvey (and coached by the legendary Ference Puskas in 1990–91), and we grew together over the next four seasons. Bruce Maclaren was in goal and I don't think any keeper in the country had better reflexes. The number of times he saved us, one on one with the centre forward, was worth five to ten points every season. For pure reflexes, he was like a cat. The fans loved his long kicking. As he was about to launch another long clearance the crowd used to wind up with a big 'Brrrruuuccce'. He regularly kicked the ball out of his hands three-quarters of the length of the pitch. In front of Maclaren was the centre half, Steve Blair. Nobody could beat Steve Blair in the air. Every now and again he might get beaten on the ground, but not too often. He was like the Rock of Gibraltar. I have a healthy respect for Blairy because although he appeared to be slow, he always positioned himself perfectly to clear high balls. If you were a midfielder playing in front of Steve Blair you never had to call for the ball because if you made position he'd give it to you with a clean, simple pass. Blairy was a 100 per cent team player. I don't think he ever got sent off. You could always count on Steve Blair to do the job.

Down the middle were Micky Petersen and I. We had a great understanding, from back in our days at Brunswick Juventus. Micky was the playmaker and I was the hard worker. If he was struggling in his defensive duties we didn't mind because we knew that any minute he could play a pass that would win us a game. Up front we had Paul Trimboli, enough said. Right down the middle of the team we had such a great blend. Mehmet Durakovic was the sweeper who would bob up everywhere, covering Blair or the full-backs and dashing into midfield. He seemed to cover 50 metres in no time at all, quicker than anyone else could cover 30. With a backbone like that, we were destined for success.

Angie Postecoglou was the captain and a great all-round full-back, able to attack and defend. That season he was brilliant at taking on players down the left. The right full-back was David Healy, the quiet achiever. He never made mistakes and was always contributing down the right, doing the little things that don't always get noticed. Danny Wright in midfield was Mr Versatile, who could play every position and often did. Up front with Trimboli, Kimon Taliadoros was the worst player in the world one minute and the most brilliant the next. The speed and power in his running always caused trouble and he was a good decoy for Trimmers. 'Gus' Tsolakis was a left winger under Puskas, although he much preferred to play as a true midfielder. He was one of those wide players who had to stay wide when he was dying to get involved. He had a powerful shot. Anywhere from 35 metres he could disturb the spiders nestling in the top corner of the goal. Joe Palatsides was another utility player, who eventually nailed down a spot at centre forward and scored a crucial equaliser in the 1990–91 Grand Final.

The squad also had plenty of talent in reserve. Paul Fernandez was a very cool defender, but he had very few chances once Durakovic arrived. There was also the young Con Boutsianis. He was something special, even at that stage. I thought he was in a different class, and what he has achieved since has proved that. I love the way he runs past defenders when he's in full flight. When I was young lad in the days of the out-and-out winger, Steve Heighway of Liverpool and Steve Coppell of Manchester United were the most exciting players around. Boutsianis has that same ability to fly past a defender and whip in a cross. It's a pity the true wingers seem to be disappearing from the modern game. It's a pleasure to watch a winger control a ball with one touch and in the same movement swerve a curling cross, so the keeper doesn't know whether to come out or stay on his line. After Trimboli, I'd rate Boutsianis at number two and Steve Blair at number three on my list of all-time greats at South Melbourne.

As for the best club team I played against in the National Soccer League, it was the 1984 South Melbourne team, who won the national championship. They were so well organised, and they stomped over everybody who got in their way. That team was like a machine. I was playing for Green Gully Ajax that season and saw first-hand how good they were. It was all about disipline, doing the same things over and over and believing it was going to work. They were so focused, as if they had blinkers on; they knew exactly what they had to do. The team was loaded with talented individuals, such as Oscar Crino, Doug Brown, Kenny Murphy and Charlie Egan, but it was the things they did as a team that mattered.

That brings me to the best coach I've played under, or, should I say, the best coach for Paul Wade. Len McKendry was the coach of that 1984 South Melbourne team and I played under him for one season at Brunswick Juventus in 1986. Len was the coach who made me aware of all my good qualities and brought them out in me. His message was always so positive, he was clear in his instructions and he could fill you with confidence. Len would convince players they were the best in the world, as long as they stuck with him and his style. Of course, as I discovered, once you leave him you're suddenly a very ordinary player, but that was the great thing about Len. He demanded, and mostly got, loyalty, and that meant his teams were always very committed. He believed in himself and his ideas.

Tough guys were found in every team when I first started playing senior soccer as a 16-year-old in 1978. Every team had a couple of hard nuts who'd run through a brick wall to get to the ball. Some of these tough guys used their elbows as much as their feet. When I started to emerge as a player I was often subjected to the rough stuff; elbows in the ribs, punches in the face and late tackles that would leave my legs cut to shreds. Only once did I come close to punching an opposition player, though. In 1983, while I was with Croydon City in the Victorian State League, a Frankston Pines player was out to stop me by any means. He punched me square on the jaw behind the play. I was shocked by the sheer audacity of it all, but I didn't find the chance to get even.

Maybe that's why Shaun Parton has spent a lifetime whacking me. Every time I've played against Shaun he's inflicted damage to my face or body. Plenty of times I've needed stitches or butterfly clips to patch up the wounds. Shaun has been around for as long as I have, with Sunshine George Cross, Preston Makedonia and Morwell Falcons. The damage usually occurs at corner kicks, when we are contesting a high ball. Without fail, his elbow finds its way into my face. I've come to believe that it's just part of his competitive nature. It's not that he's necessarily trying to hurt Paul Wade; he's just making sure his opponents know they'll be in the firing line if they try to beat him. I remember one game at Preston when we had a pleasant chat before the kick-off. I figured it might put him off, but once we crossed the white line we were again mortal enemies. It was a very muddy day and at the first corner we were jostling for position. He took two steps back, kicked mud in my face and then slapped me in the jaw before running off to the near post to try and get a header, leaving me blinded, and flabbergasted that someone who's a schoolteacher could be so callous. The worst thing is that referees never seem to see what he's doing! I just can't understand how a guy can want to hurt you one minute, then buy you a beer the next. Maybe one day I'll ask him — the Parton family lives in the same neighbourhood as the Wades and our daughters attend the same kindergarten!

Soccer stadiums around the world are all the same in one way: if they're full of fans, they're great, but if they're half-empty, they're lousy. That's why the old Middle Park Stadium was my favourite club ground in Australia. The atmosphere of the Blue and White Army made up for the facilities, which were pretty antiquated. Olympic Park in Melbourne is another one of my favourite stadiums, again because the Blue and White Army made the atmosphere so good. Without doubt the best stadium I've played in is the Olympic Stadium in Seoul. It was brand-new when the Socceroos played there as part of the President's Cup in 1987. It was 12 months before the Olympic Games and when we played South Korea in the final there were 50,000 fans. It was a very hot day and I couldn't handle the conditions and was eventually subsituted. The South

Koreans did what they always do; they played at 300 miles an hour, but couldn't score from one yard out. They battered us and in the end won the President's Cup in a penalty shoot-out. It wasn't a great day for the Socceroos, but I'll never forget the atmosphere and the sheer size of the stadium. It was modern and the most spectacular stadium I've seen.

The River Plate in Buenos Aires is memorable when there are 65,000 screaming Argentinians inside, but as a facility it's a very ordinary, rundown pile of concrete. It's almost a national disgrace for Argentina that the nation's Mecca of soccer, the venue where the country won a World Cup on home soil, is almost in ruins.

Goals are what make stadiums buzz and goals are what soccer is all about. I've never been a prolific scorer — the figures tell the story. Forty-eight goals in 299 NSL games means I score about once every six games and my average for the Socceroos is about the same. The best goal I've ever scored was in the 1989–90 season, playing for South Melbourne against Parramatta Melita Eagles at Middle Park. Paul Trimboli was in possession after a build-up on the right wing. I'd made a run from the halfway line, following the play. I ran towards Trimmers and called for the ball and with his instinct for knowing just when and where to deliver a pass, he placed it perfectly. I was running hard and hit my shot from 25 metres out. I caught it right on the bootlaces, just the way the textbooks say. The ball went through the legs of the defender trying to block the shot and went like a rocket into the top left-hand corner. What a beauty! One reporter called it arachnophobia, which is a fear of spiders. We always joke that spiders live in the top corner of the goals and my shot sent them packing. As an added bonus I beat one of my old Slavia team mates, Parramatta's goalkeeper Alex McPherson, who always gave me heaps for never being able to score past him. The match report in the *Herald–Sun* said my effort must be goal of the year, but on the ABC TV coverage, John Kosmina didn't even put it in his top five.

My best goal for the Socceroos was a header against Sweden at Olympic Park in Melbourne in February, 1992. At set pieces I had to wait on the edge of the 18-yard box and then peel off towards the far post. Ned Zelic was supposed to chip the ball into that area, directed at me. We'd had three or four free kicks, but it wasn't working, and the Swedes had worked out the plan. This time I made a run to the near post instead of the far post and Ned played it perfectly. He just put it in an area where three or four of us could attack the ball. My timing was spot on, and it was a perfect header. Most of the time in a pack of players the ball comes off the back of your head or hits you half on the nose, half on the eyebrow. This one smacked right off my forehead and sailed gracefully and hit the stancheon at the back of the goal. The goalkeeper didn't get near it and we won 1–0.

The goal that gave me the most pleasure was my winner for Brunswick Juventus in the 1985 Southern Division Grand Final against Preston. It wasn't spectacular or technically difficult, but it was the winner in a Grand Final. There might have been only 2000 Brunswick fans, but to see people jumping up and down, going wild because of something that you've done, gives you a feeling you can't put a price on.

T HE BEST COUNTRY I'VE visited is the United States of America. The Socceroos went to Orlando, Florida, to play the USA in June, 1992, and from the moment we arrived everything was perfect: the transport, the hotel, the training facilities, the stadium, the food, the lot. Everything was 'bigger than Texas', as they say. Having spent 10 years touring with the Socceroos, I was pretty hard to please, but from the first morning, even the hotel breakfast was unbelievable: there were mountains of food, everything you could think of eating for breakfast and a bit more, like cakes and trifles. We thought it was a plot to make us sick before we played them. We were training on a gridiron pitch that was as flat and smooth as a billiard table.

The game was played at the Citrus Bowl. It had the biggest dressingroom I've ever seen in my life. It was made for gridiron teams, which have dozens of players and loads of gear. When 20 Socceroos arrived to get ready, we couldn't get over how big and clean the dressingroom was. In the middle was a huge table with fruit, water, sports drinks, beer, wine, coffee, tea — everything was laid on. Another table had strapping tape and other medical bits and pieces. Nothing was too much trouble for the organisers and we made sure we had a good time.

We won 1–0, thanks to a Warren Spink goal from a Micky Petersen free kick. The American commentator said it was a shock result, but we'd have been the ones who were shocked if we hadn't beaten them. We didn't rate them at all. I'll always remember that game for the weather. A few minutes before half-time a thunderstorm blew up and there was some lightning. The referee blew the whistle and called the USA captain and I together and suggested we halt the game until the storm passed. I said, 'Look, it's only a thunderstorm. We get these in Australia all the time, so let's just get on with it.' The referee looked hard at me and said, 'I don't want to worry you, but lightning strikes in Florida kill more people than car accidents.' With that I was straight off the ground, with the rest of the team not far behind me. That was the only time I've ever gone off because of the weather.

I've been lucky to visit Europe, Asia and South America with the Socceroos — travel is one of the best things about soccer. Seeing different cultures and eating different food is great. I generally eat anything that's put in front of me, but on one of my first tours I went hungry instead. In November '86 we went to China.

Most of the food served to us was very Western, but one day in Shanghai we were served traditional Chinese food. One of the dishes was duck. The eyes were still in the duck's head and it was completely plucked. I swear it moved. There was no way in the world that we could eat it. The waiter assured us it was the finest cuisine that you could get anywhere in Shanghai, but these Aussie guys were not going anywhere near that duck. Pedro Ruz, the Socceroo physio, and Dr Brian Corrigan tried a little bit, but the rest of us decided we weren't hungry.

Shanghai was memorable for the people; there were millions of them. How do they live in cities overflowing with people like that? The traffic jams make Melbourne's peak hour look pleasant by comparison. Athens is a place of rock and rubble with not a blade of grass to be seen. I remember Tel Aviv and Rome airports for the frosty reception from security guards with sub-machineguns. On the other hand, the Americans, with their fast food, fast service and 30 TV channels, leave you feeling exhausted, as if you're being rushed through life to make way for the next generation.

I believe we live in the most beautiful country in the world — Australia. If only soccer was the No. 1 game here, as it is almost everywhere else on the planet! Then Heaven would be the only thing that could top Australia.

Above left: The four Wade children, Claire, Phil, Mike and Paul (aged eight), in St Helens, England. We boys are wearing the strip of Everton football club, but not long after, my mates convinced me I should be supporting Liverpool.

Above right: The future Australian captain, all of two years of age, honing his skills in a park in the north of England.

Left: Our second home in St Helens, the pub car park, where many a soccer match was played. We used to aim our shots at a fire hydrant valve on the pub wall (behind the black car).

ALL THE
BEST

Right: Wearing the No. 6 shirt in my one and only appearance in English league football, a guest spot for Barnsley reserves in 1980–81.

Left: Saluting the South Melbourne fans after our victory over Melbourne Croatia in the 1990–91 National Soccer League Grand Final.

Opposite page: The South Melbourne squad that won the 1990–91 NSL Grand Final. Back (left to right): Con Boutsianis, Mehmet Durakovic, Danny Wright, Paul Trimboli, Kimon Taliadoros, Joe Palatsides. Middle: Haris Micheil, Paul Fernandez, Mike Lilikakis, Steve Blair, Paul Wade, Micky Petersen. Front: Jim Pyrgolios (assistant coach), Steve Tassios, David Healy, Ferenc Puskas (coach), Angie Postecoglou, Pete Tsolakis, Mike Michalakopoulos, I. Nagy (masseur).

Right: After defeating New Zealand in 1993. Players pictured (left to right): G. Arnold, R. Slater, myself (I didn't play because of a virus), A. Tobin, M. Durakovic and A. Vidmar.

Below: The team that faced Argentina in the first leg of the 1993 World Cup qualifier. Back row (left to right): M. Bosnich, R. Slater, M. Ivanovic, A. Tobin, N. Zelic, T. Vidmar. Front row: J. Van Blerk, P. Wade, M. Durakovic, G. Arnold, A. Vidmar.

Just four of the many champion footballers I have faced during my career as a Socceroo.

Above left: Ukrainian midfielder Alexei Mikhailichenko, a dominating figure during the 1988 Olympics.

Above right: The great goalscorer, Gary Lineker, England's captain when they toured Australia in 1991.

Far left: Roberto Donadoni, of AC Milan and Italy, who played so well when Milan came to Australia in 1993.

Left: Abel Balbo, after scoring Argentina's goal at the SFS in 1993.

ALL THE
BEST

In Argentina they call me the 'Dancing Aussie', a result of the marking job I did on their captain, Diego Maradona, in both legs of the World Cup qualifier in 1993. The photo at right shows why! In the shot below, Mehmet Durakovic has control of the ball, while I'm more concerned with staying close to Maradona (though it mightn't look like it).

It took a while, but I
eventually managed to get
the shirt Maradona wore
in the second half of the
Sydney World Cup
qualifier. And once I had
it, it was a long time
before I took it off!

ALL THE
BEST

Above: In the first game of a three-match home series against Ghana in 1995, I found myself with this fabulous chance to get myself on the score sheet — and missed it!

Right: The Wade family (left to right): Emma, Paul, Brianna-Lee and Valerie.

THE BLUE AND WHITE ARMY

M Y VERY FIRST EXPERIENCE with South Melbourne Hellas was in the car park at VFL Park, the Aussie Rules stadium. In early 1983, Rale Rasic, the former Socceroo coach, rang and said, 'I'll be happy to sign you to play at South Melbourne.' I was playing for Croydon City in the Victorian State League and Rale had just taken over as South Melbourne coach. We arranged to meet in the car park of VFL Park at Mulgrave because I worked nearby in North Clayton and it seemed like a convenient place to talk without being overheard or seen. I'm not so sure now about not being seen — there are acres of clear, open land around VFL Park and we were in the open, talking soccer. When Rale had called, I thought, 'What's the story here? He has players like Alan Davidson, Oscar Crino, George Campbell and Steve Woodin from New Zealand. Why me?' South Melbourne was like the Liverpool of Australia, the biggest and most professional club around.

But for little Paul Wade of Croydon City it seemed just too big a jump. I listened to what Rale had to say and agreed to meet the South Melbourne committee. A few nights later I went to the boardroom at Middle Park Stadium. George Vasilopoulos, now the club president and an ASF Commissioner, and Billy Georgantis, who's still on the board, were there, I recall. At the time I didn't know any of them, and I figured they didn't know me. I took my dad because I was dealing with the big time. I was earning no more than $100 a game at Croydon, but I knew South Melbourne would pay its players a heap more. Bill and George were answering any questions my dad asked and the meeting was very pleasant and professional, but in the end I thought moving to South Melbourne was too big a step at my age. I was 20 years old and I just didn't feel confident enough to go. I left the meeting on good terms and played the rest of the year with Croydon City.

In hindsight, I still think it was the right decision, because I learned so much about being a professional playing at Croydon with Jimmy Rooney, the 100-game Socceroo midfielder. The next season Jimmy was coaching Green Gully Ajax in the National Soccer League and I followed him.

I played against South Melbourne plenty of times over the years, but it wasn't until 1987 that the club showed interest again. Pierre Pallas, who owned a hairdressing salon, was the team manager. He arranged a meeting and said, 'I hear that you're not very happy at Brunswick.' He was right. I was negotiating a new contract with Len McKendry, the coach of Brunswick Juventus, and he was playing hard ball. Len said there was no way I was going to get a one-year contract and that a maximum transfer fee clause was totally out of the question. I had had a maximum transfer clause in every one of my contracts since signing with Croydon City in 1981, six years earlier. The main reason was to avoid being tied down to a club and have my career controlled by a bunch of people trying to make money out of selling me. I'd never signed for more than one season at a time, for the same reason. It was important to me, so I held firm in my talks with Brunswick.

The issue came to a head in a meeting with Joe Caruso, the team manager and later chairman of the VSF, Len McKendry and me. I gave them one last chance. 'Are you sure you won't give me a one-year contract and maximum?' They shook their heads. 'As far as we are concerned, you can leave the club, because we're not going to put up with that.' It seemed to me that Len was pulling the strings at the club. I'd never had a single problem with the club in two seasons.

Pierre Pallas came along at the right time. I told him I'd love to sign for South Melbourne because Brunswick certainly weren't going to make an acceptable offer. I went to the Glen Shopping Centre on Springvale Road, in Waverley, and signed a contract in his hairdressing salon with a press photographer on hand to record the moment. I got my one-year contract and a maximum transfer fee. There was no bargaining or anything, no problems whatsoever. The club wanted Paul Wade, the footballer. It was a very straightforward deal.

The funny thing is that a few days after signing for South Melbourne, I got a phone call from Domenic Tenuta, who at the time owned a strip club in Brunswick called Crystal T's. He had taken over as president of Brunswick Juventus. 'I don't know what the other guys have actually told you, but as far as I'm concerned I want you to be a Brunswick player and I'm willing to give you your one-year contract and a maximum. Can we sit down and talk about it?' I told him I had signed for South Melbourne and mentioned that Caruso and McKendry had told me they weren't going to change their minds. A day later Len McKendry rang. 'I've spoken to the committee and I hear that they have offered you a one-year contract and a maximum. I want you to know I'm happy for you to come back on those terms.' Obviously he didn't know I'd signed for South Melbourne, or maybe thought I was bluffing. 'Oh, that's kind of you to offer me that sort of thing now, but I have just signed with South Melbourne.' The line was silent for a moment, then Lennie let fly. 'It's players like you who are going to kill the game in this country. You are just bleeding this game to death.' He then hung up in my ear. I didn't feel too fussed because when they had the chance they didn't want to sign on my terms.

I was happy to join South Melbourne, four years after that first opportunity in 1983. By 1987, I'd played three seasons in the NSL, won a championship medal in '85 and made my debut for the Socceroos. I was ready to play with 'Liverpool'. I had a lot of respect for South Melbourne and what the club had achieved by winning the championship in 1984. With their history, I thought it was a great move for me. On the other hand, I was also sad to leave Brunswick, because we had had a brilliant year in '86 under Len McKendry, who had crossed over from Middle Park. But South Melbourne was right for me: my career had always rolled along, sort of taking care of itself, and the way South Melbourne signed me gave me a good feeling about the place.

I TURNED UP AT South Melbourne halfway through pre-season training in 1987 — my wedding and honeymoon had to come first. Brian Garvey was the new coach, having crossed over from Heidelberg United where he'd done well with a young team.

The previous season, 1986, had been pretty poor by South Melbourne standards. The club didn't make the final five and that was in the days of the Northern and Southern divisions of the NSL, when the big clubs had to make a complete mess of things to miss the finals. There were some big-name players: Charlie Egan, Garry McDowall, Stuart Stevenson and Danny Crainie. Peter Laumets in goal had lots of experience and I knew Richard Miranda, who'd tranferred from Brunswick a year earlier. There was a lot of experience and a few great guys, like Carl Halford and Bobby Russell, who would become good friends of mine.

And Brian Garvey was such a gentleman. He never swore at all, which is unusual for a football coach, but he moaned a lot, and that's what the players hated. I naturally had expectations of more success at South Melbourne and I made a brilliant start. We played Sunshine George Cross in the wet at Middle Park on the opening day of the season. I scored twice on my debut and we won 3–0. I'm not a prolific goalscorer, so to score two goals on debut for South Melbourne was special. My relationship with the club and the fans of the Blue and White Army was off to a great start, and the romance continued for eight seasons.

However, it wasn't a happy debut season for Brian Garvey. We had too many volatile characters under a coach who was too nice a guy. Danny Crainie, for instance, was a really fiery character. He was also very, very skilful, in the same way as Chris Kalantzis in his Sydney Olympic days and Steve Corica, when he was at his best for Marconi. Danny seemed to glide past opponents. The difference was that he had a sharp tongue as well, and knew how to verbally dish it out. Stuart Stevenson was another one with loud opinions. Richard Miranda, both on and off the park, also spoke his mind. They were all street-wise, and that didn't make for a good blend with Mr Nice Guy, Brian Garvey, and all his moaning.

Brian, like all coaches, had his little idiosyncrasies that the players would make fun of, but in '87 it went beyond taking the mickey out of the coach. Senior players started telling Garvey where to go. It was player power at its worst. Brian Garvey regularly had to send players off the training track as he tried to get some discipline. I thought, 'Maybe this is the real world of football. Maybe I have been wrapped in cotton wool for too long.' The teams I'd played in had plenty of fiery characters and plenty of niggles, but nothing like what I experienced at South Melbourne in that first year. Sometimes Brian would join in small-sided games at training and some players used to hammer him with tackles, put him on his bum. They wouldn't even think twice, wouldn't even pretend it was an accident. It was hostile and it was out of control.

Brian didn't feel comfortable with his authority being constantly undermined and he just didn't know how to handle it. Players would say things that you should never say to a coach; they would just walk away while Garvey was talking, saying, 'You f...king idiot.' There was no respect whatsoever. For example, at Easter we turned up for training and Brian bought us Easter eggs. Each player got a chocolate egg. You can get away with that with an under–11 team, but among these street cats, that sort of thing didn't go down well at all. He used to make us take turns at leading the training warm-up. He was trying to get some leadership qualities out of people. At the end of the stretching session he would say, 'Richard Miranda, I think you controlled that session beautifully. Here's a Mars bar.' The boys were looking at each other in disbelief. All the jokes would start. When someone scored a goal in a game, it was, 'Yes, I'll get a Mars bar on Tuesday night!' As you can imagine, the tension between Brian Garvey and the players destroyed any chance of winning the championship. We finished sixth and missed the finals. For a big club to miss the finals two seasons in a row was a disaster. Too much time and effort went into the in-fighting.

We had a chance to salvage something from the wreck when we qualified for the Beach Fashions Cup final, the NSL knock-out competition. It was a two-legged final with the first game against Sydney Croatia in Sydney. We lost 1–0 to a goal from Robbie Slater, who, of course, has gone on to win an English Premier League championship medal with Blackburn Rovers as well as star for the Socceroos. The second leg was at Olympic Park in Melbourne and we were confident of overcoming the one-goal deficit. The game was played on a freezing Melbourne day. There were half a dozen models in bikinis to promote the sponsor. When women's nipples become erect, the boys call them the long studs. The girls definitely had the long studs in that day!

It was miserable for us for other reasons as well. Sydney Croatia had a clever player/coach called Vedran Rozic, and he worked out a defensive plan that totally frustrated us. We just couldn't get going and the only goal came from Graham Arnold, another Croatia player who would later move to Europe. We were beaten in front of our own fans and didn't do ourselves justice. It was another low spot in a terrible season.

Despite all the hassles, I had scored eight goals from midfield, so personally I was having a good time. I remember Len McKendry always saying, 'Once you leave me, son, you will never be the same player again.' In 1987 I scored two more goals than I did in 1986 under Len, so I felt I had proven that not all the McKendry theories are right, although after that my goalscoring tallies started to fall. Maybe Len would have said, 'I told you so.'

What I liked immediately about South Melbourne was the sense of being a club. At Brunswick there was no social side to the club and the players did their socialising away from the supporters. Brunswick played at Olympic Park No. 2, which doubles as Melbourne's greyhound track, and there was a sort of dungeon under the grandstand where we would go after a home game. There weren't too many people who hung around. Even when we won the national championship the hard-core support was never much more than 2000 people. Olympic Park No. 2 could easily hold 10,000 so, as you can imagine, the atmosphere was pretty ordinary.

South Melbourne, on the other hand, had the most passionate fans around. They were delirious if we won, but depressed if we lost. Soccer meant so much to those people, and it made me feel a real obligation to perform. In that first year, I started a habit that stuck. Whenever I scored, I would acknowledge the Blue and White Army. These fans, with all their banners and a trumpeter to lead the chants, would gather at one end of the grandstand. I'd celebrate the goal and then point to them, to say, 'I did it for you.' When we were on a roll, the cheering of the fans made us feel unbeatable. Middle Park was a tight little stadium, and with 10,000 fans the atmosphere was electric. No wonder so many opponents rated Middle Park as the hardest place to win.

South Melbourne had a social club at the back of the grandstand. It wasn't luxurious, but whenever South Melbourne won you couldn't move in that club room. The fans would be happy and would treat the players like heroes. You felt you were part of something big. It would be packed and noisy. Of course, whenever we lost, you could swing a cat and throw it from one end to the other and you wouldn't hit anybody. The Greek fans are a fickle lot and that used to bug the players quite a bit. I have vivid memories of supporters saying, 'Wade, good on you, Wade.' It was always Wade this, Wade that. They never used my Christian name. It's one thing I will always remember about the Greeks. At first I was offended by it, because it seemed impolite, but I quickly got used to this Greek custom.

Some customs, however, took longer than others to get used to. On the rare occasions when I made runs down the wings I would hear my name among a flurry of Greek words. You pretty soon work out what the Greek swearwords are. 'Wade, you malaca' was uttered a few times over the years. The other funny one was the Greek hand sign, the big palm with all the fingers spread. The first time I came across this one I figured that the fans thought I was alright, you know, like a Greek high five. Not quite. Its message is exactly the opposite. You could be a hero one minute, and a villain the next. I didn't get too much stick because the season had been a good one personally, but it had been a disappointing one for the team. The fighting between coach and players had to stop. That meant someone had to go.

For the 1988 season, South Melbourne's board decided to back the coach. That started one of the biggest clean-outs ever seen at the club. Garvey went to the committee and told them to get rid of the 'troublemakers'. Six players were kicked out, no questions asked. Players I considered to be big names:. Charlie Egan, Peter Laumets, Richard Miranda, Danny Crainie, Stuart Stevenson and Garry McDowall were all given the boot. Carl Halford asked for an improved contract, but he was knocked back and also shown the door. That left Bobby Russell as the senior player of the club, along with Steve Blair and Angie Postecoglou, who had played in South Melbourne's '84 national championship team. Seven top players just disappeared from the club and I wasn't happy about that. I had left a successful team at Brunswick for a team that had had a very ordinary year, and now the best players were being kicked out of the club. I was getting ready to make a move myself. I didn't want to leave, but I sure didn't want to play in a struggling team.

Brian Garvey went for a youth policy, signing players from the Australian Institute of Sport and other NSL clubs. David Healy, Danny Wright, Paul Trimboli, Peter Tsolakis, Paul Foster and Paul Fernandez were among the signings. Steve Tassios, who had joined from Heidelberg the previous season, was another of the young brigade. Instead of being surrounded by senior players, I was one of the oldest, at 25. At least we still had Bobby Russell, the lovable

Scot, a consummate professional and the biggest optimist you could ever meet in your life. He must have been 32, and was now surrounded by all these young pups. For him, it wouldn't have mattered if we were losing 4–0: he would still be encouraging the lads and asking them to give a little bit more. Nothing ever depressed Bobby Russell, and he was as much a part of the new Garvey mix as all the young blood. The average age of the team went from around 28 to about 20. We were dubbed the 'Baby Blues'.

The atmosphere in the dressingroom changed completely. Instead of all the bitching and slagging of '87, there was a real feeling of being a team again. All the new players were from the same generation and the older guys — Blair, Postecoglou, Russell and I — got along well with them. The atmosphere was superb. The attitude of '87 had been, 'Let's get on with it, get our money and get the hell out so we can hit the town for a few bevvies.' It was pretty much the same with the younger generation as far as getting out on the town, but before the game it was much more relaxed; the players actually enjoyed each other's company. Trimmers was always on about his favourite AFL club (North Melbourne) and David Healy and Danny Wright were into the Aussie Rules as well. All the talk was about the footy or the cricket or whatever was going on at that time. The boys brought an AFL footy to the dressingroom and we used to hand-pass that around before a game. You wouldn't have thought we were playing in the National Soccer League, it was so casual.

Trimmers likes to relax before a game. He's not one for getting himself fired up running around the dressingroom, as I tend to do. He sits there making sure his boots are clean while he laughs and jokes about whatever happened on the weekend. Brian Garvey would allow that to go on until half an hour or so before kick-off, and he would then go back to his moaning self. Even so, the team went out feeling calm and relaxed.

Training sessions were made up of 'shadow' games from the halfway line to the goal, with 11 players and no opposition. The moves would start from wide positions, go into the midfield, then back out wide before someone would take the ball down the line to get a cross in. A forward would lay it back for a shot. It felt as if there were 55,000 moves before you had a shot at goal, but it was all about fluency, being able to pass the ball and keep the ball moving at all costs. That was Garvey's method, and it worked. The players responded and the team was playing some great football. I was again having a good time. The stand-out players were Blair, Tassios, Postecoglou, Trimboli, Healy and Wright. Everyone started to play without fear.

In '87 anyone who made a mistake was slaughtered, but in '88 there weren't any hotheads. Players could try things and play quite freely. Things clicked automatically, and my fears of the team struggling were soon forgotten. My own form was solid throughout the season. The Frank Arok pre-season torture test for the Socceroos meant I had plenty of stamina and sharpness. I was constantly playing and training, either with South Melbourne or the Socceroos, so my touch was improving all the time. We went right through to the last game of the season in the top one or two positions. All we had to do to win the minor premiership was draw or beat Adelaide City in Adelaide.

It was a very wet and muddy day, which didn't suit our running and passing game. We played at the Olympic Sports Field, Adelaide City's home before they moved to Hindmarsh Stadium. To get to the pitch you had to go through a tunnel which went under the running track. In the tunnel we were so confident. We were a young team and the season had gone so well for us. We all started singing the club song, 'Hello, hello, we are the Hellas boys', and it echoed in the tunnel. It was a magic sound. But that was where we left the magic. We were battered by Adelaide City, who weren't in the hunt for the finals. Adrian Santrac was playing his last game for Adelaide City and scored from 35 metres out with a shot that didn't get more than six inches above the ground. It went like a missile right into the corner and that was it, we lost 1–0. That meant we slipped down to third place behind Wollongong City, who won the minor premiership, and Sydney Croatia. Adelaide City finished sixth.

We came back down to earth in a real hurry. If there's one thing this game does, it is kick you in the teeth the moment you think you've got it sussed. We went into the finals series on a bit of a downer and lost both games. In the Qualifying Final, Sydney Croatia beat us 2–1 and then we lost 2–1 to Marconi in front of our fans at Olympic Park in the Minor Semi Final. All season long we were in the running for the championship, but we finished with three straight defeats. Even so, the 'Baby Blues' had made their mark.

At the NSL awards Brian Garvey was named coach of the year, I won the NSL player of the year award and Paul Trimboli won under–21 player of the year award. It was all achieved with a team of youngsters, unknown at the start of the season. It was a brilliant year for me. In 1988 the Socceroos had some tremendous results in the Olympic Games and the Bicentennial Gold Cup, so internationally, it was the best year that I'd ever had. My form at club level was very good, but not brilliant. I thought I played better in 1984 at Green Gully Ajax when I won the *Soccer Action* player of the year award. But I can't complain about 1988. It was a year when it all happened for me.

BRIAN GARVEY STAYED AT South Melbourne for his third season in 1989 and everyone around the club thought we would go the extra step and win a trophy. The squad was strengthened by the signing of Micky Petersen, my midfield partner from Brunswick. I knew he would fit perfectly at South Melbourne, because the team was full of attacking ball-players and Micky would be able to orchestrate the whole thing. Instead, we slipped backwards. One of the problems for Brian Garvey was Socceroo commitments, which kept Micky and me busy for most of the first three months of the season.

The 1989 season was the last winter season before the NSL went to a summer format. That meant the league games started in late January and the finals were in July, to allow the players a couple of months rest before the inaugural summer season. The trouble was that the Socceroos were involved in World Cup qualifiers in March and April. I was also having injury problems with the pelvic complaint that had blown up in late 1988. I don't know what went wrong with the team because I wasn't playing for most of the time. A week after the 1–1 draw with Israel in Sydney ended our World Cup hopes, I was back in Sydney for a league game with Sydney Croatia. It was April 23, round 14 of the competition, but I had played only four games for the club. After the bitter disappointment of the World Cup campaign I was ready to focus on club football and help South Melbourne get back on track.

This was one NSL game I'll never forget. The nightmare started at Melbourne airport. All the way up on the trip the boys were giving me heaps about the way I was dressed. I had a pair of light grey sandal-type shoes with my navy blue club blazer and trousers. Fashion was never my strong point and the boys kept saying, 'You just don't wear those sort of things with a suit.' They bagged me from the time I turned up at the airport to the time I took the shoes off in the dressingroom. I had always enjoyed playing at Sydney Croatia's ground and at the start of the game I was having a great time: the pitch was wet and I was covered in mud, throwing myself around in midfield, enjoying myself. The ball was cleared by Alan Hunter, Sydney Croatia's big centre back, and it came to me on the edge of the penalty area. My first touch was the usual Paul Wade first touch that went just too far away. Being the competitor I am, I chased it and thought I'd have a crack at goal. I had to make up some ground and then stretch to connect with my left foot. Croatia's Ante Rumora closed me down and blocked the shot as my left foot came through. I kicked the underside of his boot. There was nothing malicious in his challenge, it was just one of those things. Boy, I knew I was in trouble. I had broken my leg.

I just lay on the ground and the ball was cleared to the other end of the park. Tony Franken, the Sydney Croatia goalkeeper, asked if I was okay. 'I think I've broken my leg.' Tony started shouting to the referee, other players and the club doctor. I was shaking. It was shock from the pain. I couldn't stop myself. I remember Graham Arnold of Sydney Croatia bending over me saying, 'Wadey, relax, relax, take it easy, calm down.' I was thinking, 'Arnie, it's hard to be calm when it feels like someone has driven a six-inch nail into your shin.' There was a lot of pain. I was stretchered off and fairly soon loaded into an ambulance. When we were about to leave, I heard people shouting, 'Hey, hold that ambulance!' Tony Franken had done his knee and it was only because I was in such pain that

145

they took me straight away. I don't know how Tony Franken got to hospital, but that was the end of both of us for a while.

At the hospital I had X-rays that revealed a tibia broken about three inches (7.5 cm) above the ankle. The doctor said it was a clean break and would heal stronger than ever. My shin pad had prevented the impact from shattering the bone. My leg was plastered and it was decided I could fly back to Melbourne that night. By this time the players had come to the hospital after the game, which we had lost 2–1 to goals from Hunter and Manis Lamond. I was still in my playing strip. Now a broken leg is something every footballer dreads, but did I get any sympathy? No way. They all wanted to carry on with the jokes about my sandals. 'You're not putting those sandals on. You can put a sock on or something, but you're not coming back to Melbourne with those horrible things.' Postecoglou and Trimmers were leading the charge. The abuse was relentless the whole way back.

Two days later I went to see a specialist. In his opinion the best form of recovery for a clean leg break was to get back on it almost right away, gradually putting weight on it. The theory is that if you put weight on your leg it starts the circulation around that area and helps the healing process. There was also some doubt about whether the break had been set properly. Having the original plaster removed was almost as painful as breaking the leg. The doctor was sticking pliers down the inside of the plaster to cut it and every single millimetre I moved my leg I could feel the break as if it had moved. An SBS TV News crew had come to do a story. I agreed to let them film because I thought changing the plaster would be a routine thing. Instead, I nearly bit a hole in my lip trying to cope with the pain. It probably looked as if I was bunging it on for the cameras, but it was one of the most painful things I've ever gone through.

I found out later that while I was in agony on the pitch at Sydney Croatia, Micky Petersen, my long-time Socceroo room mate, had the ball at his feet. Everyone except Micky P knew I was in trouble. He kept dribbling while all the other players were telling him to kick the ball out so the doctors could come on. It seemed to take forever before Micky booted the ball out. We have a laugh about it even today. He says he was getting even for the time he had knee injuries at Brunswick. Having the attitude that you just ignore injuries and work through the pain, I had told him to run it off. I advised him to run a few laps because I have done it with several injuries in my time. Four days later he was in hospital having cartilages out in both knees! He always reminds about that, saying I should have just run a few laps at Sydney Croatia that day.

In fact, for four months I didn't run at all. I was getting about on crutches with my left leg in plaster. Fortunately, ABC TV stopped me going mad by offering me a job doing special comments on the NSL 'Match of the Day' coverage. In 1989 I ended up playing only five games — and watching about

30. South Melbourne finished eighth, a very ordinary effort from a team that went within one game of the minor premiership the season before. Believe me, watching is always harder for a footballer, and watching South Melbourne struggle was a nightmare. My mum was right. I'm a bad spectator.

THE FAILURE OF THE TEAM in 1989 was the undoing of Brian Garvey, who wasn't reappointed for the 1989–90 season. It was the first season of summer soccer, but there was something even bigger happening at Middle Park. South Melbourne invited Ferenc Puskas to be coach. The players were too young to know much about Puskas, but the older people around the club were awe-struck. They treated him the way today's generation would treat Diego Maradona. To anyone who watched football in the '50s and '60s, Puskas was a legend. On the first training night there must have been 1500 people there, just to get a look at Puskas. We hadn't seen so many people at some of the away games we played!

My first impression of Ferenc Puskas was that he was a gentle, old and very large grandfather figure. He wasn't like any coach we'd seen before and he certainly didn't carry on as if he was a famous footballer. Puskas never spoke about himself or his achievements, but the club wanted the players to know all about the Puskas legend. We were shown a video of the 1960 European Cup final at Hampden Park in Glasgow when Ferenc scored four goals for Real Madrid, who beat Eintracht Frankfurt 7–3 in front of 100,000 fans. That's when the players began to realise Puskas' place in world football. The man is a legend, up there with Pelé and Maradona. Of course, he could walk down any street in Melbourne and not be noticed, but Australia is probably one of the few countries in the world where that would happen.

It took time in the early weeks under Puskas to work out how to treat him. Here was one of the world's most famous footballers, coaching a semi-professional club in a city where the AFL is the big time. It didn't seem right, but I got the feeling Ferenc didn't mind; in fact, he seemed to enjoy keeping a low profile.

At the outset, my priority was to make a comeback from my broken leg. I had heard from other players that the first few weeks back on the training track are the most scary. It's not until somebody gives you a good clout on the leg that you mentally accept that your leg is no longer broken. It's human nature to try to protect the injury and it weighs on your mind. Of course you don't go looking for hard tackles, but I knew pretty soon I'd go into a 50/50 tackle and have to test the leg. It came in a practice match against Preston. The ball was there to be won and coming at me was Ian Dobson. You probably couldn't find a guy who goes in as hard and as fair as Dobbo. I'd played with him at Croydon City and against him in the NSL, and I knew he was as hard as nails. He was also best man at my wedding. But Dobbo had played professional football in England and I knew there would be no favours. I went down low into a slide tackle thinking, 'I hope you go for the ball, Dobbo.' There's a tendency, when you know it's going to be a 50/50 tackle, to lift your boot a little bit higher than you should. Fortunately, Dobbo went in hard and fair and there was a loud whack as our two feet hit the ball at the same time. I got up, and I knew I was back in business. Even though the doctors had reassured me that my leg was stronger than it was before it was broken, I had all kinds of doubts until I came through that first tackle.

Not that Ferenc Puskas was too worried about how I tackled. We quickly discovered that you don't do much tackling at a Puskas training session. In fact, you don't do much running either. Ferenc spoke only a few words of English, but we were to hear the words, 'Two to a ball' over and over during his three years. He instructed each pair of players to knock the ball back and forwards. Then we'd move around, knocking it backwards and forwards, all at a leisurely pace. There were about 20 of us spread over the ground, knocking the ball backwards and forwards for ages. Then he would get us to kick the ball up in the air and trap it and run off for two or three metres. It was all about individual skill, things like controlling a ball on your chest and then turning at the same time, things that you do in a game, but rarely practise. Well, until then we hadn't.

Most senior coaches concentrate on fitness and team skills. The attitude is, 'Let's see how fit you are, boys. Let's see how many minutes out of 90 you can keep running.' During a break in one of the early training sessions under Puskas, I said to him, 'We have never done this before.' He just shook his head and mumbled, 'Maybe that's why Australian soccer isn't where it should be; because you don't work enough with the ball.' Even though it was pre-season we could go for an hour without any real running. It was all ball work, with no emphasis on how fast things were done. At one session when it began to rain, he ordered everyone to go inside to avoid catching a cold.

Very early on, before one of the first practice matches, we realised Ferenc wasn't big on team talks, either. He didn't give specific instructions. 'Shoot the ball' was his favourite saying. 'You must shoot the ball, boys.' Whether it was 25 metres or five metres, just 'shoot the ball'. He worked on the theory that if you shoot at goal, there is always a chance it is going to go into the back of the net. Puskas just loved shooting. We'd seen from the videos that he was a great shot himself in his day. His favourite drill would involve players running towards him on the edge of the 18-yard box. We would play the ball into his feet and he would either flick it up so that we would have to volley or he would lay it off to the side so that we could have a first-time shot. Most coaches would have rotated players in the role of flicking or laying off the ball, but not

Puskas. He wanted to show that he still had the skill. He always used to wear runners, never boots, and a big black tracksuit that had the brand name BOSS written across the front. 'Boss' was the name that stuck, not so much out of respect, but because of his big black tracksuit. In any case, Puskas was the boss, as we found out.

On our first interstate trip he declared that the pre-match meal would be consommé and steak. That was what Puskas ate before games when he played, so that's what we'd eat. When word spread that we were to eat steak two or three hours before playing, the boys were horrified. Steak was too heavy and took too long to digest, not to mention all the advice we'd been given about eating a pre-game meal with lots of carbohydrates — pasta, rice, potatoes and bread. Puskas wouldn't hear of it. The pre-match steak dinners were on the menu for seven or eight weeks, until enough players complained for him to let us eat what we wanted. And it wasn't as though Ferenc didn't like pasta; far from it.

After playing at Marconi, we were invited to the social club. Marconi has a great set-up, and the club treated us to some beautiful Italian food. A huge plate of pasta was put in the middle of the table, but the waiter made the mistake of putting it close enough for Puskas to reach. He pulled the plate towards himself, picked up his knife and fork and started hoeing into the dish. There was enough on the plate to feed a dozen people. It was embarrassing, but none of the players dared tell Puskas to share. Luckily, the waiter came back and tapped him on the shoulder to explain the plate was for the entire table, not just him. Puskas reluctantly scooped some pasta onto his plate and pushed the tray back into the middle. We often wonder if he would have polished off the lot! He weighed 20 stone (127 kilograms) or more and obviously had a big appetite.

Because of his emphasis on skill rather than running, our pre-season hadn't really prepared us physically for the NSL season. We began brilliantly by beating Sydney Croatia 4–0 at Middle Park and that made us think Puskas was right, that skill is all that matters. The following week we lost 2–0 away to Sunshine George Cross, and doubts returned. Our form was erratic over the first couple of months. We had a 100 per cent record at Middle Park, but struggled in away games and the boys were still concerned about our fitness levels. In the fourth away game of the season we travelled to Marconi, still looking for our first points away from home. We were still learning to train and play the way Ferenc wanted, so there was plenty to sort out. Things didn't go too well at Marconi and we were a little bit lucky to get a 0–0 draw. The game was 'Match of the Day' and John Kosmina, the former Socceroo captain, was the special comments man for ABC TV. He described us as the most unfit South Melbourne team he had ever seen.

Even Jim Pyrgolios, the assistant coach, was worried about our lack of fitness. Jim was from the old school, where pre-season was about running and getting fit. Jim was in charge of the warm-ups at training and because he knew that we weren't fit he would make us run hard. Within a few minutes of starting to run hard, we'd hear the big whistle from Puskas. He would give the signal to slow down and then tell us off for getting too carried away with running. We all knew we were far short of our usual levels of fitness. I was struggling. One of the things that John Kosmina had pointed out was that there were a few South Melbourne players who couldn't get up and down the park any more. Hence my guilt.

Puskas was a football purist, I guess. He was completely into playing football in the classic way. That's why he was never bothered with detailed tactics, restrictions on individual players or the team's fitness. The answer was simply to play better than the opposition. I know that Ferenc would infuriate the media with his post-match comments. His most common replies were, 'The ball is round' and 'There are three possibilities; you win, you lose or you draw.' No one could ever work out quite what he meant. Under Puskas there were few team tactics, except with the forwards. Then there were unbreakable rules. The right winger, usually Kimon Taliadoros, had to stay out wide on the right. The left winger, usually Peter Tsolakis, had to stay out wide on the left. The centre forward, Paul Trimboli, had to stay in the middle. Once the ball was up front they could do anything they liked, but when we were defending, or building up the play from the back or in midfield, they had to be in their positions or else.

We gradually picked up fitness from playing games. The club had strengthened the team by signing Mehmet Durakovic and Joe Palatsides from Footscray JUST. Things started to click and we played some fantastic football. We were the most attacking team in the country and in the second half of the season we strung together some great results. We made the NSL Cup final against Sydney Olympic. It was played midweek at Olympic Park in Melbourne, where we'd lost to Sydney Croatia three seasons earlier, in 1987. This time there was no disappointment. Micky Petersen scored an unbelievable goal, sitting on his bum about 15 metres from goal. The ball rolled along the goal line and into the back of the net from what looked to be an impossible angle. We thumped Olympic 4–1, with Taliadoros, Tsolakis and Trimboli also on the scoresheet.

That's when the Blue and White Army really turned on the celebrations. On that night the far grandstand at Olympic Park became my favourite spot to celebrate a goal or a win. The whole side was packed with South Melbourne supporters. When they're on your side and you score a goal it's such a magical feeling. I'm a Liverpool fan and always thought the Kop was the ultimate, but Olympic Park with the Blue and White Army is Australia's equivalent. The atmosphere they created that night was incredible, the 6000 or 7000 fans made the noise of 100,000.

Puskas wasn't too fussed about big occasions. In fact, before the NSL season we won the Dockerty Cup, the knock-out competiton for Victorian clubs, beating Altona Gate 1–0 in the final. We were jumping up and down in the dressingroom when Puskas walked in and said, 'That was rubbish. Complete rubbish.' We stopped in our tracks and looked at each other, stunned. I was thinking, 'Hang on a minute, Boss. We have just won the cup. Does it matter how we won it?' Ferenc was never satisfied, and often would tell us he'd rather see the team play good football and lose than play poorly and win. That was the way of Ferenc Puskas.

For most of the 1989–90 season we were able to keep everyone happy, by playing skilful soccer and winning games. We finished second in the league behind Marconi, scoring 42 goals in 26 games. We went into the finals full of confidence, but luck wasn't on our side. In the Qualifying Final against the Melbourne Knights we lost in a penalty shoot-out after a 1–1 draw. A week later, in the Minor Semi Final, we went down 1–0 to Sydney Olympic, who went on to win the championship. In 1988 we had bombed out of the finals in two games and now we'd done the same thing under Puskas. That leaves a sour taste. No one gives a damn about the good soccer in the regular season if you blow it in the finals. No one, that is, except Ferenc Puskas. How you play the game is what matters to him.

Puskas was back for the 1990–91 season and by now we knew him a little better, although with his limited English it was hard to get close to him. We had a very settled team, which was another Puskas method. Once he made up his mind at the start of the season, something drastic had to happen before he made changes to the starting eleven. When everyone was available, the team picked itself. Bruce Maclaren in goal; David Healy, Mehmet Durakovic, Steve Blair and Angie Postecoglou at the back; Micky Petersen, Danny Wright and myself in the midfield; Tsolakis, Trimboli and Taliadoros up front. Going forward we would run riot and destroy teams, but we'd also concede silly goals. Lots of coaches would come down to Middle Park and watch us train. Kenny Murphy was one and I can remember him saying, 'I can't believe the success you're having if that's the way you train.' He couldn't believe that we would stand around for 45 minutes juggling a ball or in pairs knocking it to each other and finish the session with half an hour of shooting and crossing. Jim Pyrgolios was trying his best to sneak in some running at the start, but we didn't dare try to change the Puskas attitude to training.

Within the NSL we were getting a name as the team with the kamikaze defence; you know, where everyone charges forward trying to score and forgetting about stopping the opposition from scoring. We sat down for a meeting and brought it up. 'Boss, it's just not working. We'd like to try playing a 4–4–2 formation.' We were all enthusiastic about it, and various players put the reasons for it to him. Basically, we wanted one of the wingers to come back and help defend when we lost the ball. Puskas sat and listened, and we thought we might have convinced him. When we'd finished he just shook his head. 'We will play the way I want to play.' That meant 4–3–3. 'If the opposition scores eight goals, fine, let them score eight goals, but we will score nine goals.' That was his attitude. He didn't care about how many we conceded. He was one of the first coaches in the NSL to throw three up front. Not too many coaches would do that on a regular basis, for fear of getting beaten. It wasn't so much that Puskas didn't care about winning; it was just that he believed if we had the ball, the other team didn't, so they couldn't score. It sounds almost too simple, but that was the Puskas way.

It was the same with his favourite warm-up exercise. He would stand with his legs apart with his hands up in the air and arch his back. The physio would tell us that this hyper-extension is probably the worst thing you can do for your back, but Puskas used to love doing it. He just waved away the physio. 'Boys, I have been doing it for 40 years and I've never had a problem.'

In 1990–91 we again won lots of games and scored a heap of goals. Melbourne Croatia won the minor premiership and we were second, having scored 45 goals and conceded 33 in 26 league games. Those numbers summed us up perfectly. We were always scoring goals, but copping plenty as well. In the Qualifying Final we had to play the third-placed team, Adelaide City, at Olympic Park in Melbourne. At that stage South Melbourne's record in the play-offs since I had joined the club in 1987 was pathetic: played four, lost four. Even though one of those defeats was on penalties, we were getting a bad reputation. We just had to beat Adelaide City and we did, in style. The final score was 4–2 in our favour and we felt we were going places. The next week we played Melbourne Croatia in the Major Semi Final, with the winner going straight into the Grand Final. It was a tough game, but Croatia won 1–0. That left us one more chance, in the Preliminary Final against Adelaide City.

To make things harder, the NSL officials decided the game should be played in Adelaide, which wasn't really fair because we had finished higher on the ladder. That just made us more determined to win and have another crack at Melbourne Croatia in the Grand Final. To this day our 1–0 over Adelaide City at the Hindmarsh Stadium ranks as the best finals performance from any South Melbourne team during my time. We were tough and committed and, thanks to a goal from Paul Trimboli, we were in the Grand Final.

Croatia had a very good team. Their midfield — Alan Davidson, Branko Milosevic and Josip Biskic — was top class. Up front, Ivan Kelic and Francis Awaritefe were two of the tallest strikers in the country. It was a special day. Olympic Park was packed with about 23,000 fans. We had a bad start when

Croatia's Andrew Marth scored from long range after 18 minutes. Not long after Awaritefe missed an absolute sitter. Croatia had us on toast — we weren't even in the same class. We weren't playing our best, but we hung in there. With about two minutes to go, Trimmers did what Trimmers does best. He turned two defenders inside out and slotted a pass through for Joe Palatsides, who scored the equaliser. I was on the far side right in front of the South Melbourne fans and I didn't even bother chasing Joe to congratulate him because he just took off into the far corner with Angie Postecoglou chasing him.

I turned around and looked at the 12,000 or 13,000 South Melbourne fans going crazy on that far side of Olympic Park. The sun was beaming down on them. I stood there with my hands up in the air and thought, 'It can't get better than this.' It was an unbelievable feeling. We were two minutes away from defeat in the biggest game of the year and in a split second Trimmers and Palatsides brought us back from the dead. The funny thing was that about 20 minutes before that goal, Palatsides was going to be substituted. He saw Jim Pyrgolios with the sub board with his number on it. Pala ran over and blasted Jimmy and said there was no way he was coming off, so Jimmy went back to the bench and Pala stayed on to score that crucial goal.

That was the thing about South Melbourne in the Puskas era: we were unpredictable. A number of times that season our fans would be leaving the ground early because we were losing. We might be 3–1 down and playing poorly, and the fans would listen to the radio on the way home and find out we'd drawn 3–3. The Grand Final was no different. I spoke to dozens of South Melbourne fans who'd given up. Some were in the car park when they heard the roar when we equalised, only to rush back into the stadium. Some had left their seats, with perfect views on the halfway line, and had to watch the extra time and the penalty shoot-out stuck up behind the corner flag. That'll teach them to give up on us!

The extra time belonged to us. Palatsides hit the crossbar and we were putting all sorts of pressure on Melbourne Croatia. That equalising goal changed everything. The day was ours from that moment on. When the penalties came I knew we could win. The pressure was enormous, but we were pretty focused. The penalty shoot-out order was sorted out as usual: 'Who's first? Wadey. Who's second? Trimmers', and so on. We were still pumped up and encouraging each other. We could see the Melbourne Croatia players sitting down. Their body language was tired, as though they were beaten before the shoot-out began. The pressure was on them. They had won the minor premiership and dominated normal time in the Grand Final. Now they were arguing about who was taking the spot kicks, struggling to get volunteers. I went up and scored the first goal and turned to the Blue and White Army. I raised my arm and pointed to them, to say, 'I did it for you.' George Hannah scored for Croatia, to make it 1–1, then

153

Paul Trimboli stepped up to take our second, and missed. Joe Biskic scored for Croatia to put them in front, 2–1. Micky Petersen was next up and I reckon the ball fell off a lump of grass and moved just as he was about strike it. The shot was saved by David Miller. I felt so sorry for Micky. The Croatia fans were going berserk, the flares were going off, and he came back to the huddle devastated.

Micky is one guy who takes everything hard. He cries even today when he watches the video. When he missed his penalty he was devastated. I went over and said, 'Micky, don't worry about it. We will just give it our best shot.' He just wouldn't look at me. Andrew Marth was next for Croatia and if he had scored they would have had a 3–1 lead. Luckily for us, he missed, but we were still 2–1 down after three penalties each. Ironically, Micky and Trimmers had been at a junior coaching clinic a few days before at Croydon City soccer club teaching the kids how to take penalties!

Things went from bad to worse, because Palatsides missed his kick. South Melbourne had missed three in a row and that meant Alan Davidson could win the Grand Final with the next kick. It would have been all over, 3–1 after four kicks each. Micky was on his back, looking as though he hated the world and himself and wanted to dig a hole and jump in. Davo was a cool customer, so it didn't look good for us. He stepped up, Bruce Maclaren dived the wrong way, but Davo's shot went wide!

Micky started to pay more attention, propping himself up on his elbows. Our captain, Angie Postecoglou, converted, to tie the scores at 2–2, but Croatia had the last kick in the compulsory set of five. We couldn't believe who they sent up. This was the penalty kick to decide the championship, and Croatia gave the job to a teenager. Mark Silic was having his first season in the NSL, and with all the pressure on him, his shot went wide. Croatia had twice been a kick away from winning, but they'd blown it. Our keeper hadn't made a save.

Now it was sudden-death. Peter Tsolakis scored to put us 3–2 ahead and Micky Petersen was back on his feet. Miller equalised for Croatia. Danny Wright very coolly converted to make it 4–3 and Micky was back among us. He had gone from lying on his back, dead and buried, to standing there, anticipating a victory. Theo Selemidis made us wait longer for a result; the score was now locked at 4–4. The tension was incredible. Steve Blair ambled down and made it look so easy. It was now 5–4 to South Melbourne. It came down to Ivan Kelic. He had to score to level the shoot-out. Bruce Maclaren was waving his arms and pulling faces. He still hadn't made a save, but maybe all the antics were just as good. Kelic smashed it over the bar and we'd won the Grand Final!

It wasn't the most spectacular way to win a Grand Final, but who cares? We were wild with joy, jumping around, hugging and kissing each other in front of the Blue and White Army. For the next eight hours we didn't stop. We went back to the social club at Middle Park and had trouble getting into the car park.

There were so many fans, standing shoulder to shoulder. The players had to squeeze themselves from the front door to the stage. It was hot, noisy and thick with smoke. The entire night the singing went on. 'Ole, ole, ole, ole, Hellas, Hellas.' Then the crowd started chanting, 'Puskas, Puskas'.

The Boss is never emotional about anything; when you look at the video of the Grand Final, everybody is going berserk, except Ferenc Puskas. I suppose if you've won the European Cup, the NSL championship ain't no big deal. But in the social club the emotion affected him. He had to ask his wife for a handkerchief and he kept putting it to his eyes to fight back the tears. It was incredible the amount of emotion in that room that night. Even now, watching the video, I get a lump in my throat. We won the championship, even though a lot of people would probably say that we didn't deserve to. Looking back at the 90 minutes we probably didn't, but there are games all over the world every single day of the week where the team that has more of the play doesn't win. The 1990–91 Grand Final was our turn.

Aʟʟ ᴛʜᴇ ᴇxᴄɪᴛᴇᴍᴇɴᴛ ᴏꜰ the championship masked a few fundamental problems at South Melbourne. The players were sick and tired of the Puskas training methods. There was no stimulation, nothing new. All we did was 'two to a ball'. In fact, midway through the 1991–92 season we were praying that Puskas would leave the club, because we were fed up with those words, and with all the hours of kicking the thing back and forwards on autopilot. Jim Pyrgolios was good at reading the players' minds. After two seasons, we needed some changes. We told Jim how we felt and he had a word to Ferenc. We had to get fitter and be more flexible on the park.

The magic of the Puskas motto of 'attack and don't worry about defending' had worn off. Three years is probably the most a coach could stay with the one set of players at the one club. Frank Arok once told me that teams have to keep changing. It's either the players or the coach who must go and Arok was smart enough to keep a regular turnover of players so there was never a chance for the team to grow stale.

South Melbourne had very little turnover of players under Puskas. The Boss wouldn't listen. He insisted the formation with three up front was successful for him and that he wasn't going to change. It was the same with the training routines. The boys were bored with soccer towards the end. We knew exactly what we were going to be doing at training. It was the same 'two to a ball', the same shooting routines, the same Puskas back exercises. It was four nights a week of boredom. In a strange sort of way the training meant we really wanted to play come the weekend. We could hardly complain about being physically worn out. Mentally, it was a different story, though. We finished in third place, but only because we had some of the best players in the country.

There was a flicker of hope when we beat Sydney Olympic 2–0 in the Qualifying Final, but the following week Croatia paid us back by winning 5–3 on penalties in the Major Semi Final. We still had a chance in the Preliminary Final against Adelaide City. The game was played in Melbourne and the kick-off was put back to the early evening so the South Melbourne fans could celebrate the Greek Easter before watching the soccer. There really wasn't much to celebrate. We were flat and uninspiring. It was one of our worst performances under Puskas. Adelaide City beat us 2–0 and by the end of the game our own fans were jeering us. There was no life in the team, no fight. We handed over the championship crown without a whimper.

That was the end of Ferenc Puskas. It was said that his wife wanted to go home to Hungary; the collapse of communism had made that an option. The public story was that Puskas left of his own accord. I asked Puskas and he indicated that the committee hadn't asked him to stay. I said, 'Would you stay if you were asked?' He nodded his head, but he wasn't ever asked. I think it was the right decision for everyone involved. In three seasons under Ferenc Puskas, the crowds were up, we won the NSL Cup and the national championship. It was the most successful period for South Melbourne since the establishment of the national league in 1977, but it was time to move on. I think Ferenc Puskas, the gentle grandfather, knew that, too.

JIM PYRGOLIOS HAD THE support of the players when he was appointed coach of South Melbourne for the 1992–93 season. He'd been the assistant to Puskas for three years so he knew the team inside out and he knew the problems. Jim was popular among the fans because he'd been a top striker in the '60s. For the last three years, none of the South Melbourne players had really worked hard on the training track, but that was all about to change.

Jim worked us so hard for so long that towards the end of that season the boys were saying, 'Come back, Puskas, all is forgiven.' The words 'two to a ball' sounded superb, 'shoot the ball' sounded like sheer bliss. Instead, it was 50-metre sprints, lots of push-ups and exercises with medicine balls. Ferenc would have had a fit if he had seen what was going on. It just shows what a fine balance it is trying to get players in the right frame of mind and at the right peak of fitness. The appointment of Jim Pyrgolios wasn't the only change at Middle Park.

The Australian Soccer Federation had decided to ban ethnic names for soccer clubs in the National Soccer League. We were no longer South Melbourne Hellas, merely South Melbourne. Melbourne Croatia became Melbourne CSC and later the Melbourne Knights. The fans still shouted 'Hellas' and 'Croatia', but the ASF was hoping those names would just disappear. It was wishful thinking. The changes continued for the playing staff. A few weeks into the season our goalkeeper, Bruce Maclaren, told the club he couldn't afford the time to train four nights a week, so he was forced to retire. Fortunately, the club had signed Dean Anastasiadis, a goalkeeper from Fawkner in the Victorian Premier League. Kimon Taliadoros transferred to Marconi for $43,000 and the club bought Francis Awaritefe from the Melbourne Knights for $28,000.

I was facing a big change, thanks to Steve Blair. Big Blairy had a run of injuries and I had to fill in at centre back. It's a big change when you go from the midfield, where you're doing lots of running up and down the ground, to centre back, where you're doing very little running. The job usually involved marking one player and lots of one-on-one clashes, but you end up watching most of the game. Playing stopper was a breeze, not a problem at all. At times it was even fun.

We played Marconi at Middle Park in front of a packed house. My opponent was Kimon Taliadoros, who was playing against us at Middle Park for the first time since his transfer. I'm sure Kimon will remember it for years. The South Melbourne fans treated him like a traitor. Every time he got the ball he was booed. The fans were whistling and hissing at him from the time he walked into the stadium. The fans would have been sick if Kimon had scored, so I had to make sure he had a miserable day. I was so tight on Kimon at one stage he punched me in the chest because he was getting so fed up with me hanging on to his shirt tail. I did my job and we beat them 2–0. 'Gus' Tsolakis got the first, from the penalty spot, and Awaritefe scored a great goal for the second. There were flares everywhere when we scored; it was a great atmosphere.

I was watching some brilliant football being played by the South Melbourne midfield and I was reasonably happy with the job Durakovic and I were doing at the back. We were winning games and scoring plenty of goals, as we did under Puskas, but our defence was far more solid. Jim changed the formation to 4–4–2 and introduced a more flexible approach, just as we had wanted Puskas to do. We were on top for most of the season and won the minor premiership quite comfortably. There was no doubt Jim's hard training and more flexible tactics had made us a better team. In the end we scored 51 goals, but conceded only 23. In the championship year under Puskas the figures were 45 for, 33 against, so on that basis we were a better team.

Towards the end of the regular season the Socceroos went to Hong Kong for two friendly internationals against Kuwait. I was doing extra training for the upcoming World Cup qualifiers and wanted to make up for any loss of sharpness from playing in defence for South Melbourne. In the humid conditions I picked up a bug and ended up with pneumonia, as I've outlined in Chapter Four. I'd been feeling so excited about South Melbourne's chances in the finals. In fact, I really believed another championship was on the way. We had to play Marconi in a Major Semi Final two-legged tie, under the NSL's new Top Six format.

The first leg was at Olympic Park in Melbourne. On the morning of the Marconi match I woke up feeling very sick. I had severe flu symptoms and no energy whatsoever. The club doctor gave me something and I felt a lot better, but there was no way in the world I could play. I was named as a substitute and was stripped and sitting on the bench, more in hope than anything else. My illness was the first disaster that day. About 10 minutes into the game Micky Petersen hurt his Achilles tendon and had to come off. Marconi played a very clever defensive game worked out by Frank Arok. He played his two strikers out wide and left a huge gap down the middle for Steve Corica to exploit with his runs from deep in midfield. On the hour, right on cue, Corica killed us with one of his trademark solo runs to score the winning goal. To cap off a rotten day, Con Boutsianis hurt his ankle in the last 10 minutes. It was Frank Arok 1, South Melbourne 0.

Frank had not only beaten us with his tactics, but he'd won the mind games with his comments in the media. He said, 'If South Melbourne don't win the title this season, they should start selling players and building a new team.' Was that directed at me? Was it Frank just playing games? Maybe both. In any case, things got worse for Paul Wade. I was diagnosed with pneumonia and told to rest for a couple of weeks. Great! Rest for a couple of weeks in the middle of the finals with the World Cup qualifiers a month away! I sat at home feeling lousy all week as the boys prepared to play Marconi in Sydney.

I was sitting in my lounge room on the Sunday afternoon and finally decided I'd better turn on the radio to find out the score. Greg Blake was calling the match from Sydney and the first few comments I heard gave South Melbourne an awful lot of stick. I thought, 'Blakey, you're a Melburnian, the least you could do for us South Melbourne supporters back here in Melbourne is cheer us up a bit.' He kept slaughtering South Melbourne. Then I found out why. He announced the score and I almost fell over. It was 4–0 to Marconi, with half an hour still to play. It was the most depressing 30 minutes I have ever spent listening to a football match. In the end we lost 7–0 and had Mehmet Durakovic stretchered off with concussion, thanks to a shirt front by Glenn Johnson. It was a total disaster.

That's when the 'Colliwobbles' thing started — Collingwood AFL team almost always lost their big finals games. Since beating Sydney Olympic in the Qualifying Final the previous season, South Melbourne had lost four finals games on the trot. We had to play Adelaide City in the preliminary final at Olympic Park and the build-up all week was, 'Are we going to see the Colliwobbles again?' I wasn't 100 per cent fit, but I made myself available. Just to show it wasn't our year, Sergio Melta scored an unbelievable goal after about five minutes. We didn't need a kick in the head, but Melta gave us one, anyway. He had no right in the world to score that goal. He was 25 metres out and somehow hit this dipping volley into the top corner. Melta's shot hit the goal in a place where the spider webs are rarely disturbed! Not long after that, Trimmers was clear in the Adelaide City box and was cut down by Robby Zabica, the Adelaide City and Socceroo goalkeeper. Not only did we not get a penalty kick, but also, Trimmers hurt his shoulder in the fall and had to go off. We had so much bad luck in that finals series. We went down 3–1. Damian Mori smashed in a shot from close range and the third goal came after Mori ran past me and placed his shot underneath Dean Anastasiadis. Even if I had been fully fit, Damian Mori would have been too fast for me, but a few observers said I shouldn't have played because of the pneumonia. Socceroo coach Eddie Thomson was among them, but I felt good enough to be out there.

It was all over for 1992–93 and the crowd got nasty. Jim Pyrgolios had won the NSL coach of the year award, but the South Melbourne fans were screaming abuse at him. We couldn't help feeling that injuries and illness, not lack of ability or preparation, had destroyed us. In the league season we had been by far the best team in the competition, and were favourites for the championship. But it was another one that had got away. The media had a field day with the stories about us losing five finals game in a row.

My career move from midfielder to defender became permanent for the 1993–94 season. Steve Blair had been given a promotion in his work for the RACV and told the club he couldn't train four nights a week. The club said it was all or nothing, so Blairy retired. The club signed Andrew Marth, from the Melbourne Knights, as a defender to replace Blair, but before the season started Marth changed his mind and went back to the Knights. George Vasilopoulos, Bill Georgantis and Jim Pyrgolios called me to a meeting. 'Wadey, we want you to play for this club for another five years, not another two. We don't think you can go on in the midfield much longer so we want you to play at the back.' I wasn't happy. I wanted to play in midfield because I wasn't going to be picked for the Socceroos as a defender. But at the end of the day, the club is the employer and I realised we had players like Petersen, Tassios, Tsolakis and Angie Goutsioulis competing for spots in the middle. The club was also negotiating to buy another midfielder, Jason Polak, from the Newcastle Breakers. The club was short of experienced defenders, so I had to do the job. On top of the positional move, I was named captain.

The trouble was, I was still in the middle of a World Cup campaign. We had played New Zealand and Canada during the NSL off-season, but the games against Argentina were coming up and I was desperate to get back my spot as a midfielder in the Socceroo starting eleven. I said to Jim Pyrgolios, 'I understand that you want me to play at centre back and I'm quite happy to do that, but please do me a favour and let me play the early games in the midfield so I can get myself ready for the World Cup games.' Jim agreed. I played in midfield during the pre-season friendlies and in the cup matches before the NSL league season started. I really needed those games to get my first touch and my vision keyed in to the midfield role. It's very different at the back when all the play is in front of you.

After the World Cup games against Argentina I was back at Middle Park as a defender and we had a reasonably successful year. The Melbourne Knights won the minor premiership and we were six points behind in second place, positioned for a shot at the championship. But once again the 'Colliwobbles' struck. Mehmet Durakovic hurt his ankle on the Thursday night before the Major Semi Final against the Knights and we had to reorganise the defence. Kevin Muscat took over as the sweeper, but in the wet conditions he made a mistake and Adrian Cervinski scored for the Knights. In the reshuffle I ended up playing more of a defensive midfield role. We didn't play very well, and Cervinski scored a second. At 2–0 we were in deep trouble, but Trimmers scored with a header to make the final score 2–1, giving us some hope for the second leg.

For that game I stayed in the midfield, proving there was life in the old dog yet! I was loving it. The wet conditions were perfect for me: everybody comes back to the field, nobody's quick any more — it's just a matter of how big your heart is, and that suits me right down to the ground. I was running as hard as I could and things started to happen. I was marking Joe Biskic, the Knights captain. He'd played midfield all season, so if I stuck to him, he would carry me through. We were 1–0 down to a Mark Viduka goal and the Blue and White Army was pretty quiet. Steve Tassios made a run out on the right-hand side and I took off towards the near post. Steve chipped it into the middle as I ran into a gap and there it was on the end of my head. I nodded it into the back of the net and ran straight to my favourite spot in front of the South Melbourne fans. I was throwing my arms up and saying to them, 'Come on, get behind us.' They went berserk and the atmosphere was superb.

We started to take over the game. We had lost the first leg 2–1, but at 1–1 in the second leg it was 3–2 overall. Awaritefe came off the bench and scored, making it 3–3 overall. We were on fire, but not for long. With about three minutes left, Fausto De Amicis hit a shot into a pack of players. It was going to hit me, but Zoran Trajcevski ducked and it flicked off his back and into the far corner of the goal. I just sank to my knees and thought, 'What do we have to do to get to win a final game?' The second leg finished at 2–2, but we lost 4–3 on aggregate and it ripped the heart out of the team.

The next weekend in the preliminary final, Adelaide City did their usual trick and beat us, for the third year in a row. We had played eight finals games without a win. It's times like that you think, 'Maybe we are the Collingwood of the National Soccer League, maybe we just haven't got the bottle.' The worst thing in football, or in life, for that matter, is wasting opportunities. Over the first eight years I was at South Melbourne, we had a team good enough to win the championship four times. Instead, we won it once. The most sickening part of it all was getting eliminated in the preliminary final year after year and not even being there on Grand Final day. I played in four preliminary finals for just one win.

In years to come, people won't be able to remember the good times with those great sides — because they didn't win grand finals. South Melbourne fans will always remember the 1984 team under Len McKendry and the 1990–91 side under Ferenc Puskas. Who will remember the 1988 team under Brian Garvey, the 1991–92 Puskas team or Jim Pyrgolios' minor premiership side of 1992–93? Well, I will. I'd just like a few more trophies to go with the memories from my first eight, happy seasons at South Melbourne. And what of my ninth and final season at the club? That's where Frank Arok comes in.

Between Arok and a Hard Place

WHEN FRANK AROK, the former Socceroo coach, arrived at Middle Park to take over as coach of South Melbourne for the 1994–95 season, I thought we would win the championship in his first season. Frank was going to be the missing link for the club. We had a team that had finished first and second in the previous two regular seasons, but got the Colliwobbles and bombed out in the finals. We were overdue for a championship. We had half a dozen players with international experience. Frank's ability to motivate players and get his teams to peak in finals, having coached St George and Marconi to Grand Final wins, was going to make the difference.

The regular season started off superbly. The opening fixture was the Greek derby against Heidelberg United at Middle Park. It was also the farewell game before the stadium was demolished to make way for the Grand Prix track around Albert Park Lake. The atmosphere was the same as it always is for a big game at Middle Park: absolutely brilliant. With 10,000 fans packed in, Middle Park was something special. After playing for most of the previous two seasons in defence, Frank moved me back to centre midfield. It was only a couple of minutes into the game when Con Boutsianis gave us the lead. The Blue and White Army was going crazy. Before the interval Heidelberg equalised from the penalty spot after Jason Polak, the Socceroo midfielder, handled the ball on the goal line. Polak was sent off, so we went off at half-time down to 10 men, and with the scoreline 1–1.

It was a big test for Frank and the players. All the club wanted to farewell Middle Park with a win. The situation was made for Frank. He was ranting and raving, and the lads were fired up. We went out and wiped out Heidelberg 4–1. It was a great performance, the sort of 100-miles-an-hour attacking stuff that

South Melbourne was famous for. On the final whistle the fans were going wild. As captain, I was very proud of the way we had responded. My belief that we were good enough to win the championship had been confirmed. Everybody had said that we were too hot to even put any money on for the championship; our odds were so short you wouldn't get your money back. I already had two championship medals and I thought I was on my way to a third.

But that's where the story ends as far as success goes for this season — round one. South Melbourne fell in a big, big hole. There wasn't any one thing you could put a finger on, but dozens of little things kept going wrong. In that Middle Park farewell game, Mehmet Durakovic hurt his groin. Yuggsy and I had formed a pretty solid defensive partnership over the previous two seasons. He was an excellent sweeper, the spare defender who covers everyone else and fills in the gaps. Yuggsy also found time to attack, but he was missing when we travelled to Brisbane the next weekend and it was a big loss. The sweeper is the most important defender. I was moved from midfield to centre back in a reshuffle and we were hammered 3–1 by the Strikers. Without Durakovic, Gary Hasler had moved from full-back to sweeper, but after copping three goals we couldn't say the move was a success. The trip up north is always tough!

In round three we were playing our first game at our new 'home' ground, Olympic Park. The club had to vacate Middle Park, and our new Lakeside Stadium wouldn't be built until the start of the 1995–96 season. The fans weren't that thrilled about the move to Olympic Park. Car parking is always a hassle and, worst of all, we'd lost quite a few important finals games there. The fans thought there was a bit of a hoodoo on the place. Morwell Falcons were the visitors and if you were looking for omens, they were all bad. Frank made more changes to the defence. This time Micky Petersen moved from midfield to sweeper and I went back into midfield. It was a filthy night, wet and windy. We were chasing the game all night. The Falcons scored first, so we were always playing catch-up. We'd equalise, then give away another goal. To try to get us going Frank made more changes at half-time. Gary Hasler ended up playing sweeper again and Micky went back into midfield. It was like musical chairs. We kept conceding goals. In the wet Hasler miskicked a ball and it went straight to Morwell's Brian Bothwell, who scored, giving the Falcons a 3–2 lead. It was only a late goal by Paul Trimboli that saved us from defeat, but in the penalty shoot-out for the extra point (an innovation introduced for the 1994–5 season), the Falcons came out on top.

For the second week in a row we had conceded three goals. I couldn't remember the last time that happened, not even in the Puskas days when we were an all-out attacking team. But look at the choice of Gary Hasler as sweeper: here is a guy who is a centre forward, transformed into a full-back, then thrown into a sweeper's role. I believe that a sweeper has to have the biggest mouth on the park because he has to organise the back line. This situation was tough because Gary was thrown in at the deep end and expected to perform, not only as a playmaker from the back, but as the player in control of the rest of us. I was getting frustrated that he wasn't talking and he was getting frustrated because he was caught between trying to adapt to a new position and being expected to be a leader in defence. It was a totally frustrating period for everybody involved.

Things hit rock bottom in round four. We went to Wollongong on a Friday night with yet another revamped defence. This time, Steve Mangos, a young guy signed from the Victorian State League, was the sweeper. That meant we'd had four different sweepers in four games. To add to the changes, Frank dropped the goalkeeper, Steve Mautone, and put in Dean Anastasiadis. It's no wonder the defence was in chaos. I was once again in midfield. The game was a disaster. Kevin Muscat was given a red card for a pretty harmless shoulder charge, and Gary Hasler was given his marching orders for arguing with the referee. We finished the game with nine men and lost 3–2.

We were starting to fall miles behind the league leaders. The team was a mess. Every week we had three or four players missing through injury or suspension. By round four we'd had three red cards, and usually we wouldn't have so many in a whole season. Frank was getting frantic. The fact was, we weren't playing particularly well and all the red cards and injuries only made things worse. I know from experience that when players are first coached by Frank Arok it is a little bit different from anything they've seen before. Frank is very professional and very passionate about everything to do with football, but it can take time to get used to him.

There were a few guys at South Melbourne asking Paul Trimboli, Micky Petersen and I about what Frank Arok was on about. What does he mean when he says this? What does he want when he says that? Frank was making so many changes that we didn't know the answers ourselves. The crisis was so unexpected. We were fit at the start of the season, and all the players were revved up. Kevin Muscat and Con Boutsianis were playing out of their skins in the early games. Because we were so optimistic in the pre-season it made it even harder to cope when things went wrong. We lost Steve Tassios because of chronic knee problems. Angie Goutsioulis walked out after round five because of a disagreement with Frank. Durakovic's groin injury was to be a long-term problem, and morale was getting pretty low. From the very first game, when Durakovic hurt his groin, it seemed that we would lose a defender to injury or suspension every game. The back line was changing every week and we were conceding lots of goals: 10 in the first four games.

In round five we had a bye, thanks to the late withdrawal of Newcastle from the NSL. That gave us some breathing space, and we all thought we'd start afresh in round six. However, Frank was still experimenting in defence. For the round six game, away to West Adelaide, Mike Valkanis was to be sweeper. Five games, five different sweepers. We lost 2–1 and the bad results affected everybody's form and confidence. We were second last. So much for being championshp favourites!

Construction work on the Albert Park Grand Prix track meant we had lost our training facilities at Middle Park. We had to find a new place to train, which was another disaster. For a month we trained across from Olympic Park on a cricket oval with a turf pitch in the middle. The curator would put up barriers around the centre wicket area and we had to train around it. There were no soccer pitch ground markings so it was impossible to do any meaningful work on tactics or team formations. The club then found another training venue in Brunswick, but that was a football oval with a couple of soccer goals in the middle of it. The arrangements were terrible for a national soccer league team.

F RANK AROK DOESN'T TOLERATE failure. South Melbourne was scoring goals as freely as ever before, but conceding many more. For the round seven game, at home to Adelaide City, Frank picked me as the sweeper, the sixth player to have the job in six games. He also resorted to some pretty unconventional methods of plugging the defence: he demanded that every player had to pick up a specific opposition player when we lost the ball.

I didn't think it would work. It went against every principle that I, as a midfielder, had been taught for the whole of my football career. In midfield you can't just mark one man and think you've done your job. Sometimes you have got two or three jobs to do. If one of the wide midfielders gets beaten and you're in the middle, you can't just watch and say, 'Well, that's not my man. I'm going to stay with my man and it's your job to mark the guy with the ball. You're the one to blame.' What does that achieve? Frank seemed to think his idea of man-marking would work because players would be so scared of their opponent doing some damage that they would be more desperate to stop them. When things went wrong in defence he would be able to point the finger at one player and say, 'You were the one who caused that goal on the weekend.' It seemed that he wanted to be able to blame somebody and say, 'Right, this is the reason you have been dropped this week.'

The idea was crazy. How can you play and express yourself if you're filled with the fear of making a mistake? In any case, it's a team game. If a team is playing badly, it's up to the team to put things right. Frank's idea of blaming individuals was only going to cause more trouble. If the player you were supposed to be marking scored a goal or sent over a cross that created a goal, what could you say? Sure, your opponent has scored, but who was marking the guy who passed the ball? Where do you stop? Frank was also keeping a tally of how many times each player gave the ball away with a bad pass or a mistake. He'd be on the bench scribbling away every time something went wrong. Realistically, you just can't run a team that way. Football is a team versus a team, not eleven individuals against another eleven. You could put eleven Maradonas out there and the team would probably get thumped by an eleven who had less ability but who played as a team.

I was trying to do what Frank wanted, but I knew it wouldn't work. In the early games we had Angie Goutsioulis, who is a naturally attacking player, and Kevin Muscat, a defender who likes to go forward, in our back four. Obviously, if one of them goes forward and our attack breaks down, somebody, usually the sweeper, has to go and cover. When the sweeper goes to mark an opponent, the full-back furthest from the danger has to tuck in and become a sweeper. It all might sound a little bit complicated, but my junior coaches in England taught me how to balance in defence when I was 10. It's just a matter of players being aware of what's going on and working as a team.

Our defensive record didn't get any better against Adelaide City. We again lost 2–1. That meant we had conceded 14 goals in six games. Frank and I had a couple of disagreements on the training park about the way we were defending. He still insisted we pick up man for man. I, as sweeper, was saying, 'You can't pick up man for man, because we have to cover for each other.' I was trying to play more of a zone defence. Most midfields operate on a zone defence; it's the most effective way to defend. Someone has to attack the ball and the rest pick up the opponents in the most dangerous positions.

It became a bit of a showdown between captain and coach. I asked myself, 'Am I being stubborn? Am I thinking as a midfielder and trying to use all the midfield principles in the back four?'

I tried and tried, but Arok's system just wasn't working. We were getting beaten every week.

After the loss in Wollongong we lost another three in a row: to West Adelaide, Adelaide City and then 2–0 away to Parramatta, conceding six goals in the process. After seven games we were second last, with one win, one draw and five losses. That was enough proof for me that Frank's plan wasn't working. We were conceding silly goals while missing glaring chances at the other end. Our defence was becoming a joke. Frank was making changes every week to try to find a winning combination. He even dropped Paul Trimboli, the most talented footballer at the club, for no other reason than it might change something.

We were really just hoping things would change for the better, without really having a plan.

Frank was full of ideas, as usual, but for once in his career things weren't working out. Several times Frank told the media, 'I've never had a season like this, not in 40 years.' When we came to play Sydney Olympic in round nine, we were absolutely desperate for a win, after four straight losses. I was the sweeper for the third game in a row, which was something of a record. Trimmers gave us an early lead, but in the second half Joe Bacak scored for Olympic, with a shot that took a deflection off my foot. It was just another example of the way everything was going against us.

Fortunately, the players' relationships survived the strain. That was the one good thing that came out of it. As captain I have always said that no matter how many things were going wrong on the park, the boys had to stick together off the park. I knew that it would all turn around at some stage. I have bad memories of other teams I have been in, at both junior and senior level, where you started getting cliques within the team, people blaming each other and arguing off the park. Then you are in real trouble. At South Melbourne there was none of that whatsoever off the park. We had huge arguments on the park, but never any off.

T HE CRUNCH CAME IN a vital league game around Christmas. We had to play the league leaders, the Melbourne Knights, away. We hadn't won a game since the opening day of the season in October and now we were in the last week of December, with a record of one win, two draws and six losses. In the week before the Knights game Frank had gone all out to strengthen the defence. In effect, he'd given up trying to make things work with the existing players. The club signed Alex Kuzmanovic from the Melbourne Zebras for $28,000. Alan Davidson, the former Socceroo full-back, was signed on loan from his Malaysian club Pahang, and was rushed into the team after arriving on the morning of the game. Mehmet Durakovic was back in the team after eight weeks out injured. With three defenders available I was back in midfield.

What a game for me to go back into the middle of the park! It was blowing a gale and the Knights were really fired up because their supporters love to see South Melbourne getting beaten. Alan Davidson was playing a defensive midfield role and Micky Petersen was the playmaker. I was, supposedly, the engine room in midfield. Not a bad combination, all of us with international experience, but the Knights were one of the top teams in the country and their midfield was very mobile and very quick. It was tough. The Knights were all over us, but we defended quite well. We survived at 0–0 until half-time, but not long into the second half disaster struck.

Dean Anastasiadis, our keeper, threw the ball to the right full-back position. I had just made another covering run into defence and was thinking, 'Phew, that's another attack we've stopped.' The ball went over my head to Davidson, who was out wide. I don't know whether he missed it or the Melbourne Knights won it back. All of a sudden the Melbourne Knights were coming at us again.

Their left back, Fausto De Amicis, had a shot and it cannoned off Durakovic. The ball somehow found its way back to De Amicis and this time he scored.

The next day I read in the *Herald–Sun* that I had failed to clear a ball, which led to the goal. All I remember was the ball flashing past me in the penalty area. In a matter of five seconds we had given away possession and conceded a killer goal. The game had turned and the hundreds of thousands of newspaper readers were told it was my fault!

After that goal, we went downhill. Kuzmanovic was sent off with the score still at 1–0. We were obviously going to have to push forward a little bit more to try and get back in the game. That's not easy in midfield when you're one short against players as quick as Spiteri, Pondeljak, Silic and Tiatto. They also had Mark Viduka, the league's top goalscorer, up front. It was tough in midfield, because we were trying to push up and give the forwards some support, but our back line was another 50 metres behind us. Davidson had dropped back to fill in for Kuzmanovic, so Micky Petersen, Jason Polak and I had to cover a lot of area. It was my first game in midfield for a couple of months and I was finding it pretty tough to keep the engine ticking under all the pressure. With 20 minutes to go it was, 'No. 6, your time is up.' I thought, 'Fair enough, Frank's obviously seen that I've been working flat out and I'm a bit knackered.' I came off, and I was a little bit disappointed. The Knights scored another two goals and we were well beaten 3–0.

The following Thursday Frank Arok called me aside at training. He said, 'Listen, Wadey, I am in total chaos at the moment. I just don't know what to do next. I have tried everything. I have tried you at sweeper, I have tried you at centre back, I have tried you in the midfield. You've been involved in almost every goal we've conceded lately. I have decided to leave you out this week.' I didn't like what I heard, but I accepted Frank's decision. I thought I was being left out the way Trimboli was — to see what effect it would have. It was as though Frank was just shuffling his players and it was my turn to miss out. I was club captain, but if Frank says you're out, then that's it. The next morning in the *Herald–Sun* there was a story with Frank announcing his team for the next game. He was quoted as saying, 'It is my best eleven who will play the next game, and anyone who wants to get in is going to have to work really hard.' Suddenly I wasn't in the best eleven at South Melbourne, after eight seasons as a regular. I didn't mind that because everyone deserves a kick up the bum sometime. I wasn't playing badly, but it was hard for any of us to play consistently well the way we were being moved around. It was still a shock, though. I had never been dropped at national league level before.

In 1983 I was left out of the Croydon City team for arriving late and in 1984 Jimmy Rooney took me off during a game. Both events had the desired effect — I worked harder. I did the same with Frank. I attacked the problem head on: 'What do I have to do to get myself back in this team?' He said, 'Well, Wadey, I don't think you are quick enough, for a start. And I'm not happy with those boots you are wearing.' It was a fairly sweeping criticism. For a start, I've never been a speedster, but that misses the point. My game is built on stamina, not sprinting. As for the boots; I was wearing Blades, a new and revolutionary football boot. Instead of having studs, the boots had blades at 45 degree angles. The technology was developed to help players avoid ankle and knee problems. Blades boots give the wearer stability and comfort and a greater ability to turn at short notice, without studs fixing into the turf, creating an injury risk.

In the off-season before the 1994–95 campaign I'd had operations on both ankles. Over the years I'd hurt my ankles many times, and the joints had taken a battering. The injury in Chile during the World Cup campaign was the final straw. When the specialists took X-rays they showed how many bone spurs and bone fragments were in the joints. Dr Siri Kanangra, the Socceroos' doctor, said he'd never seen anything like it. David Young, the surgeon, said he couldn't believe I was still running around with such bad ankles. He removed lots of shrapnel. Frank Arok wasn't happy I'd come back so quickly. It was about eight weeks after the operation that I played for the Socceroos on tour in Malaysia and Japan. As far as I was concerned, the Blades boots were the smart option. On top of all that, the Blades company was one of my sponsors. I had a contract to wear those boots, and now my coach says they're part of the problem!

I said, 'Okay, let's do a test. I will wear a pair of normal studded boots for a while and we'll see.' After talking at length to Frank about what he saw as my problems, I committed myself to extra training sessions. I asked Frank to help and, to his credit, he didn't hesitate for one moment. These special training sessions were to sort out my problems, as Frank saw them: being too slow, and my first touch not being good enough. After the first training session he said, 'There you go, you see. Today I thought you were much quicker and sharper on your feet in normal boots.' I thought any difference he saw was due to the fact that training on your own means you are bound to be buzzing that little bit more because you're under the microscope. I certainly didn't think the boots had anything to do with it.

We worked on speed by running down a hill and keeping my strides short. This meant I was actually moving faster than I would on flat ground, and my legs had to go quicker to keep up. If I was going to run down the hill and not go head over heels, I had to pump like crazy. There was lots of repetition and it made sense. We did this exercise for two or three sessions. There were other drills where Frank would blast the ball into an area and I would have to chase it, bring it under control and knock it back to his feet as quickly as possible. I was working hard.

This went on for three weeks, with two or three morning sessions in addition to the four nights a week with the team. I could feel my fitness and sharpness improving. It helped my attitude, too. Instead of feeling left out, I felt I was doing the hard work that would get me back into the team, but my omission coincided with the start of a winning streak for South Melbourne. In the first game after I was dropped we lost 2–1 away to Sydney United, but then scored our first 'home' win at Olympic Park, beating Marconi 2–0. Obviously, you don't change a winning team. We then won three in a row. I was happy the team was winning because it's easier to play well when the team is in good shape, and I was sure I'd be back in the starting eleven soon. You must have a positive attitude or you're finished.

Of course, it's not every day that the national captain sits on the bench. There was plenty of talk about Paul Wade being good enough to captain Australia, but not good enough to play for South Melbourne. I never thought of it that way, but I was starting to wonder when I'd get back into the team. The weeks passed and I started to feel that something wasn't quite right between Frank Arok and me. At the start of each week I would pull Frank aside and ask how I was doing. I genuinely wanted to know exactly what he was thinking. We were over the hardest part, which comes when a coach drops a player. I had accepted his decision and was working hard to get back. You can only go on hoping and trying for so long, though, without some sign that you're on the right track.

My big chance came along when centre back Mike Valkanis was suspended. According to my previous discussions with Frank, I was the understudy. The *Herald–Sun* soccer reporter, Peter Desira, began his match preview of the South Melbourne/Brisbane Strikers game on the Sunday night with the news that 'Paul Wade is expected to play his first full game for over a month'. I never took anything for granted, but I had a feeling that Frank would pick me. I felt I deserved a recall. I was fit and I knew I could do the job at centre back. I had played there for almost two seasons, 1992–3 and 1993–4. Mehmet Durakovic was still struggling with his groin injury and had again been off the training track for a couple of weeks. Alan Davidson was playing sweeper and Kuzmanovic was one of the central markers with Valkanis. While I had been on the bench, the team hadn't lost a game, and anyone who's ever played under Frank Arok knows it's harder to get out of the team than into it when things are going well. The Valkanis suspension was the break I'd been waiting for, or so I thought.

At the main training session for the week, I got a nasty shock. All the players were in a group waiting for instructions. Frank began handing out training bibs to all the youth players and the guys not in the starting eleven. It was common to have a full practice game with the first eleven against the rest. Frank was working his way through the group, handing out coloured training bibs to the youth and reserve players. I was about to jog over and join the first team when Frank handed me a bib and moved on, without saying a word. I was stunned. Something had gone wrong. This couldn't be right. I could hardly believe my eyes when I looked across and saw Mehmet Durakovic in the first eleven. Yuggsy hadn't played since that fateful night against the Melbourne Knights in December. All the time I'd been training six or seven times a week, he'd been out injured. After patiently waiting for my chance, it was unbelievable to think he was back in the team ahead of me. He hadn't trained all week and now, in the final session before the game, he appeared in a position I thought was mine. Inside I was boiling. I was furious, but tried not to show it.

When I spit the dummy I don't stand there and sulk. I get mad and I tackle harder. I take out my frustration on the training track. The practice match started and I was fired up. I was running as hard and as fast as I could. Every time I won a tackle I stood up and I looked Frank Arok straight in the eyes. I might have been 30 or 40 metres away, but I looked him straight in the eyes. Under my breath I was saying things like, 'Stuff you, Frank Arok.' I felt Frank had deceived me. I had been through too much. It wasn't a case of Paul Wade demanding a game, far from it. In fact, Mehmet Durakovic should have been given that spot ahead of me, if he was fully fit. I have always said that Alex Tobin and Durakovic are the best man markers this country has ever had. The thing was, Yuggsy was far from fully fit. He was on one leg. He could only jog laps with the physio for the week before this training session. You can imagine how incensed I was with the whole ordeal.

I was going through players, winning the ball and letting them know I was not happy. Frank could tell I was angry and on several occasions when the 'stiffs' had won the ball and were attacking, he stopped the play. That made me even more mad. I wanted to batter the first team, Frank's so-called best eleven, to show him they weren't invincible and that I still had it. When I gave him the evil eye during one of the stoppages, he said, 'This game is not put on for your benefit.' While Frank was saying his bit to the first team, I kept thinking about how stupid it was to pick Durakovic. Players know instinctively when other players are unfit. You didn't have to be a doctor to know Mehmet Durakovic was crook. The more I thought about it, the madder I got. I may as well have been playing against Argentina the way I was going in this training session. I was desperate to win absolutely everything. The session finished with some short sharp sprints.

As the lads were walking off I said, 'Excuse me, Frank, can I have a quick word with you?' Frank has always been approachable. I have never had a problem talking to him, and now I had something serious to talk about. 'What am I not doing right now?' I thought it was fairly obvious what I was talking

171

about. 'I don't know what you mean', he replied. I put it to him bluntly that in my opinion Durakovic wasn't fit and, by the way, whatever happened to me being a centre back in line for Mike Valkanis' spot? Frank replied, 'Look, as far as I'm concerned, having Mehmet Durakovic out there is an inspiration to everybody else.' I looked down at the ground. And what does that make me? I was still club captain, and I was Socceroo captain. I'd done everything right. I hadn't whinged about being dropped. I had worked overtime to improve my fitness and touch. I'd been patient and, if I can say so, professional.

I was running my fingers through my hair, dying to say exactly what was on my mind. It was clear to me that Frank Arok didn't want Paul Wade in his team. He was shafting me. I held it in. Instead, I asked, 'Look, let's get this straight. Mehmet hasn't played for over a month and you can see he can't run. I am busting my gut, so tell me, what am I doing wrong? Am I quick enough?' 'Yeah, I'm happy with the fact that you have increased your speed', said Frank. 'Am I looking sharp?' 'You're playing very well. You're playing better than anybody else at training.' 'Am I talking enough?' 'Nobody's doing better than you at the moment, nobody. I can't point the finger at one thing that you're doing wrong.' 'Then why haven't you picked me?' 'Look, Mehmet Durakovic has a certain presence out there that I need now.' What? I couldn't believe it!

The last thing I said to Frank before walking away was, 'I can't believe you are doing this.' I was ready to explode. I was being overlooked because there's a half-fit player who has 'presence'. I was so frustrated. I went home with my head in a spin. Frank Arok had just kicked me right in the guts. I couldn't eat that night. My wife Val could tell the difference in me. I was getting depressed. I had given Frank Arok plenty of reasons to put me back in: good form on the training track and a positive attitude despite all the frustration. I honestly thought, 'This is the end. Frank Arok doesn't want me at South Melbourne.'

Despite feeling furious, I sat on the bench against Brisbane and we won 1–0, thanks to a goal from Micky Petersen. Four days later we played Heidelberg away on Australia Day. I was still on the bench and the lads were struggling a bit against the Bergers, who were at the bottom of the league. The score was 1–1 when I came on in midfield and sent over the cross for Con Boutsianis to score. I am not saying I was the difference, but certainly a fresh pair of legs helped, and all of a sudden the boys were buzzing again. Paul Trimboli scored, and we ended up winning 3–1. I had made a big impact on the game and judging by the reaction, I figured everything was set for a recall to the starting eleven.

The next morning I rang Frank and said, 'Are you doing anything? I only had 20 minutes against Heidelberg yesterday and I want to have a session this morning.' Frank wasn't feeling the best, but agreed to come. A lot of coaches probably would have said, 'Stuff you, Wadey, I will see you at training tonight', but Frank didn't. I never gave up hope of regaining my spot because Frank Arok was going out of his way to help me to do these extra training sessions. Surely he wouldn't let me waste my time and his?

Our next game was only three days away, against the Morwell Falcons in the La Trobe Valley. Micky Petersen didn't come to the final training session because he was ill. It was another chance for a recall. This time Frank put me in the first eleven for a training game and I felt I was turning the corner after weeks of hell. We travelled to Morwell together on a bus. Micky was still not 100 per cent, but when Frank announced his team an hour before the match, Micky was in the starting eleven and I was on the bench again. I was devastated.

As they had in the first round, Morwell made the running. We were losing 2–1, with 10 minutes remaining, when I got the call to go on. I received the ball in midfield, inside my own half, and hit a searching pass into the Morwell penalty area. There was a challenge and the ball fell perfectly for Ivan Kelic to tap in for a very late equaliser. Once again, I had done my job off the bench, but I was running out of time. I hadn't played a full game for seven weeks and I needed a 90-minute run to get some match fitness. My immediate concern was my place in the Socceroos. The first game of a two-match series against Colombia was only eleven days away.

The next morning I rang Frank and asked to play in the youth team for the next round. It was my last chance to play a full game before going into camp with the national team, and I didn't want to spend another night sitting on the bench, waiting for a 10-minute run at the end of the game. Frank refused to play me in the youth team, claiming he needed me on the bench for the first team. I pleaded with him to see my side of things. 'Look, you don't need me. If you needed me you would have put me in by now. Just let me play in the youth game.' I was told to ring back the next day. He finally agreed, and I turned up the next day to play for the youth team against Preston Lions at Olympic Park, the curtain-raiser before the South Melbourne versus Wollongong City game. Another senior player, Giancarlo Lucchetta, was also playing. He had joined the club earlier in the season, as a visa player from Italy, but things hadn't worked out and the club was threatening to rip up his contract and send him home. We won by four or five goals and I set up the first two. I had my 90 minutes, but it was hardly inspiring stuff. Giancarlo and I then went over to the outer at Olympic Park where the Blue and White Army congregate.

South Melbourne was leading 1–0 in the first half, but then Francis Awaritefe had a heavy clash in the Wollongong penalty area and broke his arm. I sat and wondered what would have happened if I had sat on the bench. Would Frank have put me on in place of Awaritefe? Who knows? Anyway, I was in the grandstand and Steve Panapoulos came on. He played very well. Hindsight is a beautiful thing, but we don't have that luxury. I went home that night happy to have played 90 minutes of football.

After that weekend I went straight into camp at the Australian Institute of Sport in Canberra in preparation for Colombia series. Eddie Thomson put us through all sorts of different sessions and I was really happy with my fitness and form. Now a second opinion never goes astray, so I asked Ron Smith, the head coach at the AIS, for an honest opinion. Maybe I was missing something, maybe I was at fault. Sometimes you don't want to hear the truth and that's why you keep blocking it out. Frank Arok, by his actions, had made it clear what he thought. If somebody else said I was too slow, wasn't jumping as high as I was, wasn't getting as many headers, I'd stop and think again.

Ron watched me at training a few times. I wanted him to be brutally honest. I said, 'Don't tell me what you think I want to hear. Tell me straight.' Ron said, 'As far as I can see, Wadey, you are no different now than any other time. You still throw yourself into stupid tackles and you still won't shut up on the park. You are just as enthusiastic. You still can't hit the target from six yards and as for your crossing and passing? Well, you could never do those things before, so nothing's really changed.' Said in the nicest possible way, of course. I felt reassured, but I soon had a constant reminder of my troubles with Frank Arok.

Eddie Thomson called Mehmet Durakovic into camp, but from the first day Yuggsy was taking training sessions off. I felt sorry for him, because he's a bloody good player and he was still being crippled by injury. The doctor told him to have two weeks' complete rest — do absolutely nothing, not even have sex. And this is the same player that Frank put in ahead of me! Yuggsy was sent home to rest. Thommo didn't even consider playing him, which confirmed my view that Frank was wrong to pick him.

Despite all the hassles at South Melbourne, Eddie Thomson had kept his faith in me. I played the first game against Colombia in Brisbane, but pulled a muscle in my thigh, maybe due to a lack of match practice. I had to miss two Socceroo games in the next week, against Colombia and Japan in Sydney, which was very frustrating.

THINGS CAME TO A head when I returned to South Melbourne. Before training I went to Frank to resolve my future at the club. If he didn't want me, I wanted him to just say the word, and I would leave. I got the impression Frank didn't really want to face up to the issue, but in the end he put his side. 'As far as I'm concerned, you can't play in my first eleven, because I don't want you playing at the back, you're not quick enough to be a wide midfielder and the only place you're going to play is in the centre midfield if Petersen and Polak get injured.' What? I thought I was only going to play centre back, and now it's only centre midfield.

I put it to Frank that he was basically saying that I wasn't wanted. 'No, I didn't say that', he protested. 'I said that you're not guaranteed a place in my starting eleven, but this is a full squad and we are going to need 16 players to win this championship.'

I was 33, not 23. I didn't have time on my hands. My choice was to stay at South Melbourne as a squad player with few opportunities or transfer to another club. 'I may as well go, then', I said. I felt betrayed by Frank Arok. For weeks I'd been waiting and hoping things would sort themselves out, but now I felt it had all been a waste of time. I was hurt. I asked for 24 hours to consider my decision. Frank refused. 'No, no, come on. You know whether you are going to stay or whether you are going to go. It's not a decision you are going to make in 24 hours. You already know it's not going to be any different tomorrow.' With that, I made a decision to leave South Melbourne; not because I wanted to go, but because I had to go. I asked if I could train with the boys for the last time. Again Frank refused. 'I don't want you anywhere near those guys.' Frank then called the whole squad into the dressingroom, minus Paul Wade, of course, to tell the players I was going.

It was all over. It hit me that I was never going to play for South Melbourne again. Eight years of good times and good friends was over. I waited outside, aimlessly kicking the ball around with three or four youth team players. I couldn't even go in and get my gear to get changed. After five minutes or so the players started coming out. I remember a few of them looking at me as if to say, 'Wadey, I can't believe what you have done.' If they only knew what I'd been through! I went inside to get changed. Francis Awaritefe was there getting treatment on his broken arm.

Frank had told everyone I was probably going to decide in the next 24 hours to leave the club because I couldn't get a game and that he respected my decision. He told the players there were no hard feelings. That wasn't quite right. I said goodbye to Chris Constantinou, the physio, and Joe Nagy, the masseur. I said goodbye to Francis and to Giancarlo Lucchetta. I walked along a narrow concrete footpath that skirts the training oval and the boys were playing in a small square, three in the middle.

As I was walking away, I looked over. I would never be able to kick a ball around with all those guys again. It was a very empty feeling. There were a couple of supporters on the fence and I was wondering what they would think when they found out that I had left. Would they give a stuff? I drove away feeling a bit shaken.

I rang my manager, Jim Shomos and said, 'We'd better start looking for another club because I've just left South Melbourne.' We met at The Keg restaurant on Albert Park Lake and went over everything. I was wondering if I would have changed my mind if I'd had 24 hours to think about it. I doubted it. We drafted a letter asking for a transfer. The next morning I went to see the South Melbourne president, George Vasilopoulos. I sat down in his office in the Westpac Bank in Moonee Ponds. He read the letter and asked, 'Are you sure about this?' I said I was, and he accepted my decision as final. There was no pleading to change my mind. I asked for a free transfer and for the money that I was owed, about $2000. George said it was a matter for the board to consider.

I just wanted to leave on good terms. Despite my problems with Frank Arok, I still respected him. He was the one who gave me a chance to play for my country. He was honest enough to say that he thought I wasn't fast enough. He put in a lot of time and effort in one-on-one training sessions. I can accept the fact that a coach, be it Frank Arok or anyone else, thinks that I'm not good enough. I just wish Frank had told me his true thoughts much earlier. When you are 33 and captain of your country, sitting on the bench with little hope of a regular game is not an option. How long could Eddie Thomson keep me in the national team if I wasn't playing regular club football? I didn't want to find out.

All I wanted to do now was play football regularly and that wasn't going to happen at South Melbourne.

To make sure my point of view was put to the board of South Melbourne, I asked George Vasilopoulos if I could address the board members. In my experience, things between players and committees often go horribly wrong because there's no trust or communication. I wanted to avoid that. The meeting was at the Lakeside Oval in a run-down old building that was being used as the temporary office of the club.

I intended to go alone, but there was a mix-up with cars and in the end Jim Shomos came with me. He sat in the car park and I went inside. On the way in I met Mehmet Durakovic. He wanted a transfer to Selangor in Malaysia and, like me, wanted to make sure there were no hitches. Selangor eventually paid $130,000 for him. The difference between our cases was that I wanted a free transfer. After eight years of service I thought that was a fair thing, and it would help me find a new club.

I met Bill Georgantis, one of the longest-serving committeemen, at the top of the steps before I walked in. Billy said, 'Wadey, you're silly. Why didn't you hang on? Why didn't you just wait until the end of the season?' I told him I was a footballer and I needed to play regular football. Inside there were 17 board members, crowded around a long table. Frank Arok wasn't there. After the greetings I started my little speech. I was really emotional. Every word I was saying I meant, and I had to stop a couple of times to compose myself. Eight years is a long time when you are standing in front of people you've known for all that time, telling them why you are leaving. I explained that at 33 years of age I didn't have time to waste. My place in the Socceroos was in doubt if I didn't play regular club football. I thanked them for the chance to play for such a great club. I asked them to consider my efforts over eight years and grant me a free transfer, so I could leave quickly, without any fuss.

I'd also written a letter and asked the board to publish it in the club match program. I was so emotional I couldn't read it. I asked George Vasilopoulos to read it. It said: 'To all loyal South fans. It's very difficult to leave a club like yours especially after eight years. My decision to leave was not made lightly. My desire to play at the highest level was not being fulfilled from the bench. We've had some brilliant highs and I hope you might remember me for those highs as I finish my career elsewhere. Stability is one of South's biggest assets and I'm sure you will support the club like never before. Led by the Blue and White Army, you continue to be the loudest and most passionate supporters in the country. Yours sincerely, Wadey.' You wouldn't think so on the park when the adrenalin is pumping, but off the park I'm a big softy. Even so, I didn't think I was going to choke as much as I did.

I thought I'd put my case as well as I could, so I decided to leave before I made a complete idiot of myself. As I turned to leave, a couple of board members stood up and started to applaud and then everyone was applauding. I left thinking that I'd got through to them. I was open and honest and I felt they would see it my way. I wanted to be able to sit with South Melbourne people or walk into the Lakeside Oval in years to come and reminisce about the good times.

I didn't want to leave on bad terms. Friends of mine, Carl Halford and Bobby Russell, had left on less than happy terms. When David Healy left, South Melbourne effectively kept him out of the game by asking for a $12,000 transfer fee, even though he wasn't going to a national league club. He just wanted to play. I knew Healy had a bad taste in his mouth over that. The standing ovation made me think I would be able to avoid any bitterness.

Mehmet Durakovic was still in the car park, complaining that the club was going to be difficult with his transfer. I went back to my car, where Jim Shomos was waiting. I told him they were going to make a decision and he asked when. With all the emotion, I hadn't asked exactly. So I went back to the office, this time with Jim. We wanted to know right away because the transfer deadline was two days away. George Vasilopoulos said, 'We can't let you go for free because that wouldn't be in the interests of our supporters or sponsors, but we will let you go to Heidelberg on loan for free.' I was stunned. Heidelberg was at the bottom of the league. I wanted to play in a club that could make the top six play-offs, so I could play as many games as possible to keep fit for the Socceroo games against Ghana in June.

There was lots of talking. Steve Sirkos, the club doctor, and Peter Matrakis, the solicitor, were saying more than anybody. This time Frank Arok was sitting in the meeting. The whole time he must have been sitting next door listening to

177

the meeting. In the middle of all these committeemen talking I pointed to Frank. 'Just listen to your coach. He doesn't need me.' Frank didn't respond. One of the committeemen said that if I wanted to transfer to a club of my choice, then fine, but that club would have to pay top dollar. No figure was mentioned, but I imagined they would have been thinking of something in the region of $20,000. No club was going to pay as much as that for a 33-year-old two days before the transfer deadline and with only six games of the regular season remaining.

Now I was getting mad. Matrakis was getting steamed up as well. He said, 'I don't know what you take us for, Wadey, but can you imagine what we'd look like if we let you go to another club, like Morwell Falcons, and that club gets into the top six at our expense? Can you imagine what we would look like to our supporters and sponsors? You must take us for idiots.' I kept waiting for Frank to say something. I told the board, 'You put Frank in charge of the team for three years. He's the one in charge and he doesn't need me.' Frank was reluctant to say too much. The whole time my manager was in the corner. Finally, Frank spoke. 'If this was St George (the Sydney club Frank coached and managed for 10 years) you wouldn't be here right now. It wouldn't be an issue. You'd be gone. But I'm just the coach of the football team and I have no say in how the board runs the club.'

That made me even more wild. I had a go at the board. 'I can't believe you people. You want me to play for the bottom club, just to save you any embarrassment.' Things were getting out of control. George said all seventeen board members agreed with the decision. 'Players are always taking from this club. You must think of the club. Just hang on until the end of the season and then we'll give you a free transfer to anywhere', said Georgantis. It was starting to get nasty.

George Vasilopoulos decided it was time to call it a night. I pleaded for them to reconsider. 'Would any of you go and serve on the board of Heidelberg? Think about that when you're sending me to Heidelberg.' It had nothing to do with the people at Heidelberg. I just didn't want to play for the bottom team with no chance of playing in the finals. George ushered us out of the room and said he would call us on the mobile phone in 10 minutes or so. Jim and I went for a walk around the lake. It was 1 am.

I couldn't believe they were doing this to me. I felt I had given so much to South Melbourne. I had busted my leg trying to win a game for the club. For eight years I had shed plenty of blood and sweat, and all for what? I said to Jim, 'I'm not going to Heidelberg. I'm not ready to disappear yet.' Peter Tsolakis, a former team-mate, had gone there from South Melbourne at the start of the season, and his career had gone nowhere. The same had happened to Bobby Russell. Heidelberg was like quicksand. If I stepped into it, I'd sink as well. Now was the time when I had to keep in mind my long-term goal of playing for the Socceroos.

Twenty-five minutes later, the mobile phone rang. They told us they had reconsidered, but had still finished up with the same position. I drove home cursing all the way. It was either a free loan to Heidelberg, the so-called sister club at the bottom of the league, or I would have to back down and stay at South Melbourne.

I had some contact with the Melbourne Zebras and the Morwell Falcons. Both clubs were interested and both were still in the running for the play-offs at the time, but Matrakis had made it clear I wouldn't be going anywhere that might backfire on the board. I'd made my decision. It was over. The umbilical cord had been cut. I was out of there.

I kept thinking of the Ghana games. At least Heidelberg would give me six league games. Andy Bozikas, the Heidelberg coach, was happy to have me, so that was it. I had no other choice. I remember standing outside the club rooms at the Olympic Village, Heidelberg's ground. I was wearing the Heidelberg strip because Channel 7 had come to do an interview and take a few shots. The transfer deadline was 5 pm and at 4.30 I was still waiting for an official to come and sign the papers. I was thinking about the quicksand. Heidelberg didn't have a very good reputation.

But all credit to the Heidelberg players — they were great, and made me feel very welcome. My first game was away to Brisbane. We scored first and were playing quite well. Then we conceded a goal, and I realised why I hadn't wanted to go to Heidelberg. As soon as the Strikers scored, the heads dropped. The morale plummeted and we were getting torn apart. On top of this, the strained thigh that had kept me out of two Socceroo games in February, against Colombia and Japan, was bothering me, so I was pretty down.

As it turned out, Heidelberg only lost twice in six games during the time I was on loan, against Brisbane away and against Sydney United away. Over that time the morale improved and the Bergers showed a lot of pride, even in very difficult circumstances, but still they finished dead last.

On my 3AW Radio spot, Mal Brown, the Richmond AFL club manager, put me on the spot. He asked what I would have done if I was South Melbourne president and the club captain came and asked for a free transfer to a rival club. I said I would have let the player go. Mal laughed. 'Let's say it right here and now, you'll never make a president of a football club.' Maybe South Melbourne, as a business, did the right thing.

My argument was that after eight years and more than 200 NSL games, it wasn't just business. I had shown loyalty and dedication to the club. When I was dropped, I didn't make a fuss. For two months I had tried to regain my place — until it became obvious that it wasn't going to happen. For whatever

179

reason, Frank Arok didn't have a place for me in his plans. At that point, my Socceroo career was under threat. I honestly believe I had no other option.

Goodbye, South Melbourne, and thanks for the memories. And thanks to the Blue and White Army. For the best part of nine seasons you inspired me to greater efforts. I did it for you.

A GAME OF PASSION

O N AUSTRALIA DAY, JANUARY 26, 1995, I was awarded the Order of Australia Medal. The commendation read, 'For services to Australian soccer and to the Quit Smoking campaign.' It is a great honour, and something I cherish. It recognised all the work I've done promoting the game, especially the work with school kids.

That's why I was so disgusted by the allegations made about me by John Johnson, the father of Glenn Johnson, now a Sydney Olympic player, at the Senate inquiry into Australian soccer. He gave evidence to the Senate inquiry, which was established after the Stewart Report alleged all sorts of misconduct in Australian soccer. The Stewart Report had been commissioned by the Australian Soccer Federation in 1994 to inquire into a range of issues related to Australian soccer that had been raised in the media.

I wasn't named in the Stewart Report, but serious allegations were made against Socceroo coach Eddie Thomson, his assistant, Les Scheinflug, and several other leading people in the game, including Frank Arok and Rale Rasic, both former Socceroo coaches. The report recommended that Thommo be sacked for helping Ned Zelic negotiate his transfer from Sydney Olympic to Borussia Dortmund in Germany in 1992.

I still can't work out John Johnson's motivation for criticising me. In April, 1995, under oath, he told the Senate Inquiry that he believed certain players, coaches and officials lacked the courage to come forward and give evidence to the investigation. A little later he told the Senators that if he was ever offered the Order of Australia he would refuse it because of 'some of the people that have got it'. Then he used me as an example of a high-profile soccer person who had been awarded the Order of Australia.

Every time I recall those words I get so angry. What right has he got to say those things? The inference is that I had information that could incriminate somebody, but that I was refusing to come forward because I wasn't a 'man'. What a load of crap. His comment about the OAM just made me sick. I'm captain of the Socceroos, I've played more times for my country than anybody else and I've been honoured with an OAM, and a guy I've never met goes before the Senate inquiry and the TV cameras and tries to destroy my reputation.

For the record, I will make the following statement. I have not withheld evidence from the Senate inquiry. I have co-operated fully with the Senate inquiry and I hope that this inquiry can help make Australian soccer a better sport. The fact is, the Senate inquiry heard all the evidence, and cleared Eddie Thomson of any wrongdoing. And yet John Johnson not only decided Eddie Thomson was guilty, he accused me of covering up the evidence. There aren't words to describe how I feel about an accusation like that when my whole football career has been based on honesty.

In any case, I know absolutely nothing about the Ned Zelic transfer and the events surrounding it. I wasn't in the Barcelona Olympics team. How could I know? Just because I had a close working relationship with Eddie Thomson, and Thommo was then subjected to unproven allegations, people put two and two together and come up with five. John Johnson thinking I'm covering up for Eddie Thomson is so far off the mark it's not funny. I wish he had the guts to repeat his allegations outside the Senate inquiry. I promise him a writ and a day in court. Now that the Senate has cleared Thommo, John Johnson owes me nothing less than an apology. If he were a 'man' he would do it.

Again, for the record, here is what I know about overseas transfers. Israel Moaz, one of the agents named in the Stewart report, approached me in early 1989 and said he wanted to be my manager. He claimed he had a club in Belgium interested in buying me. I asked, 'What are the terms of the contract?' I had to pay my own airfare to Europe, supposedly be reimbursed for it by the club, and stay for a two-week trial. It sounded suspect. I figured if a club wanted me they would find the $2000 for an airfare. I didn't return any of Moaz's phone calls and that was the last I ever heard of it.

The only other time I had any connection with a transfer to Europe was in March, 1989. It was rumoured that Trevor Francis, the former England international, was going to watch me play for the Socceroos against Israel in a World Cup tie. Francis was then the manager of Queen's Park Rangers, the English Premier League club. After the game there were more rumours — that Francis was happy with the way I had played and he would call me. So much for rumours. There was never any official contact.

What I can tell you about overseas transfers is that, in my very limited experience, the system we have is totally inadequate. It's a clear example of how the game on the park has outgrown the game off the park. I don't wish to offend any current Australian soccer officials, but we are still extremely amateurish in our dealings with agents and overseas clubs. We have to start protecting the young players because they don't know what they're getting themselves into. I don't know how many players have blown $2000 on airfares on the off chance of getting picked up by a European club. I don't know how many thousands of dollars Australian clubs have missed out on by selling players too cheaply.

Because we didn't have a system or much knowledge in dealing with agents, it often fell to Eddie Thomson to give advice. The best players were in the national teams and he was the coach, so it was obvious he would have some contact with player agents. He has a lot of contacts in Europe, which is how he is able to organise so many games. Eddie Thomson has personal relationships with people like Frank McLintock, the former Arsenal great, and it is in his interests and the interests of Australian soccer that he keeps in touch with these top people in European football. The fact that Frank McLintock is also a player agent doesn't mean his relationship with Thommo has been all to do with transfers. I never thought anything of it — Thommo knows a lot of people. Do we expect the national coach to go overseas and stay alone, locked in his hotel room? I've got no reason to protect Eddie Thomson or anyone else, as alleged by John Johnson. I have not withheld information about Eddie Thomson or anyone else, as alleged by John Johnson. That's the truth. The Senate has reviewed the Stewart report and found there is no evidence to back up the allegations. No one can call me a liar.

SOCCER IS A GAME of opinions, which is both the best and the worst thing about it. It's good because it means the world's best coach can have one opinion and the humble supporter on the terraces can have another and nobody is really right or wrong. Everyone can feel a part of the game because soccer is not a science with definite answers. Soccer is also a game of passion, some would say religious fervour, so when football arguments happen, they can very easily become heated. Go anywhere in the world, from Birmingham to Buenos Aires, walk into a bar, and chances are people will be talking and arguing about soccer.

Best of all, soccer mirrors life in so many ways and the lessons you learn by playing it will stand you in good stead. I found out the hard way about the volatile mix of opinion and passion in 1989, the year I broke my leg. I was facing four months in plaster, watching soccer, unable to play. It was hell — I'm a terrible spectator.

One day I bumped into Peter Gee, the ABC TV soccer commentator. The ABC had taken over soccer coverage from SBS at the start of that season and Peter invited me to do some commentary. I was happy to have a go, but the first problem was the TV scaffolds, which were about 10 metres high. It was only with a great deal of difficulty, and after a good 15 minutes, that I would get up to the top of the scaffolding. Somebody would pass my crutches while I bounced on one leg up the ladder. Once the commentary began, the real fun started, trying to pronounce names correctly, sound intelligent and make 'expert' comments.

South Melbourne had given me the go-ahead, but it meant I didn't see them very often. I was watching Preston almost every second week because they were having a good spell and featuring on 'Match of the Day'. It was when I was combining working as a commentator and watching South Melbourne that I got myself into trouble. The ABC cameras went to Chaplin Reserve in Sunshine, which is not a very hospitable place at the best of times. South Melbourne was playing Sunshine George Cross and it was a thrilling game. The score finished at 5–2 for South Melbourne, after two Sunshine George Cross players had been sent off.

The referee was Dennis Voutsinas, who happens to be of Greek origin. The Sunshine supporters come mainly from the Maltese community and you can imagine what they were thinking when a referee with a Greek name sent off two of their players against South Melbourne Hellas, a Greek-supported club. The Sunshine George Cross people are not the most forgiving. They let you know what they are thinking, either by actions or by words. In their opinion, the referee had crucified them. The game was over and Peter Gee and I had signed off the commentary. As far as I knew, the cameras had gone off and the microphones were dead.

As the referee was making his way off the ground a group of fans began throwing full cans of beer at him. In their opinion he was the cause of their defeat. A few other so-called supporters ran onto the ground to abuse the referee and the police were trying to hold them back. The crowd was going berserk near the players' race, spitting and throwing things at the South Melbourne players and officials as well as at the referee. It was just another bad episode at Chaplin Reserve and I'd seen my share. My mum and dad had refused to go to Chaplin Reserve for years because of the bad behaviour of a minority of the crowd. When I was playing for Croydon City in 1983, one of our players was punched by a fan who jumped the fence. Six years on, nothing much had changed, and the sad side of our game was on show again.

I was caught up in the excitement of the game. It had been a thriller and I was getting so frustrated that the crowd trouble was spoiling such a good contest. I said to Peter Gee, 'Just have a look at them. They're animals. They should have collars and leads. They're absolute animals. It happens every single time I come to this ground.' Peter just watched the crowd in disgust. I was sitting up the scaffold with my broken leg and my crutches beside me, tidying up my papers. The next thing I know there's all this shouting going on at the bottom of the scaffolding. Then the scaffold started to rock a little bit. Peter and

I wondered what the hell was going on. We looked down and there were half a dozen irate fans, shouting abuse. 'Wade, you come down. I kill you, you bastard!' I couldn't work out what was wrong, but there were six blokes really going off their heads. I figured that they were abusing me because I was a South Melbourne player. The guy who was leading the charge was huge. For a moment I couldn't work out what was worse; having the scaffold tipped over or having to face the mob. But I couldn't stay on the scaffold forever, so I hopped down. I copped heaps of abuse, but fortunately an official chaperoned me into the South Melbourne dressingrooms.

I don't know how I got past those half a dozen people without getting whacked. I was in the dressingrooms congratulating the boys when Les Carter, one of the Sunshine players who was a team mate of mine at Green Gully, came in. 'Wadey, don't go out there. They're going to kill you. You've said something that's upset them, called them dogs or something.' Oh no! How could they have heard? The mikes were off. 'The telly was on inside the club and they heard every word you said.' Even though the transmission was over, the pictures were still going back into the club. I wasn't going to get out of there alive. It was suggested that I should wait there until everybody had gone home, but that was going to take all night. So they backed a car up to the dressingrooms and I quickly jumped in and sped off. Until that point I was fearing for my safety.

And that wasn't the end of the matter. Two weeks later I was covering a game at Somers Street, the home of the Melbourne Knights. Sunshine George Cross had hired the ground for a game against Wollongong. I caught a cab from home in Rowville to Sunshine, a good $60 or $70 fare. I arrived at the gate and said, 'Hi, I'm Paul Wade. I've come to do the commentary for the ABC.' Alf Zahra, the George Cross president, was waiting for me. 'No you're not,' was the reply. 'Not after what you said about this club's supporters.' We argued, with the cab meter ticking away. After about five minutes I convinced him to at least let me go and tell the ABC director about the problem. Sunshine supporters who had seen me arrive at the TV van started abusing me. The ABC people were starting to get concerned about how hostile these people were becoming, so they called the police. Two divvy vans turned up. By now I was wondering what the hell I had gotten into.

After listening to the club and the ABC, the police said, 'Paul, we think it would be best for everybody if you leave now.' I still had the cab waiting — it was my lifeline and I made sure he wasn't going anywhere. In the end I didn't need to be convinced that I should get the hell out of there. I went home. The cab fare was $190 for the round trip. Luckily, the ABC was paying and, even more luckily, I still had the job the following week.

The television work was great fun, apart from that episode at Chaplin Reserve. The amazing thing was that six years later, in 1995, the same Alf Zahra offered me the job as player/coach of Sunshine. I turned him down, but only because I wasn't ready to coach. It just shows that time heals all wounds and that his opinion of Paul Wade had changed! I'm not so sure about the supporters. I figure they love you when you're in their colours, but watch out if you're against them.

THE ONE-OFF INTERNATIONAL between Australia and England in June, 1991, was another example of differing opinions causing drama. I was the English-born captain of Australia and I remember sitting in a taxi with Socceroo coach Eddie Thomson and two other players, travelling to the England team's hotel for a media conference. I was thinking, 'Why the hell do we have to travel to THEIR hotel to do a media conference?' It was another example of Australian soccer's bad old habit of respecting our opponents more than ourselves. I walked into the conference and was stunned by the crush of media people. I'm talking 150 people in the room, with cameras, lights and microphones everywhere. Gary Lineker, the England captain, Graham Taylor, the manager, and Tony Dorigo, the Adelaide-born English full-back, were already there.

I'd heard so much about the Fleet Street press that I almost feared them when I walked into the room. I took my seat and waited to be bombarded with dirty questions, but none came. Everything was sweet. One English reporter asked, 'If you're going to score a goal against England, where do you think it will come from?' I said, 'I bet you it won't be from a corner', which got me a laugh. Two weeks earlier, at Wembley, England had conceded a goal against Brazil from a corner, and I assumed they would have then worked on that at training. It was just a throwaway line, but the media latched onto it. The press conference finished with everybody happy about the way it went.

Of course the English media were interested in my background because I was born in England, and four or five reporters wanted to ask some more questions. We went off to a corner of the room and they gathered around, asking questions in a really nice way. I thought, 'What are Lady Di and the Royals complaining about? These Fleet Street guys are okay.'

After I'd finished those inteviews the photographers wanted a shot of Gary Lineker and me together. They were trying get us into a certain position and they were man-handling me. I thought they were just being fussy, so I tried to oblige. Then one photgrapher tried to do the same thing to Gary Lineker, to push and manoeuvre him into position. Well, as soon as he touched Lineker, Lineker snapped. 'Take your f..king hand off my arm.' There were about 20 people gathered around waiting for these shots and they all took a step back. From then on it was, 'Mr Lineker, could you just put your head to the left a bit. Thanks very much.' That's how Gary Lineker handled Fleet Street! I thought I'd done okay, and John Tully, then marketing manager for the ASF, agreed: 'Wadey, if you can handle a press conference like that, you can handle anything.'

Some people might think I had some sort of soft spot for England because I was born there. Well, I do, but not for the English team when they're playing Australia. The Poms probably had more support than we did, even though the Socceroo faithful were there shouting their lungs out. I said to a few of the guys, 'Why won't the Aussies come out and support us? We're playing the old enemy at home and the Aussies are outnumbered.' It was very disappointing. The game itself was very tight. David Platt missed a couple of chances for England, but Lineker didn't get a kick. Mehmet Durakovic did a great job marking him.

I had a new experience that night. I'd never feared 50/50 tackles since recovering from my broken leg, but for the first time in my life I took a couple of short steps so that I wouldn't get to a 50/50 contest. Coming the other way was Stuart Pearce, the England left back from Nottingham Forest. He's as solid as a rock and is a mean character on the park. I'm told his nickname is 'Psycho Pearce', even though he's a very quiet guy off the park. His build reminded me of Manchester United's (now Chelsea's) Mark Hughes. That's the way a footballer should be built, solid and athletic, not like me, all skin and bone. When Pearce was coming the other way I'm glad I didn't make the 50/50 because he connected with the ball with so much power, my leg would have gone with the ball.

We had a couple of great chances to win the game. Ernie Tapai had a couple of good scoring attempts and Graham Arnold was threatening, but in the end we got the ball into our own net. Ian Gray was very unlucky to be the last man to connect with an England cross and 1–0 was the final score.

After the game I was back facing those 'nice blokes' from Fleet Street. They asked what I thought of England. After a couple of questions along the same lines I said, 'To tell you the truth I was a little bit disappointed.' John Salako, the Crystal Palace winger, had done some magic things; he was in a different class from what we were used to. The rest were nothing special. They are on our TV screens every week in the English football highlights and they're built up to be legends, but up close they weren't so much better than us. That's what I was saying to Fleet Street. It was mild stuff really, and it hardly rated a mention in the Australian media.

But a couple of weeks later my relatives in England sent some newspaper clippings. The big headline on the back page of the *Sun*, a paper that sells in the millions, said in huge letters, 'I don't give a XXXX for England'. The first paragraph was something along the lines of 'Aussie captain Paul Wade thinks the English team is crap and badly needing John Barnes and Peter Beardsley to spark them up.' There were other quotes attributed to me that also slagged the English team. That was supposedly what I said! I realised how vicious the Fleet Street pack could be. I felt really bad, because I didn't slag them, but in the opinion of Fleet Street I had. All I'd said was that I was a bit disappointed, that I expected a bit more, then the press took the key words and made a meal of it. In the end I got so upset with what they'd done that I rang Laurie McMenamy, England's assistant coach. I got his answering machine and said, 'I hope I haven't caused you any heartache, but you know I didn't slag your team like that. I hope there's no harm done, I meant nothing by it.'

Looking back, it was probably true that I didn't give a XXXX for England, but at the time I'd been captain for less than 12 months and wasn't so sure of myself. It was Fleet Street being Fleet Street and I was just another sucker.

WHEN THE SOCCEROOS RETURNED to the River Plate in Buenos Aires for the second leg of that World Cup play-off, we found out all about the passion of South American football. After the final whistle, I rounded up the players to go and applaud a small group of Aussies waving Australian flags. I said, 'Let's go over and give them a clap and let them know that we appreciate that they were brave enough to wave Aussie flags in front of 65,000 Argentinians.' We all jogged over to the touchline and started applauding, and couldn't believe it when the thousands of Argentinian fans in that area started applauding us. It was an incredible feeling. Arnie and the boys suggested we go over and do the same on the other side of the stadium. Again, the Argentinians gave us a big cheer and applause.

Afterwards, we were told that opposition teams are never applauded by Argentinian crowds. Everyone was so touched by the battlers from the other side of the world who had come up against the might of Argentina. The next afternoon a few guys were having a hair of the dog — we'd had a long night of drinks after the game. A young local approached Raul Blanco, the only Spanish-speaker among us, and said, 'I would like to offer you my watch. I'm not very rich, I haven't got many possessions, but on behalf of all the young people of Argentina I would like to give you my watch as a gift for teaching us humility. Sometimes we forget and become arrogant as a nation and as a people. You taught us how to be humble last night when you went over and applauded the crowd.' Raul couldn't tell him we were really applauding the Aussies with the flags, but we were all touched by the sentiments he expressed. After quite a while, Raul convinced the guy to keep his watch.

I had only a few hours sleep the night after the game because I had a commitment the next day. Austrade, the government agency that promotes Australian exports, had appointed me as a tourism ambassador. The Austrade office in Buenos Aires was sponsoring a local school, so the idea was for me to make a visit. I'll never forget those kids. Within minutes of arriving I was surrounded by school kids standing thirty deep. There were hundreds of them. Thanks to Austrade there were lots of posters around the school, pictures of the

Sydney Harbour Bridge and so on. I was asked to say a few words to the kids and as they were translated into Spanish, they'd start cheering. In no time my words were drowned out as they started chanting 'Australia, Australia'. It felt really special. These kids had a genuine affection for Australia and were treating me like a hero. Here I was in Diego Maradona's backyard, getting mobbed by hundreds of children.

It lifted me out of the doldrums. Instead of thinking that we failed to reach the World Cup, I was feeling that a lot of good had come out of the campaign. The public's support for the Socceroos and soccer in general during the Sydney game was fantastic, and now on another continent I could see what being Australian meant. We left behind such a good image of our country in Argentina, and in Chile before that. It made me realise that there are bigger things in life than the outcome of a soccer game.

It made me wonder what would have become of my soccer career if I hadn't left England at age 11. My claim to fame in European football was when I returned to England as an 18-year-old to visit relatives. I trained with Barnsley, a professional club in the English Third Division. Norman Hunter, who made his name as a defender for Leeds United, was the manager. For a month I trained with Barnsley's reserve team and had a great time. When it came time to return home to Melbourne I thanked the club for their hospitality. They couldn't believe I was leaving and insisted I played a game before going. The reserves were playing a Wednesday night game at Oakwell, Barnsley's ground. I played and was named man of the match in the newspaper.

Then again, St Helens was a pretty rough area, and maybe I wouldn't have ended up a footballer. Guys I knew were getting into gangs and fighting, and a few were getting into drugs, pinching cars and all sorts of mischief. I might have become a professional footballer, but could just as easily have been playing for Her Majesty's Pleasure at one of her establishments, never able to play away from home. So when I do wonder about what might have been, it's a very short thought.

THE NIGHTMARE SHIRT IS part of daily life for the Socceroos. Each day on tour or in camp, one player is awarded the Nightmare shirt for doing something really dumb. You can win it for anything. The trouble is, the Nightmare shirt is a tatty yellow T-shirt and the rules are that you can't wash it. It has the words, 'I had a bloody nightmare' on the front and 'I am an idiot' on the back. It has to be worn everywhere, even to official functions.

My favourite Nightmare shirt nomination was Scott Ollerenshaw, who played in the NSL with St George and Sydney Olympic, and later went to England. At the Seoul Olympics we had to play one game outside Seoul. We were flying down to Pusan and, as usual, we were running late. Scott was sitting on the bus and, for a joke, a few other guys asked him if he'd brought his passport. He is a very quiet lad and didn't suss out what was going on. Within a few minutes he was convinced he needed his passport, so he jumped off the bus and ran as fast as he could through the Olympic Village, up 16 floors (the lifts were always slow), got his passport and frantically rushed back to the bus, with Frank Arok and all the tour officials glaring at him. When Frank asked him where the hell he'd gone, Scott explained that he had forgotten his passport and at that moment everyone cracked up. The boys were killing themselves laughing. It was a classic! You had to laugh, because the next day it might be your turn. Thanks to the comedians you find in every soccer team, there's never a shortage of Nightmare shirt nominations.

It's the same with nicknames. My first nickname was 'Westgate', because Jimmy Rooney used to nutmeg me so often that the lads reckoned my legs were as wide apart as a span of the Westgate bridge! Then Micky P named me 'HB', because my frame was about as skinny as a lead pencil. Later that became 'Milk Bottle' because my fair skin doesn't take a suntan too well. What I do is go red, peel and then go white, hence the name. This Captain Socceroo ain't no bronzed Aussie. When I first made the Socceroo squad, Charlie Yankos called me 'Skeletor', again in reference to my body.

The latest nickname, given to me by Paul Trimboli, is 'Chopper'. 'Chopper' Read is a notorious criminal, exactly the opposite of my character, according to Trimmers. One day at South Melbourne he made sure the name stuck. When I was captain my No. 6 shirt had a white armband sewn onto the sleeve because the elastic armband would always slip off my skinny arm. Trimmers, in his wisdom, decided that this white armband should have a bit of colour, so he got a big Texta and wrote 'Chopper' across the armband so that TV viewers could see and, Trimmers hoped, ask questions about 'Chopper' Wade. I must have a clean image, though, because no one said a word!

BEYOND 2000

THE FUTURE of Australian soccer can be found in any schoolground in the nation. As an unofficial youth promotions/development officer I see the 'future' almost on a daily basis. All the young kids, boys and girls, running around in the schoolground are the ones who matter to our game, whether they play soccer or not. They are the players and the spectators of the future, and we need to get them involved and interested while they're young. It's a matter of showing them the skills of the game, and selling the idea that soccer is fun. If kids walk away after an hour of my clinic with smiles on their faces, I feel I've planted a seed from which the game can grow. Sadly, however, we are not doing enough about this.

When I arrive at schools as Paul Wade, Socceroo captain, the majority of kids, even now, do not know who I am. In a class of twenty-five 10- or 11-year-olds there will be, on average, five or six who recognise me. That tells me that soccer still has a hell of a long way to go. If I'm not well known after five years as the captain and hundreds of media appearances, we've got problems. Look at all the successful sports in Australia and you'll find heroes: look at the image that Gary Ablett has in the AFL, Mal Meninga in Rugby League, Allan Border for cricket, David Campese for Rugby Union.

We have to make sure that soccer players have the same recognition, so the kids can identify with the game through someone they know and see regularly on TV. I find 10- and 11-year-olds pretty honest — they'll tell you how they perceive soccer in Australia. They generally know who the Socceroos are. As the marketing people like to say, 'Socceroos' is a strong brand name, but not enough people 'buy the product'. That comes back to identifying with individual players and wanting to watch them play. So what it is going to take to convert all these kids to soccer?

In my opinion, before we can even talk about marketing or youth development, we have to start doing the basic legwork. Stop talking about it and do the hard work. This is where we fall down badly as a sport. We have a very good message, but we're not spreading it around. My opening statement to a class of 25 schoolchildren is, 'I have been travelling around the world for the last 10 years playing soccer and getting paid to do it.' They stand there and you can see them thinking, 'Wow, that'd be great!' It's a message and an image that Aussie Rules and Rugby League can't convey.

We are the world game, for boys and girls, but how often do they hear it? In Victoria, for example, there are over 2000 schools and as I write the Victorian Soccer Federation has ONE development/promotions officer — one person to go around the schools promoting the game. Kevin Muscat, the Olyroo captain and South Melbourne defender, is that person. We may as well call his job 'Mission Impossible'. I did that job for two years, along with the former Socceroo goalkeeper Jeff Olver, so I know what I'm talking about.

The Victorian Soccer Federation's attitude to this vital area is pathetic. There is no planning or financial commitment to the task. It's as though Australian soccer feels that we deserve to have these kids supporting our game, and it will only be a matter of time before they DO starting flocking to us. I can tell you, unless we go and sell the game properly in the schools we don't have a chance. Even five development officers in Victoria would not be enough to cover all that has to be done.

A lot of the responsibility for this should also fall to the clubs and the players. Today's players don't realise how important it is for them to be out in the field, working with kids. Each club in the National Soccer League is supposed to have a development/promotions officer, but in my experience the clubs do the bare minimum. I'll use South Melbourne as an example, not because the club is in any way the worst offender, but it's the example I know most about after eight years. Before Frank Arok arrived, South Melbourne didn't have a structured youth development program, but now Frank is working hard to develop the million dollar players of the future. You have to put in years of hard work and money before you'll find a Mark Viduka, a superstar you can sell to Europe to pay for a grandstand.

The club also works hard at marketing itself to its sponsors, but what about promoting the club and the game to the general public? Clubs are always complaining that they can't afford to pay for a full-time development/ promotions officer, but in the same breath they complain that they're not getting enough people through the gate. You have to spend money to make money. What are they doing to attract more fans?

For one season Micky Petersen was named as the development/promotions officer, but he was very busy working in his bookshop, so hardly anything was done. He wasn't paid anything extra to do the job and had no background in promotions anyway. If he had a spare minute and he felt like doing it, he'd go to a school. It was another exercise in cutting corners and taking the easy way out.

The bad attitude that exists in so many clubs was on show at the OzSoccer Soccer Summit, in May, '95. A first team coach of an NSL club was one of the speakers on a panel discussing youth development, and his opening statement was, 'I don't know why I am sitting on this panel. I'm a first team coach and my job is to get results on the park, not worry about junior development.' I nearly fell off my chair. Is it a surprise that coach came from a club with the lowest crowds in the NSL?

For many years Tim White was the VSF Director of Coaching and just before he was sacked he devised a very simple but effective scheme for the VSF and the NSL clubs. Tim would join an NSL senior coach at his club's junior training sessions. In most clubs, the juniors train on the same night, so you would have a captive audience of around 300 kids. Not only could Tim help the junior coaches with a few tips, but he would also encourage the NSL coach to get involved with the kids. I remember in my junior days being coached by one of the senior players at Doveton — I still haven't forgotten Ian Sweeney and how big he was and how far he could kick the ball. Those images stay with youngsters and getting some tips from an NSL coach would be a big thrill for a 10-year-old. At the same time it might just encourage the kids to take an interest in the NSL team.

If these kids also got a free ticket to a game, their mums and dads might make it a family night out. If the family enjoyed the outing, the NSL might just have found some new supporters. You don't have to spend weeks with the juniors, just two nights in a season.

Another simple idea would be to get senior NSL players to watch at least one of the club's junior teams per season. Surely it's not too much to ask a player to find one hour on one Sunday morning to encourage the kids. And it's not hard to organise.

Tim White is no longer with the VSF. As I write, the VSF doesn't have a Director of Coaching, which is a disgrace. Steve Darby, the ASF development officer, often complains that he's getting no feedback from the Victorian clubs on the work they are doing in the community. He knows as well as I that the clubs just aren't doing enough promotional work. It's not complicated, it's just a matter of deciding that youth development and promotion are important and getting down to it. Here's an example.

Mars Confectionery is one of my major sponsors. My job with them is to promote the Snickers brand on my travels to schools and coaching clinics. The Mars public relations people make sure that before I go to a school, the local newspaper is supplied with a photograph to publicise the visit. They also encourage the paper to send a photographer to the coaching clinic. More often than not, my picture and a story appear in the local paper. That is the sort of stuff that sticks in people's minds. Is it so hard to get some photos taken, write a media release and post a package to a local newspaper?

Soccer has to become consumer-friendly and build a good image. It boils down to the game on the park having outgrown the game off the park. If we want to become a modern, professional sport we need modern, professional administrators. As much as better stadiums, we need promotion of our star players and our game's image so kids can identify with soccer. I gladly brag about Robbie Slater earning $12,500 a week and winning a championship in England with Blackburn Rovers. I give away posters of Aurelio Vidmar and tell the kids he's in the top 100 players in the world. I give away stickers of Ned Zelic and recall the miraculous goal he scored to take Australia to the Olympics. The looks of amazement say it all. We don't need a five-year plan; we just need five hard-working development officers to get out there and work their butts off.

I have seen myself how the basketball people in this country have been working flat out to promote their game. Whenever the Socceroos are in Sydney we are invited to be special guests of the Sydney Kings. They have dozens of girls giving away posters, stickers, badges, you name it. The kids swarm around to get these freebies. The basketball clubs know it's more than just the game that will bring the kids back next time. I remember doing a coaching clinic at a Melbourne school and the kids were asking me, 'Did you see we won the basketball last night?' I thought, 'I can't remember the Boomers playing.' It wasn't the Australian team they were talking about, but the Americans. They were talking about Michael Jordan! The kids are saturated with Michael Jordan on Gatorade ads and with the American NBA on commercial television. A survey showed that Michael Jordan was the most popular sporting hero among Australian 14-year-olds. Australian basketball capitalises on the Jordan thing because they promote the local NBL stars on the back of the biggest name in the sport. That's what Paul Wade is competing against.

Having said that, there are plenty of kids walking around in Socceroo shirts, but I wonder how many more would be wearing the green and gold if our promotion was anything like basketball's. I know the clubs will say they haven't got the money, but with stickers and badges you're not talking millions of dollars. If you add a good infrastructure to accommodate the fruits of that hard promotional work, bingo, you've got a commodity that sponsors will be fighting for.

As well as pushing the positives, though, it's important to handle the negatives better. We are often on the back foot because of stupid things like a scuffle at a match. Other sports have worse problems, but they can somehow kill the issue within a few days. Rugby League has had its fair share of drugs and scandals, but the problems are buried very quickly, and all anyone remembers is Tina Turner and 'Simply the Best'. The AFL seems to have the same knack of using positives to bury the bad news. Maybe they have the money and the expertise to cover it up. Soccer hasn't got the money to employ a Tina Turner, but we can learn the lessons from these other sports and do a better job selling the positives; our star players. If we believe our game is the greatest in the world, let's be proud and positive about it. Let's get out there and sell to the grassroots.

QUALIFYING FOR THE WORLD Cup in France in 1998 will get the ball rolling, but I think we are kidding ourselves if we believe that that alone will solve the long-term problems. The USA had a professional league with Pelé and Beckenbauer and a host of other superstars from around the world. They were drawing 60,000 to a game, but within five or six years the entire league went bust and disappeared. The same thing will happen here if we make it to the World Cup finals and think our problems are solved. We will be red-hot news for a month, but a year later the interest will be gone. It seems that every four years Australians get excited about the World Cup and we have a couple of sell-out crowds. Then it all dies for another four years. We have no trouble finding sponsors for the big games, but where do they go between these high points?

I think our relationships with sponsors should change. For example, the Mars Confectionery group is a worldwide sponsor of soccer, mainly through the Snickers brand. When my manager, Jim Shomos, first approached Mars, he gave them an outline of what Victorian soccer was capable of giving them as a company. There was no big game or tournament to sponsor, but he could offer a relationship between a company and a sport. I fitted their plans because my work with school kids gave me the right image, and the kids were a target group for their products. It was a matter of selling the positives of our game and demonstrating the long-term benefits.

Soccer should be bending over backwards to build partnerships with sponsors. In Australia, more kids play soccer than play any other football code. What a statistic! With the right marketing and promotion we could make sure that sponsors come into the game and don't want to go anywhere else because soccer is the best avenue for promoting their product. And yet, as I write, the Victorian Soccer Federation doesn't employ a full-time marketing manager! How can we expect to find sponsors and build a long-term base? If Terry Jones, the VSF Chief Executive, is expected to look after marketing, as well as all the other administration jobs, is it any wonder not much is happening?

The visit to Melbourne by the English Premier League club West Ham in May, '95, was a classic example. A private promoter had financed the tour and the weekend before arriving, West Ham had played a major part in deciding who was going to win the English Premier League by holding second-placed

Manchester United to a 1–1 draw on the season's final day. That gave us plenty of angles to promote the game. I was among half a dozen Victorian players who were guests on Channel 9's 'Footy Show' and on the morning of the game I invited Tony Cottee, the West Ham striker, onto Channel 7's 'Sportsworld' during my regular spot. Bruce McAvaney asked the right questions about what had happened in the English Premier League and the viewers would have thought the Victoria versus West Ham game meant something.

In the end, though, the entrepreneur lost money and there was little or no benefit for Victorian soccer. West Ham played Victoria in front of 2500 people, less than the average NSL crowd. It wasn't as though it was a bad game, either. The Victorian team played really well, but I think we were allowed to play well by West Ham. There was not the same quality of play that day as there had been seven days earlier when they had played Manchester United. We expected a little bit of a drop, but not to the level we saw. But that really wasn't the issue.

If the VSF had promoted the game through the junior ranks, for example, giving away free tickets to all the under–12 players in the State, hand-delivered to the junior clubs by the Victorian players, in lieu of a training session, maybe we could have achieved something. If we had five promotions/development officers in Victoria, it would have easily been achieved. What we ended up with was the 2500 diehards who go to the game rain, hail or shine.

Then there is the issue of touring teams holidaying in Australia at the crowd's expense. Before the game I was talking to one of the West Ham players, who confessed they'd been in holiday mode for seven days and had been out drinking until five in the morning before the match. It's not the first time a touring team has come to Australia with the wrong attitude. We keep saying, 'We'll never let that happen again', but we do. The fans paid $20 to watch a bunch of Poms, with a couldn't-care-less attitude, play sub-standard football. They are right to feel ripped off.

The ultimate insult was the West Ham bench. Peter Tsolakis, who was then playing with Heidelberg United and is a lovely guy, was called the night before the game and asked to make up the numbers for West Ham! Sitting on the bench with him was West Ham's assistant coach, Frank Lampard, who is the other side of 40. In the end, Tsolakis came on for West Ham. No disrespect to 'Gus', but the fans didn't pay money to see him playing for West Ham. If Bruce McAvaney or any of the TV viewers had gone to the game, they would have laughed their socks off. It was a farce. If we had invited some prospective sponsors to that game, we would have scared them off. Victorian soccer needs a kick up the backside. Let's tune into reality and stop dreaming.

MELBOURNE HAS A GREEK community of 300,000, I'm told, and South Melbourne, the biggest Greek club in town, averages about 5000 fans a game, not even two per cent of the community. Not so long ago, 100,000 Greeks turned up for a political demonstration in Bourke Street, Melbourne. Where the hell are they on a Sunday afternoon when eleven South Melbourne players want some support? The whole ethnic question is the most difficult dilemma for Australian soccer. We live in a multicultural nation and it's what makes Australia so unique. Martin Tyler, the English commentator, who is also a good friend, summed it up when he referred to our multicultural country and what effect it had on our soccer: 'It's such a beautiful cocktail.' Players from all ethnic backgrounds and soccer styles mix in a special Aussie blend.

But the NSL clubs were not built around the idea of being multicultural, they were built by one ethnic community. Now there's no doubt the Greek, Croatian, Italian and other ethnic communities have done great things for soccer over the years, but the fact is, they can't attract really big support from their own communities any more. People at South Melbourne would always point to the black and white pictures of the 'good old days', when Middle Park was packed every Sunday. Nowadays the club is doing well to get one 15,000 crowd in a season. Maybe the image of South Melbourne as a club for Greeks only is stopping the average soccer fan from going to South Melbourne games. South Melbourne says it welcomes any fans of any background, but the non-Greeks are not turning up in big numbers.

I don't think clubs need to relinquish their ethnic background in order to attract fans from beyond their community; those communities support soccer, and we don't want to lose them. What clubs could be saying is, 'Yes, we have a Greek heritage, but we are an Australian sporting club.' So the image the club presents to the general public makes them feel welcome, not alienated. It should be possible for clubs to have emblems and flags that reflect their history, without having political or nationalistic overtones; those overtones are hardly what sports fans want from a sports club.

The next concern is crowd behaviour. Deserved or not, the NSL has a bad reputation in the wider community. If it's your club and you see a problem with some supporters — and it's usually only a handful who cause trouble — shouldn't the club be able to pick out those people and make sure they know the club won't tolerate them harming the club's image? For example, the fans who chant 'Nigger, nigger' at Francis Awaritefe are a disgrace to their club and to the game, and should be banished. Their racist taunts were broadcast on national TV. Think of the damage they've done to the game's image in the eyes of potential sponsors and the general public. There's no doubt that crowd behaviour is one barrier stopping the couple next door and their kids coming to an NSL game.

The dilemma for the NSL clubs is that most of them are financially weak and they don't want to confront questions of the ethnic base of the club and crowd control for fear of losing the supporters they have, without gaining any new ones. They cling to the 3000 people who turn up because that crowd is better than nothing. With professional administration and more marketing and promotional effort, costs will go up: we'll need bigger crowds to pay for it all.

We should work harder at pulling down these barriers. We should have family enclosures and alcohol-free areas. There's no reason why a South Melbourne family can't sit alongside a Melbourne Knights family and enjoy the game for what it is, without worrying if they'll be caught up in some nastiness. We could establish junior supporters clubs so the 'Hellas Hooligans' can go jump up and down behind the goals and have a lot of fun, but be reminded they have a responsibility to the club not to go overboard with their language or behaviour. Hopefully, the new administration under the ASF Chairman, David Hill, can make a start on these matters.

Whenever the Socceroos play we have a multicultural support. We are all Aussies united behind the Socceroos. That's why I'm really excited by the idea of an A League, an Asian competition where instead of having the Melbourne Knights versus South Melbourne, which is still often seen as Greeks versus Croatians, it's the Melbourne Chargers versus the Hiroshima Hurricanes. Whether you are Greek, Italian or Croatian, you would cheer for Melbourne in the A League. The Sydney Stallions would get great multicultural support against the Auckland As. Take a look at what happens in the AFL when the West Coast Eagles or the Adelaide Crows play any Victorian club. All the Victorian fans want the Melbourne club to win, even if they don't normally support that club. Collingwood beat the West Coast Eagles? I'd like to see that. As a rule I hate Collingwood, but the interstate rivalry with the West Australians is great. Look at the State of Origin games in Rugby League. These are the rivalries of Australian sport. If we can replace the rivalries between the different ethnic clubs with interstate rivalries, we'll have taken a huge step forward. I think that would be a very good thing for Australian soccer.

We have to start somewhere and accept that our ethnic-based competition must become more open and more professional. South Melbourne has always had enough supporters and money to rule the roost in Victorian soccer, but there's no use being a big fish in a little pond. Soccer was the first sport in Australian to have a national club league; let's be the first to have an Asian League.

Full-time professional players must be the long-term aim. Depending on how it's handled, professionalism could be a burden on Australian soccer or it could be a huge boost. We can't yet take the European or South American approach, where players are paid simply to play and train. The economics are so different in Australia. If we are to have full-time professionals, it must work without bankrupting the clubs. In my case, being a full-time professional means a combination of paid promotional work on behalf of sponsors and a contract with an NSL club. Maybe clubs can use this method to have full-time players. It might not sound like a possibility for many now, but that is how I have played full-time soccer for the past three years. If we think we can afford full-time players now, great, let's have a go. But I fear it would be a flash in the pan and within two years clubs would go broke and we would be back to square one. However, with some careful planning and investment, and with the players as willing partners, we can find a way.

These days, most of the young guys in the NSL don't have an outside career because they're all dreaming of a full-time contract in Europe. When all's said and done, though, no scheme to go full-time can work unless we start generating more revenue; through the turnstiles, from sponsorship and TV rights.

'WHAT DO YOU THINK of Aurelio Vidmar's ploy to kick you out as the Socceroo skipper?' I've had some curly questions from the media in my time, but that question was a beauty. What did I think? I didn't know Aurelio was trying to boot me out, but when I saw what had been written by Justin Brazier of Australian Associated Press in February, '95, it was pretty clear Vidmar A. was chasing my job. He was quoted as saying I should retire immediately and let the next World Cup squad get on with the job. He kindly pointed out that I'm the wrong side of 30, and that if he were the captain he would be able pay more attention to the overseas-based Aussie players (90 per cent of the Socceroos are expatriates). The quote was totally negative towards Paul Wade.

They say there's no such thing as bad publicity, but I can tell you it wasn't pleasant having my value to the Socceroos torn apart while another player lobbied for the captaincy, something I always thought was bestowed as an honour by the coach, based on ability and leadership qualities.

Let me make one thing clear here and now. I will remain the Socceroo captain until the day the Socceroo coach says I'm no longer good enough for the job, or when I think it's time. And if that's tomorrow, at least I'll know I gave it my best shot and I'll sleep well at night knowing that. The old line about being over at the hill at 30 is not a question for me to worry about. If I'm good enough, I'll play for the Socceroos until I'm 40 and I'll give it away when I'm not good enough, not when I reach some age barrier. I know there's a danger that I could become like a lot of people before me, who have done anything to stay in the game, whether it's for the good of the game or not, but one thing I will not do is retire because someone in the media or another player thinks it's the right thing to do. That will be my decision.

For the record, I did ask Aurelio Vidmar a few questions. In one of my radio spots we rang him in Belgium. After the constant ribbing from co-hosts David Hookes, the former Test cricketer, and Gerard Healy, the AFL Brownlow medallist, I thought it was inevitable. On air I asked Aurelio to explain his comments. He admitted saying them, but claimed he didn't mean to look as if he was chasing my job. I asked who exactly had told him I wouldn't be playing in the '98 World Cup campaign and Aurelio sort of beat around the bush without giving an answer. I think he got the point.

The funny thing was that David Hookes is an Adelaide boy himself, and he took great delight siding with Aurelio. A month earlier I had been awarded the Order of Australia Medal, the OAM. Hookesy said the OAM stood for 'Only Aurelio Matters'. Nice try, Hookesy, but for now the Socceroo captain is a Melbourne boy. That doesn't mean I'm not thinking about retirement and what that will mean. Over the past three years I have built a career in promotions and the media, and by working in these areas I would like to make a living out of this game after my playing career is finished. I have learned so much about the media and marketing, and I'm sure there's a role for me in the future of Australian soccer. The ASF and the VSF have invested time and money in developing Paul Wade as a high-profile player and I don't think I'm pushing my barrow too hard if I say I have something to offer.

Soccer is always complaining about not getting enough coverage, but I have some useful media contacts through my work for Channel 7's 'Sportsworld' and the 3AW Radio sports program, and from doing dozens of media conferences and meeting radio, newspaper and TV reporters all over Australia. I genuinely enjoy all the promotions work and the school visits, and while I may not be Socceroo captain forever, I reckon I have a role to play as a soccer ambassador for a long time to come.

Before I hand over the Socceroo captaincy, there are a few things I'd like to see changed about the way the national team is run. The first one will come as no surprise after all the hassles I've had with money. There should be a representative of the national team players, maybe someone from the Players' Union, who can sit down and negotiate the money and the conditions for Socceroo players. Everything from match fees to insurance to promotional work for ASF sponsors Coke and Adidas should be set out each year. At the moment the whole thing is a headache and it's the captain who gets it in the neck. It's ridiculous for the captain to be haggling about money two or three days before a game.

Another thing that really eats me up is that too many Socceroos don't know their national anthem. Watch the Wallabies, the Australian Rugby Union team, and you'll see them standing arm-in-arm singing the national anthem, as if it might be the last time they are ever going to sing it. Too many of our guys wouldn't have a clue about the words and that is a great disappointment. Given that the singing of the national anthem always features in live TV coverage, it is a serious responsibility, and reflects how big an honour it is to represent your country. Every time the Socceroos go into camp we should make sure that every player knows the national anthem and every player realises what it means to represent his country. We have a bad enough time trying to promote our game, without broadcasting pictures of Socceroos who don't sing or mumble their way through the national anthem.

For the Socceroos, our World Cup future is in Asia and it's about time we paid more attention to our regional neighbours. We have played Japan both home and away recently, and the teams are pretty closely matched, even though we haven't played them with our so-called first eleven. South Korea has always been a tough opponent, and I can't understand why we don't bring them out here. We've always played in South Korea and in my time we've never beaten them. The new ASF Chairman, David Hill, wants the Socceroos to play 16 times a year, with 12 of those games in Australia, and I think that's the way to go. Why not have a yearly four-nations tournament with Japan, South Korea, New Zealand and the Socceroos? Surely with all the Japanese and South Korean companies that do business in Australia we could find a decent sponsor. The Socceroos have such a positive image I'm certain the fans would come to 12 home internationals a year.

The big Socceroo games stay in people's memories; they're great Australian sporting events. That's the reason I'm writing this book. If it weren't for Diego Maradona and Argentina, I wouldn't have nearly the public profile that I do. Because soccer is a game of the world, Australians feel some extra national pride in that green and gold shirt. I will never forget the feeling of playing for the Socceroos. When I think of the thousands of kids all over Australia who would love to be where I am, I feel so proud of what I have achieved. That's what keeps me going.

I have been fortunate to make it to the top in Australian soccer and I feel a tremendous responsibility to all those people who support the Socceroos. It sounds silly, but I love standing there, holding that stuffed kangaroo and singing the national anthem. I always tell kids to hang on to their dreams, even when there are bad times; keep your dreams alive and never give them up. Believe me, that's how Paul Wade, the skinny kid from Dandenong, became a proud captain of the Socceroos.

EXTRA TIME

BY KYLE PATTERSON

PAUL WADE HAS LIVED in one of the most successful and controversial periods of Australian soccer's history. Pick any major event over the past 10 years and you'll find Wadey as one of the main characters. When the Socceroos won the hearts of the sporting public by beating the world champions Argentina in the Bicentennial Gold Cup, Paul scored the first goal. When the Socceroos made the football world sit up and pay attention by beating Yugoslavia at the Seoul Olympics, Wade was among the heroic eleven. When Australia confronted Argentina again in those dramatic World Cup qualifiers, it was Paul Wade who went one-on-one with the great Diego Maradona. And when the game was plunged into the turmoil of the Stewart report and the Senate soccer inquiry, Wadey was inadvertently caught up in the hysteria.

For these reasons, Paul's memoirs are as much a chronicle of the times as a personal reflection. Paul Wade is rarely an observer of events; he's usually in the middle of them. Given that precious little of our nation's soccer history is captured in print, this book is an important publication. I hope you have enjoyed reading the Paul Wade story as much as I have enjoyed being the 'ghost' who helped him write and research it. He has been full and open in his memoirs, happy to share good times and not afraid to confront the bad. It says much about the essential honesty and integrity of the man.

I have known Paul Wade since 1978 when I was a cub reporter for the now-defunct weekly newspaper *Soccer Action*. My beat was the Victorian State League, and in that season a skinny, long-haired teenager was making a name for himself as a left back for Prahran Slavia. Then, as now, Paul Wade was an over-achiever. He possessed great stamina, running as hard in the final minutes as in the first. He had a reckless disregard for his own well-being, throwing his wiry frame into great collisions for the good of the team, emerging more often than not with his body intact and the ball at his feet. In the air he had a rare gift. He used his height and jumping ability to rise above packs of players and head the ball with great power and accuracy. For years the Socceroo set-piece plays revolved around Wadey's aerial abilities.

Yet when Paul talks about his game he's more likely to reflect on his weaknesses. Perhaps that is a legacy of a hard-to-please father. His heading ability and his prodigious heart and lungs aside, Paul was not blessed with natural skill. He was always working overtime on his ball control and his passing. In this book he makes many disparaging remarks about his skill level, the 'usual Paul Wade first touch that meant the ball went a metre or two further than I wanted'. Modesty forbids him from telling the rest of the tale; that dedication to practice and tactical discipline meant he largely overcame these deficiencies. His ball control and passing may not be spectacular, but they are efficient parts of his game. Swerving 40 metre passes are not Paul's forte, so he doesn't often make an attempt. Instead, he concentrates on what he does best; getting to as many contests as possible, winning the ball and then maintaining possession for his team.

As a result of his diligence Paul Wade has been Australia's best defensive midfielder for the past 10 years. No one can match his work-rate, his clean tackling and robust enthusiasm. Paul Wade is not meant to knock 40 metre passes like Ned Zelic or dribble at opponents like Robbie Slater. But could they show their spectacular skills without Paul Wade to balance the mix? Not likely. That's why Frank Arok and then Eddie Thomson have picked Paul Wade in the Socceroo team. He was the best 'workhorse' around, and while that tag might not carry the same prestige as 'playmaker' or 'goalscorer', you won't find Paul Wade complaining. His game is built on courage; the strength of mind to push his body when his legs and lungs were screaming for respite. That inner strength, rather than any overt display of skill, is what has made Paul Wade a player of international class. He has played to his full potential, a feat few players can boast.

Yet Paul Wade is merely an ordinary guy with an extraordinary story to tell. It's the journey of a wide-eyed kid from the suburbs who grew into a globe-trotting footballer. A battler who made his mark in the company of world soccer's aristocrats. A player who harnessed his modest ability to become the most capped Socceroo of all time. Most inspiring of all, it's the tale of a migrant kid who has shown a national spirit for his adopted homeland that makes others feel proud to be Australian. And after all this, he's still an ordinary guy, and that's what makes Paul Wade a champion in the true sense of the word.

He says in this book that he plays for the fans on the terraces as much as for himself. They're not merely trite words for the customers who ultimately pay his wages. As captain of Australia, Paul has a deep and abiding commitment to the welfare of Australian soccer and the ordinary people who support the game. They are his people and he is one of them. As Socceroo captain he has truly championed the cause of Australian soccer and along the way has treated the supporter asking for an autograph with the same respect as he would a Prime Minister. There are no airs or graces; he's just a well-mannered nice guy. His very homespun nature makes him special in the cynical world of professional sport. Indeed, Paul is sometimes too nice for his own good, but anyone who knows Paul Wade will appreciate that his naivety is one of his endearing qualities He's forever looking for the good in people, willing to give his time, to lend an ear and show interest, but the trust isn't always returned.

He remains deeply hurt by the way South Melbourne treated him. He expected a free transfer as a mark of respect for the eight years he devoted to the club and I am among many soccer people who believe he deserved it. Instead, South Melbourne demanded a transfer fee of $8000. It's not so much the amount, but the crude valuation of the worth of a loyal servant and former club captain, someone who shed blood and broke bones in South Melbourne's cause. Someone who passionately believed in what he was doing for the club.

There are plenty of players who have a cynical view of the game, and who would expect that sort of treatment; Paul Wade can't understand it. To him, the game of soccer has intrinsic values. It is a game worthy of a life's endeavours. It's a noble pursuit. Sure, the money's important, but it's not the reason the game exists for Paul Wade.

When confronted by financial matters, Paul is often bewildered by the greed and avarice he sees. His soccer wages were always handed over to his wife, Valerie, while he got on with the job of playing. This nice guy was never motivated by money — he's a footballer who has never really bothered with the trappings of success. He doesn't drive a sports car, flaunt gold jewellery and holiday in exotic locations, as many of his peers do. It wasn't until he was the other side of 30 that he was finally persuaded to hire a personal manager to capitalise on his public profile.

Now he is far more aware of the commercial realities of professional sport, but he retains very simple tastes. He lives in Melbourne's outer

eastern mortgage belt, he drives a Ford Falcon and is a devoted family man, husband to Valerie and father to Emma and Brianna-Lee. If not for the fact that he spends months away from home each year playing soccer, he'd be the perfect nominee for Father of the Year.

My observations are made after 17 years of a mainly professional relationship. For a personal insight I asked Valerie, Paul's partner for the best part of 14 years. Valerie has watched Paul play hundreds of matches and provided unqualified support for his career, even though it has left her virtually a single mother for long periods. She taught him how to dress himself. She tolerates his habit of forgetting the most important appointments, except for match kick-off times. She forgives him for silence in front of the TV and the erratic driving that comes from match-day nerves. She laughs about his total lack of ability to do the easiest of handyman jobs around the house. And she's had to cope with a social life that comes second to a soccer career.

But when Paul doesn't push his own barrow hard enough, Valerie rues the cost. 'I've come to the conclusion that he's far too modest when it comes to his ability,' says Valerie. 'He constantly underestimates his own worth. He always tells the kids at coaching clinics that he got to where he is by putting in 100 per cent effort all the time, but I think he should credit himself with a little bit of skill. In any case, I think he puts in 110 per cent effort and an awful lot of dedication. Never say die is the Paul Wade trademark.'

Valerie says that the past two years have taken a toll on Mr Nice Guy. Getting dropped by Eddie Thomson in Canada and his split with South Melbourne have caused him grief. 'When I see what he does for soccer and how much he loves the sport, I get angry at the lack of respect Paul receives,' says Valerie. 'The things that have happened over the past couple of years have changed him. It started when Thommo dropped him in Canada. I couldn't believe he was the same person when he first came home. I think that bad experience made him finally realise he had been too much of a Mr Nice Guy.'

Despite all the family sacrifices, Valerie says Paul's eventual retirement will be just as traumatic for her. 'I will miss it as much as him,' she says. 'I love to watch him play and I've missed very few games over the years. People often ask how I put up with his frequent absences and say that they couldn't tolerate that sort of relationship, but I knew exactly what I was getting into. I don't understand how anyone could prevent their partner from doing something they love so passionately.'

For another insight I went to Micky Petersen, a long-time friend and team-mate. Micky is almost the total opposite to Paul: his game is built

EXTRA
TIME

on pure skill; he has always had a cynical view of soccer administrators and the sharks who circle the game; and as a character he's as complex as Paul is straightforward. Yet Wade and Petersen formed a superb midfield partnership. They were a perfect match; Wade's work-rate combined with Petersen's skill. That combination helped Brunswick Juventus and South Melbourne win national championships. Frank Arok transplanted the pair into the Socceroo team and was rarely disappointed with the results.

Micky has nothing but respect and admiration for his partner. 'When I first arrived at Brunswick I thought, "This is brilliant. I've got Wadey to do all the running and I can just stand in the middle of the park and ping a few balls." That's the way our relationship developed, our strong and weak points balanced each other out,' says Micky. 'Without him I doubt whether I would have been as successful as a footballer. I've probably taken three years off his career because of all the kilometres he ran and the tackles he went through for me. But to say Wadey's game is only about work-rate is selling him short. He is always good a for a crucial goal and he dominates in the air.' Petersen credits Wade with helping him gain international selection. 'With Wadey alongside me, I think Frank Arok saw I had something to offer, even though the defensive side of my game wasn't outstanding. I was selected because of Wadey's compensating attributes of work-rate, stamina and commitment.'

The playing relationship spanned 10 years and extended off the park. Petersen and Wade were room-mates on countless Socceroo tours, but that doesn't mean it was all sweetness and light. 'Our relationship is really good, but there's plenty of ups and downs,' admits Micky. 'Because he's so dedicated and committed he sometimes gets annoyed at my attitude. We've had some great slanging matches on the park. He'd often say, "Do you really care, today, do you give a shit?", questioning my commitment. I'd say, "Wadey, as long as you stop giving the ball away, I'll be able to play." It would be real cut-to-the-bone stuff, but that was his way of firing me up. We'd have a good old ding-dong on the ground and we'd both lift our game, but some of the opposing club players would say, "God, those two can't stand each other. How can they be team-mates?" Afterwards we'd have a beer and forget the whole thing. With the passion of Wadey, that's the way it is.'

Micky says Paul's record number of games for the Socceroos and his five years of captaincy speak for themselves. 'You don't play over 100 games for your country and become the captain if you're not a bit of an inspiration to others,' says Micky, who is still amazed by Wade's

dedication to the cause. The kids selected to be Socceroo mascots would always end up in the Wade/Petersen room because Paul was prepared to put in the time and effort. 'In the hours before a game I'd be trying to concentrate, but Wadey would be making sure the mascot had a day to remember. That's a sign of leadership, in itself. He could see beyond his own needs. People call him naive or gullible. That's his nature. For every person who takes him for a ride there are many more who take to him and trust him.'

Indeed, it has become fashionable in soccer circles to speculate on Paul Wade's retirement. His friend has some clear views. 'If Wadey wants to go on it's his privilege and his right. I admire sportsmen who never say die. Wadey has to come to his own decision, no one else.' Whenever he does decide to retire, I trust Australian soccer will make good use of this champion. Charlie Yankos was the Socceroo captain before Paul Wade and established a similarly high public profile. Charlie also had professional marketing skills, but the ASF knocked him back when he applied for the job as marketing manager. That was a terrible mistake. I hope the game's current administration has more foresight when Paul Wade's future in the game is up for grabs. The game can't afford to lose such a champion and such a fine ambassador.

I would like to thank the following people who gave me so much support: my wife, Donna, and my daughters, Chloe and Olivia, for allowing me to goof off from family duties during the writing of this book; Lou Gautier, Laurie Schwab and Greg Blake for their help with statistical and historical research; Julie Ogle and Judy Stephenson for the hours of transcribing; Tim McKenzie for guiding my path through computer technology; Jim Shomos for putting the deal together; and Paul Wade for just being himself.

Kyle Patterson, August, 1995.

EXTRA
TIME

PAUL WADE'S

SEASON	CLUB	GAMES & GOALS		
		League	NSL Cup	Finals
1984*	Green Gully Ajax	28/4	3/2	N/A
1985*	Brunswick Juventus	22/2	1/0	5/2
1986*	Brunswick Juventus	20/6	1/0	2/1
1987+	South Melbourne Hellas	22/8	4/0	N/A
1988	South Melbourne Hellas	21/2	1/0	2/0
1989	South Melbourne Hellas	5/1	0/0	0/0
1989–90#	South Melbourne Hellas	26/1	3/2	2/0
1990–91	South Melbourne Hellas	25/4	3/0	4/1
1991–92	South Melbourne Hellas	23/7	1/0	3/0
1992–93^	South Melbourne	25/1	2/1	1/0
1993–94	South Melbourne	17/2	4/0	3/1
1994–95	South Melbourne	10/0	4/0	0/0
	Heidelberg United (on loan)	6/0	0/0	0/0
TOTALS		250/38	27/5	22/5
CAREER GAMES & GOALS		299/48		

* NSL divided into two divisions of 12 teams

+ NSL reverts to single 14-team competition

First season of summer soccer

^ NSL bans ethnic names

Paul Wade's NSL statistics were compiled by Greg Blake.

NSL Record

LEAGUE POSITION	AFTER FINALS	TEAM HONOURS
9th	N/A	Nil
2nd	1st	NSL Southern Division Champion NSL National Champion
1st	3rd	NSL Southern Division Minor Premier
6th	N/A	NSL Cup runner-up
3rd	4th	Nil
8th	N/A	Nil
2nd	4th	NSL Cup winner
2nd	1st	NSL National Champion NSL Charity Shield winner
3rd	3rd	Nil
1st	3rd	NSL Minor Premier
2nd	3rd	Nil
6th	3rd	Nil
13th	N/A	Nil

NOTE: FULL 'A' INTERNATIONALS IN CAPITALS

1984

10 October: v Tasmania 2–0 (Gomez, Senkalski) in Hobart.

1985

23 September: Australian B team v China 2–0 (Petersen, Wade) in Canberra.

25 September: Australian B team v China 1–1 (Arnold) in Newcastle.

1986

3 August: v CZECHOSLOVAKIA 1–1 (Arnold) in Melbourne.

6 August: v CZECHOLOVAKIA 0–1 in Adelaide.

10 August: v CZECHOSLOVAKIA 0–3 in Parramatta.

22 October: v Victorian All-Stars 2–1 (Dunn, Zinni) in Melbourne, charity match for Greek earthquake victims.

25 October: v NEW ZEALAND 1–1 (Arnold) in Auckland.

2 November: v NEW ZEALAND 2–1 (Arnold, Zinni) in Parramatta.

9 November: v South Australian All-Stars 21 (Maxwell, Yankos pen) in Adelaide.

23 November: v CHINA 2–0 (Kalantzis, Arnold) in Canton.

28 November: v Shandong Province (China) 2–0 (McDowall, Arnold) in Shandong.

1987

President's Cup in South Korea:

9 June: v MOROCCO 1–0 (Farina)

13 June: v Shamrock Rovers (Ireland) 1–0 (Farina)

15 June: v South Korea B 5–0 (Farina 2, Yankos pen, Crino, Arnold)

22 June: v EGYPT 0–0, won 4–3 on penalties – semi-final.

25 June: v SOUTH KOREA 11 (Arnold), lost 4–5 on penalties—final.

3 September: v NEW ZEALAND 1–1 (Zinni) in Melbourne.

9 September: v NEW ZEALAND 0–1 in Wellington.

Olympic Games qualifier:

15 November: v TAIWAN 3–0 (Arnold 2, Farina) in Taipei.

1988

10 January: v IFK Gothenburg (Sweden) 0–1 in Parramatta

3 February: v Dinamo Zagreb (Croatia) 1–1 (Arnold) in Melbourne.

5 February: v Dinamo Zagreb (Croatia) 3–1 (Kosmina 2, Farina) in Parramatta.

Olympic Games qualifiers:

26 February: v TAIWAN 3–0 (Arnold 2, Farina) in Canberra.

6 March: v ISRAEL 2–0 (Yankos pen, Farina) in Melbourne.

INTERNATIONAL RECORD

9 March: v TAIWAN 3–2 (Crino, Tobin, Patikas) in Adelaide.

13 March: v NEW ZEALAND 3–1 (Patikas, Crino, Farina) in Sydney.

20 March: v ISRAEL 0–0 in Christchurch.

23 March: v NEW ZEALAND 1–1 (Farina) in Wellington.

27 March: v TAIWAN 3–0 (Arnold, Farina, Wade) in Auckland.

Bicentennial Gold Cup:

7 July: v BRAZIL 0–1 in Melbourne

9 July: v SAUDI ARABIA 3–0 (Farina 2, Ollerenshaw) in Parramatta.

14 July: v ARGENTINA 4–1 (Yankos 2 incl 1 pen, Wade, Bozinoski) in Sydney.

17 July: v BRAZIL 0–2 in Sydney final.

15 September: v Hanyang University (South Korea) 3–0 (Petersen, Yankos pen, Kosmina) in Seoul.

Olympic Games in South Korea:

18 September: v YUGOSLAVIA 1–0 (Farina).

20 September: v BRAZIL 0–3.

22 September: v NIGERIA 1–0 (Kosmina)

25 September: v USSR 0–3 quarter-final.

12 October: v NEW ZEALAND 2–1 (Arnold, Ollerenshaw) in Dunedin.

16 October: v NEW ZEALAND 2–0 (Spink 2) in Bendigo.

1989

17 February: v Malmo (Sweden) 3–0 (Arnold, Spink, Trimboli) in Parramatta.

World Cup qualifier:

12 March: v NEW ZEALAND 4–1 (Arnold 2, Crino, Yankos pen) in Sydney.

15 March: v Apollon (Greece) 1–1 (Krncevic) in Athens.

World Cup qualifiers:

19 March: v ISRAEL 1–1 (Yankos pen) in Tel Aviv.

2 April: v NEW ZEALAND 0–2 in Auckland.

16 April: v ISRAEL 1–1 (Trimboli) in Sydney.

1990

29 January: v Torpedo Moscow (Russia) 0–2 in Sydney.

2 February: v Torpedo Moscow (Russia) 3–0 (Arnold 2, Tobin) in Melbourne.

3 June: v Hajduk Split (Croatia) 1–0 (Trimboli) in Parramatta.

6 June: v Hajduk Split (Croatia) 2–2 (Durakovic, Yankos pen) in Melbourne.

Piala Kemerdekaan (Independence Cup) in Jakarta:

20 August: v Malaysian Olympic team 3–0 (Taliadoros 2, Tapai).

23 August: v Indonesia under-23 7–0 (Zinni 3, van Blerk 2, Taliadoros, McCulloch).

23 August: v Thailand under-23 2–0 (McCulloch 2 incl 1 pen).

25 August: v INDONESIA 3–0 (Wade 2, Zinni) final.

6 September: v SOUTH KOREA 0–1 in Seoul.

8 September: v SOUTH KOREA 0–1 in Seoul.

1991

30 January: v CZECHOSLOVAKIA 0–1 in Melbourne.

6 February: v CZECHOSLOVAKIA 0–2 in Parramatta.

12 May: v NEW ZEALAND 1–0 (Milosevic) in Christchurch.

15 May: v NEW ZEALAND 2–1 (Petersen, A Vidmar) in Adelaide.

1 June: v ENGLAND 0–1 in Sydney.

President's Cup in South Korea:

8 June: v USSR B 2–1 (Zelic, Gray).

10 June: v USA B 4–2 (Gray, A Vidmar, Durakovic, Arnold).

12 June: v South Korea B 2–0 (Arnold, G Brown).

14 June: v SOUTH KOREA A 0–0, lost 3–4 on penalties — semi-final.

1992

26 January: v SWEDEN 0–0 in Sydney.

29 January: v SWEDEN 1–0 (Edwards) in Adelaide.

2 February: v SWEDEN 1–0 (Wade) in Melbourne.

13 June: v USA 1–0 (Spink) at Citrus Bowl, Orlando.

18 June: v ARGENTINA 0–2 at River Plate, Buenos Aires.

21 June: v URUGUAY 0–2 at Centenario Stadium, Montevideo.

5 July: v CROATIA 1–0 (Marth) in Melbourne.

8 July: v CROATIA 3–1 (Tapai, Spink, J van Blerk) in Adelaide.

12 July: v CROATIA 0–0 in Sydney.

Piala Kemerdekaan (Independence Cup) in Jakarta:

10 August: v Thailand under-20s 1–0 (G Brown).

11 August: v MALAYSIA 0–1.

13 August: v South Korea under 2–0 0–1.

14 August: v INDONESIA 3–0 (Edwards, Gray, Wade).

World Cup qualifiers:

4 September: v SOLOMON ISLANDS 2–1 (Veart, McCulloch) in Honiara.

11 September: v TAHITI 3–0 (Mori, Veart, Wade) in Papeete.

20 September: v TAHITI 2–0 (Veart, Durakovic) in Brisbane.

26 September: v SOLOMON ISLANDS 6–1 (Genc, Gray, Wade, Veart, G Brown, Durakovic) in Newcastle.

1993

11 February: Vitesse Arnhem (Holland) 1–0 (Arnold) in Arnhem.

13 February: v Borussia Dortmund (Germany) 0–3 in Dortmund.

16 February: v Go Ahead Eagles (Holland) 0–3 in Deventer.

18 March: v Yokohama Flugels (Japan) 2–1 (Iriarte 2) in Sydney.

15 April: v KUWAIT 1–0 (Trimboli) in Singapore.

19 April: v KUWAIT 1–3 (Wade pen) in Singapore.

World Cup qualifier:

30 May: v NEW ZEALAND 1–0 (Arnold) in Auckland.

16 June: v AC Milan (Italy) 0–1 in Sydney.

17 June: v AC Milan (Italy) 0–2 in Melbourne.

16 July: v Duisburg (Germany) 1–1 (Arnold) in Duisburg.

18 July: v De Graafschap (Holland) 0–1 in Holland.

21 July: v NEC Nijmegen (Holland) 1–0 (Corica) in Holland.

World Cup qualifier:

15 August: v CANADA 21 (Farina, Durakovic), won on penalties 4–1 in Sydney.

24 September: v SOUTH KOREA 1–1 (Mori) in Seoul.

26 September: v SOUTH KOREA 0–1 in Seoul.

World Cup qualifier:

31 October: v ARGENTINA 1–1 (A Vidmar) in Sydney.

6 November: v Colo Colo (Chile) 2–3 (Veart 2) in Santiago.

World Cup qualifier:

17 November: v ARGENTINA 0–1 in Buenos Aires.

1994

Kirin Cup in Japan:

22 May: v JAPAN 1–1 (A Vidmar) in Hiroshima.

26 May: v FRANCE 0–1 in Kobe.

8 June: v SOUTH AFRICA 1–0 (A Vidmar) in Adelaide.

12 June: v SOUTH AFRICA 1–0 (Polak) in Sydney.

22 September: v Malaysian Olympic team 3–0 (Edwards 2, Popovic) in Kuala Lumpur.

24 September: v KUWAIT 0–0 in Kuala Lumpur.

27 September: v JAPAN 0–0 in Tokyo.

1995

8 February: v COLOMBIA 0–0 in Brisbane.

18 June: v GHANA 2–1 (T Vidmar, Arnold) in Sydney.

21 June: v GHANA 1–0 (Veart) in Adelaide.

24 June: v GHANA 0–1 in Perth.

30 June: v ARGENTINA 0–2 in Buenos Aires.

Played: 113 matches
76 'A' internationals, 37 others

Scored 10 goals — 9 in full internationals, 1 in non-international

Most games for the Socceroos:

All matches:
115 Peter Wilson
113 Paul Wade
103 John Kosmina
100 Jimmy Rooney
 92 Charlie Yankos
 89 Atti Abonyi
 84 Graham Jennings

79 Alan Davidson, Graham Arnold
77 Frank Farina

'A' internationals:
76 P. Wade
64 P. Wilson
60 A. Abonyi, J. Kosmina
57 J. Rooney
50 Manfred Schaefer, A. Davidson, A. Tobin
49 Ray Baartz, C. Yankos
45 G. Arnold

Paul Wade's Socceroo statistics were compiled by Laurie Schwab.

INDEX